LAGOS

Also in the series:

LAGOS

A Cultural History

Kaye Whiteman

Interlink Books

An imprint of Interlink Publishing Group, Inc.
Northampton, Massachusetts

First published in 2014 by
INTERLINK BOOKS
An imprint of Interlink Publishing Group, Inc.
46 Crosby Street, Northampton, MA 01060
www.interlinkbooks.com

Published simultaneously in the United Kingdom by Signal Books

Library of Congress Cataloging-in-Publication Data available

ISBN 978-1-56656-919-4

Cover image: Lolade Adewuyi

Illustrations: Lolade Adewuyi pp. 81, 109, 209, 246, 251; Armet Francis p. 99; courtesy Kaye Whiteman pp. 83, 121, 147, 158, 179, 192, 213; Wikipedia Commons pp. i, 11, 21, 54, 72, 134, 140, 166, 173, 220, 235, 240; drawings by Nicki Averill pp. 25, 46, 51, 65, 69, 72, 138, 223, 228; maps by Sebastian Ballard

Printed and bound in the United States of America

To request our 48-page, full-color catalog, please visit our websire at www.interlinkbooks.com, call us toll-free at: 1-800-238-LINK, or write to us at: Interlink Publishing, 46 Crosby Street, Northampton, MA 01060 email: info@interlinkbooks.com

Contents

Foreword by Femi Okunnu

When in early February 2012 Kaye Whiteman proposed to me in London (a few days before the end of my holidays) that I should write the foreword to *Lagos: A Cultural and Historical Companion*, I thought momentarily of the punishing program ahead of me in Lagos. I was nonetheless persuaded that it was a challenge I could not refuse. Kaye gave me a very tight deadline for when the foreword was needed.

I accepted the challenge primarily because history was my first love, not law. And I am part of the history of modern Lagos in many ways. Lagos, in any case, is my birthplace. In between my activities as President of the Ansar-ud-Deen society of Nigeria and other social and charitable work, I had to find time to meet Kaye Whiteman's deadline.

And what a tour de force this book is for all lovers of history and those interested in Nigeria's political and socio-economic development and her future role in the world economy. For the book is not only about the history of Lagos—it has many vignettes of history, including the colonial administration—but also covers its topography and physical planning, its art and culture and its political and social life. I knew Kaye as a journalist; I did not know the pub crawler side of him, though that is part of the life of a successful journalist.

The book starts with the Portuguese connection, and the naming of Eko as Lagos. Kaye at times interchanges Isale Eko with "Eko" or Lagos Island. It is worth emphasizing that Isale Eko is only that part of Lagos Island where Iga Idunganran (the Oba's Palace) is situated. Isale Eko is the "heart" of Lagos, as Lagos remains the "heart" of Nigeria, in spite of losing the Federal Capital status.

The original inhabitants of Lagos were the Aworis, but the dominant ethnic group in Lagos remains the non-Awori Yorubas from the hinterland. Kaye highlights, quite rightly, the settlement of the Binis in historic Lagos; the role of the Nupe as a dominant force amongst the early settlers, as well as the Saros and the Amaros after the abolition of the slave trade. The book discusses the reception of Christian missionaries, but could have had more on the earlier reception of Islam by a large section of the Eko community.

From its governance under the British Consulate, Lagos (coterminous with the present Lagos State) became a British colony in 1861 by virtue of the controversial Treaty of Cession. At first it was part of the colonial administration in Freetown, later part of the then Gold Coast, and finally it was placed directly under London's control until Lagos lost its independence when it was merged with the Protectorate of Nigeria in 1906.

In his "Prominent Personalities" Kaye includes many names, but omits to bring into more prominence others like J. H. Doherty in commerce and Chief Tijani Oluwa who fought the British administration successfully in the Privy Council in the famous Apapa land case.

The history of the creation of Lagos State, in which this writer played a part, should have featured more prominently in the book. And in Chapters 2 and 3, where the development of the ports (Lagos, Apapa and Tin Can Island) and the railways are chronicled, little is said about the highways, bridges and interchanges of my creation, comparable to those found in most cities of the world. The tramway and Carter Bridge are properly in place in the book.

Arts and music feature very well, including Portuguese/Brazilian architecture, which in Brazil is called "colonial" architecture. And Fela Anikulapo Kuti deserves his place in the book. One chapter gives me special pleasure: Chapter 10 "Streets of the Imagination: Everyday Mysteries of the City." The author describes in minute detail the characteristics and social life in the major streets of Lagos. Kaye knows his onions. Though now in his seventies, he is a Lagos "boy."

Lagos Island or Eko has now become one sprawling market, from Isale-Eko to Olowogbowo, from Ehingbeti to the Brazilian Quarter and Epetedo, from Ita Faji to Oko-Awo and Idunshagbe, with residential buildings dotted here and there. The Central Business District of Ehingbeti and Oluwole is enjoying a sort of renaissance. The residents of Lagos Island are like squatters in a large marketplace.

But the reality of Lagos State becoming a mega-city is taking shape on Victoria Island, Ikoyi and along the Lekki corridor to Epe, and from Iganmu along the rail/road highway (under construction) to the Benin Republic border, replacing the old Badagry Road. And that is for a start. That is Lagos, with the new Carter Bridge and Eko Bridge of the Gowon era; the mega-city with the long third Mainland Bridge which merges with the Lagos-Ibadan ten-lane expressway. It is the link with the rest of Nigeria.

What, then does tomorrow hold for the city of Lagos? Yes, Lagos has a "soul," but it is more than a "state of mind." Lagos is alive. It is this extraordinary life and creative vitality contained within its bounds that will make it a true world city of the future.

A Personal Message from the CEO of BGL

After many visits and my student years at Kings College Lagos, I began my professional life in Lagos back in 1988. In many ways I can say I owe my career progression to the unique collectives of people that only Lagos could have agglomerated within its large population: the intellectuals who inspired my analytical bent and an application to detail; the entrepreneurs who revealed that a "Nigerian Dream" is more likely to be Lagos-based than anywhere else in Nigeria; and the regulators who over the course of my career have gone from the rather inflexible bureaucrats of the military rule period to the dynamic, often diaspora-influenced proponents of private sector-led economic development currently steering the ship of Financial Services guidance.

My peregrination within Lagos—an area tiny in size but huge in strategic importance, human capacity and economic potential—has seen me personally take in the working-class hubs of the mainland, the hard-driven, fast-paced, can-do bustle of the three Islands and the under-appreciated green areas that still dot the thorough modernity of the metropolis. I am grateful to be one of the many officers of BGL PLC whose dint of hard work has taken him or her "from Mainland to Island."

From my own humble beginnings living happily, but very modestly, in Ogudu and plying the bracing bus-routes from the typically rowdy but entertaining Oworonshoki bus-stop via the Third Mainland Bridge to CMS bus-stop/Marina, I have seen Lagos' transport system evolve from Danfos to BRTs. My career path has in many ways mirrored the occupational and figurative course of tens of thousands, even hundreds of thousands of professionals and entrepreneurs to whom Lagos has given the opportunity to change their circumstances individually, even alongside their contribution to the finances and development of the metropolitan community.

Speaking of community, this is one of the most remarkable features of the Lagos Metropolis. The fact that it is small but densely populated means that you are never far off from the people whose lives you have touched or vice-versa. However, the frenetic pace of Lagos also means that you could be literally minutes away from a friend, family member, contact or acquaintance and not even catch a glimpse of each other for years! This is why technology integration involving telephony and the Internet is faster in Lagos than anywhere else in the country (and perhaps even the sub-continent). This is why the thriving social scene of Lagos, fueled by a representative melting pot of peerless and often timeless artists, poets, musicians, broadcasters, media practitioners and entertainment impresarios is of such crucial importance. From our social clubs and parties (our *owambes*) to our ubiquitous places of worship, the hard-working and often rather bedraggled swell of Lagosians are offered the opportunity to remind ourselves that a common humanity is what matters the most, even as we strive to make a living. I am convinced that this social cohesion is what has made Lagos—a place that appears to be virtually bursting at the seams sometimes—somehow defy the doubters and thrive, despite the many challenges it faces.

Albert Okumagba

Preface and Acknowledgements

Even in my most exotic creative imaginings, I had not thought that Lagos, even as a city that I have known well for a long time, would be the subject of the first full-length book that I would write, above all in the middle of my eightieth decade. So when Michael Dwyer of Signal Books approached me in 2005 with the idea of writing a book about the city by the lagoon, the notion came as something of a shock.

I first visited Lagos in 1964, and have been a regular visitor ever since. However, it was only the fact that I had just spent two vitally important years of my life living there in 2001-02 that caused me first to entertain the idea of writing a book, warm to it and then embrace it. From having been a regular visitor who still saw the city as a backdrop to political and journalistic encounters, I had become a "Lagos boy." I guess that it was the concept of Lagos as a "city of the imagination" that clinched it for me. For the most immediate impact you can receive from Lagos is from its creative energy, that which fuels the imagination. I can still recall the rush of adrenaline that hits you any time you arrive; the existential awareness that each new day is completely different from the last; the contradictions of philistine aggression and cultural wonder, and of the shockingly perverse alongside the unexpectedly serendipitous.

The historical, topographical and social background is fundamental to understanding what has led to the development of this peculiar force. Nigerian readers should forgive me for dwelling at length on the two-stage British takeover of the city—the bombardment by a Palmerstonian gunboat in 1851 (along with the deposition of the Oba) and the humiliating Treaty of Cession ten years later. The text of this makes such painful reading that I have included it as an Appendix. In spite of all the forces at work in the three preceding centuries these two events were seminal in the configuration of the city we know now, and in the making of Nigeria itself.

For me, however, the core of this book is the impact that the genius of the city and its astonishing melting-pot has had on the creative output of its people, and to a much lesser extent on those from outside who have been drawn into its vortex. Lagos is above all a triumph of imagination over reality. This makes the two chapters that deal with literature, music and the cultural environment central to the idea of the book. Few cities have inspired so many in so short a time. Odia Ofeimun's recent volume *Lagos of the Poets* alone is evidence enough of the city's creative passion.

It has also been my concern to write of particular, if arbitrarily chosen, incidents; and of a number of prominent citizens and "Lagos boys." I chose, too, to take journeys through especially evocative streets, highways and quarters of the imagination. This may sometimes have led to repetitions in more than one place and yet illustrates, perhaps, the confused nature of the city, which can be seen through so many prisms.

Since the conception of the book I have had twelve visits there, all between 2005 and 2010, as well as two major surgical experiences, the latter which has prevented me more recently from undertaking long distance travel. My last visit was in 2010. The visits I made permitted me to engage in a series of essential researches even while busying myself with other activities, some of which involved simple breadwinning (an elementally Lagosian activity). But over this seven-year period I have sometimes felt I was engaged in producing a blockbuster like the film *Ben-Hur* which was also seven years in the making. I began to feel it was one of those books that are treated as a joke and end up never being written. The publication before you is proof to the contrary.

ᘒ

There are a number of valuable works, notably by Akin Mabogunje, Professor Ade-Ajayi and Dele Cole, to which I have often referred. For the history, Richard Burton and E. D. Morel have given me some valuable quotations. Apart from the research into secondary sources the book depends on many interviews and conversations, as well as long years of distilled experiences. Because I have not been in Lagos since May 2010 some of the material may already seem out of date, but that is the nature of the place. I have also often drawn on my own writings and introduced an unavoidable subjectivity verging on the autobiographical; although to claim ownership of such a place looks seriously pretentious, this is my Lagos.

Even enlisting the eminent Lagos elder Femi Okunnu in writing the foreword of this book involved me in exciting and careful negotiation, perhaps an indication of arguments to come with the publication of the book. He made me aware of the pitfalls in writing about Lagos and heightened my awareness of my own lack of insight into the mysteries of the city, for which I thank him. I also accept his reproach for not including figures like Doherty and Oluwa; my only defense is that there are many other eminent Lagos figures also deserving inclusion. Such selection is an onerous, arbitrary exercise. Although I have tried to scrupulously check facts, there are probably many that I have been unable to alight on. These mistakes are my own and for these I plead indulgence, for there are many people out there who know more of the city than I do, who have lived with the idea of Lagos all their lives, an idea often only articulated through creativity. I also regret that for reasons of space I have not included much detail of the three major towns of Lagos State: Epe, Badagry and Ikorodu.

In all these endeavors I have been immensely assisted by support from the BGL Group headed by Albert Okumagba, without which this book could not have been completed. Albert's message, which precedes this preface, is testimony to the group's support. I wish to thank BGL and in particular their head of research Olufunso Oke for his belief in the book, a belief which he communicated to his colleagues, and for his patience faced with all the delays experienced. A description of the activities of BGL can be found on p.263.

I must also thank my old friend and fellow alumnus of the Queen's College, Oxford, Hadja Abdulaziz Ude, who has at various times in my career given me encouragement, and in the case of the book provided me with an important introduction to His Majesty Akiolu I, the Oba of Lagos who has taken valuable time to explain to me some of the complexities of the traditional city. He put me on to a number of key figures such as Alhaja Habibatu Mogaji, supremo of all Lagos markets, and Professor Kunle Lawal of Lagos State University, and I thank him. Governors Tinubu and Fashola also readily agreed to be interviewed at length. I am also indebted to Tayo Akpata, Philip Asiodu and Francesca Emanuel for many helpful ideas and insights. John and Jill Godwin, Brits who have made Lagos their home for over fifty years, have been consistently helpful, pointing me in all sorts of useful directions and correcting the gaps in my own knowledge.

I must also mention Stanley Egbochuku and Freddie Scott, who brought me out to Lagos in late 2000, providing me with the two-year experience of the city at first hand without which this book could not have seen the light of day. Frank Aigbogun and the staff of *Business Day*, who have over the past ten years given me a continuing foot in the door, also deserve to be included among those who have helped make this book possible. I must likewise thank those two "cultural landscapists" Jahman Anikulapo and Toyin Akinosho for helping me to discover the "havens in the wilderness" like those run by Bisi Silva and Bolanle Austen-Peters, of a kind that flourish joyously all over the city. Jahman, as well as Professor John Peel, Olly Owen, the Godwins and Giles Omezi, have all read parts of the book and given freely of their comments.

My irrepressible friend of twenty-five years Tunji Lardner has helped me to understand the Lagos mentality (both of Mushin and Ikoyi), and his one-time colleague at Wangonet, Paul Kalu, proved an unrivaled guide to the highways and byways of Lagos during my two years' adventure at the beginning of the new century. Chike Nwagbogu of Nimbus fame and his brother Azu, as well as Lagos Boys Osagie Oyegun, Valentine Okogwu and Uchechi Ogwo, all formed part of that learning curve. I have a debt to many others in this incredible place too numerous to name, all of whom have been important in providing a deeper and wider-ranging appreciation of a city that has all too often been portrayed to the outside world as being a hell-hole of crazy slums, endless traffic jams, con-men and chaos when it is so much, much more.

Kaye Whiteman

To my family, Marva, Simon and Joshua, with all my love

Introduction

"The town of Lagos is certainly one of the most unhealthy spots on these malarious shores."

> Sir Richard Burton, *Wanderings in West Africa* ,1863

"The inner life of Lagos is a dark and often times incomprehensible mystery."

> Editorial in *The Observer of Lagos*, 6 August 1887

"Lagos is chaos theory made flesh and concrete."

> Lonely Planet *Africa*, 30th Anniversary Edition, 2008

"I know there is a logic in Lagos that shouts itself to victory; it is loud
And riotous with colours; it wants to be heard
And it means to be seen..."

> Afem Akeh, from the poem "Bodies"

"Lagos is a state of mind."

> Kunle Adeyemi, OMS Rotterdam, 2006

This work is a quest for the soul of the city, and like most quests it is doomed to be ultimately unfulfilled even if it still gives satisfaction in the questing. Some cities are cold and unforthcoming. Lagos, for all its confusion, is full of emotional warmth, often shocking or misdirected, sometimes bleakly humorous, often too tragic for tears, but always full of raw intensity; above all it is a city of people. It is almost impossible to set the parameters of the quest, since the subject, as vast as the city itself, could cover so much. There is therefore no point in apologizing for not using up a lot of printed space on pressing infrastructural issues such as water supply or sewerage, health services or crime rates, although they are bound to figure in places. This limitation applies even more to the issue of traffic and roads, integral parts of the city's daily drama which could fill a book, and are a fundamental part of its persona. It may be unfair, but to link any of these in one phrase with Lagos—as in "Lagos water," "Lagos sewerage," "Lagos traffic" or "Lagos roads"—is to sound oxymoronic.

Because this book is intended to be a "cultural and historical companion" rather than a more routine kind of guide book, the work includes, indeed feasts on, a variety of references to and quotations from those who in various periods have written about Lagos. These quotations range from the European visitors of the nineteenth century such as Sir Richard Burton, who presented a particularly vivid picture of Lagos in the early 1860s, to the academics, along with the politicians and public servants. both Nigerian and non-Nigerian, but above all the Nigerian writers—the novelists, the poets, the journalists. They dominate the two long central chapters on the literature and the musical and artistic culture of the city. Without them this book would have had much less substance. This "feasting" makes it more of an empirical adventure, and not so much a scientific study with any academic pretensions. Hence there are no footnotes although I have tried to provide a comprehensive bibliography for further study. Readers of this impressionistic maze are also asked to excuse that I have engaged in a measure of authorial self-indulgence, and they may find reference to some of my own writings, drawn from material published over the past fifty years. I hope these occur only where they positively illuminate both the text and the wider purpose of the book.

Telling people that you are writing a book about Lagos produces some unusual reactions, ranging from a pitying look, suggesting that you are not quite normal, to downright astonishment that you are taking on such an uphill struggle. For there are still probably few international cities with a worse image. The normally admirable Jan Morris, in her book *Cities*, published in 1963, included only Accra and Kano as West African cities worthy of her creative attention. This is disappointing as her narrative skills might have come up with some interesting descriptive passages. However, the disparaging remarks about "Westernized Africa" that introduce her frank essay in admiration of Kano suggest that she too, despite her fine writing, would join those who put down Lagos as not worth consideration by serious "travelers." Lagos has only been dwelt on as part of a pursuit of the "other," as defined, for example, by Ryszard Kapuscinski, who has his own take on Lagos, even if most of those travellers who are often genuinely curious beings end up self-indulgently chasing after exoticism. The same dismissal of Lagos as not worth serious attention is implicit in its ruthless exclusion from *The World's Great Cities* published in 2008 by Lonely Planet, a giant glossy tome which reveals its own superficiality in preferring to embrace the relatively characterless and still unformed Abuja to Lagos. A more judicious approach came from Morley Safer, of the US CBS-TV program *Sixty Minutes*, who once (in the early 1980s) described Lagos as "a city like no other." This was perhaps double-edged, but even Lagos aficionados would not disagree with him.

Apprehension about the place, leading to a certain rejection, is not a recent state of mind. It goes back probably five centuries to the first Portuguese explorations of the coast and was one reason why they were deterred from further investigation there for more than two centuries. The first known written account of a visit is that of the German Andreas Ulzheimer in 1603, full of interesting detail, but there are scarcely any other records until the eighteenth century. Even then there was little to excite the traveler. Barbot in his *Voyage to Guinea* (1732) noted only the perennial problem of the "bar," the sandbank at the mouth of the network of lagoons that lay behind the long straight coast. The bar was one of the main problems that exercised visitors over the next two centuries (see Chapter 2).

In the first part of the nineteenth century, although the settlement was already evolving, the climate and the ambiance of what by then had developed as a slaving center was so insalubrious that even by mid-century it was in some ways surprising that missionaries, and then the colonial forces, were keen to move in. By that time, however, it seemed to be a focal point and a magnet, offering challenges both for those seeking to profit from trade and for others hoping to spread God's word. This study has dwelt at probably too great a length on the period of the mid-nineteenth century when the two-stage British takeover of the city happened. This was, however, an event of profound importance when everything changed, and I felt it needed a more profound exploration.

In the course of the text the reader will find quotes, not always complimentary, from the likes of Sir Richard Burton, Giambattista Scala, Mary Kingsley, Lady Glover, E. D. Morel, Sir Frederick Lugard, Margery Perham, Elspeth Huxley and John Gunther, but Lagos was never to my knowledge the subject of an expatriate novel, although there are novels on Nigeria such as those by Joyce Cary, which were a source of irritation for budding Nigerian writers such as Chinua Achebe. Lagos never had a foreign writer to do for the city what Lawrence Durrell did in *The Alexandria Quartet*. Books of memoirs like *Dark Subjects* by H. L. Ward Price (1939) occasionally have passing descriptions of what Lagos was like, but it was not on the whole a place to stay or reflect. Occasional external comment has continued, however, most of it from journalists, much of it still not flattering, very little of it comprehending.

Big cities, it is true, have often in history had a hostile press, and have been a favorite subject for excoriation. For, example, London in the eighteenth century, in a period of disorderly growth, was called the "Great Wen," a source of all manner of social evils. The Industrial Revolution created many more cities in what was still an essentially agricultural world, and they had a bad reputation, somber subjects for writers such as Dickens and Zola who nonetheless painted unforgettable pictures of London and Paris at that time.

Nigerians have been writing about Lagos since the first flowering of newspapers in the 1880s, often in the form of social comment. M. C. Echeruo in his much-appreciated book *Victorian Lagos* (1975) made a point of going through newspapers of the last twenty years of the nineteenth century: a similar exercise could be done with those of the twentieth, a subject filled out in Chapter 4, and vital commentary on some of the glories and follies of the city has continued, for example in Metro sections of daily newspapers.

There has, of course, been much more to the recent literature of Lagos than simply journalism. Great cities need their writers, although Nigerian writers of that marvelous generation that came to flower in the two decades after the Second World War often had ambivalent or even hostile feelings about the city. The background to this ambivalence was the massive rural exodus in Nigeria, which has been so recent and so accelerated that there have survived all manner of bonds between the urban sprawl and the mass of villages in the interior. But the critics often became those who in fact, in spite of themselves, sang the city's praises.

One still feels, however, that Lagos has not yet quite found among Nigeria's own writers its Charles Dickens or still less its James Joyce, or, for a more pertinently related fictional experience of a city, its Naguib Mahfouz (the novelist who has been the true bard of contemporary Cairo). A seminal piece "Imagination and the City" by the poet and social commentator Odia Ofeimun in *Lagos: A City at Work* points the way to the possibilities of this line of exploration. His elegant essay is, in fact, an essential pointer for those trying to understand the soul of Lagos, or to look for what Ofeimun calls the "citiness" of the city. The section of

Chapter 4 which deals with Lagos in literature is fruitfully informed by some of his material, including his important recent anthology *Lagos of the Poets*, but in a typical rambling and adventurous Lagosian manner his subject matter extends well beyond simple interpretation of the written word into history, society, philosophy, culture and other subject matters.

One example taken from Ofeimun's "Imagination and the City" gives an idea of his unique contribution:

> …there is in Lagos a certain openness, showiness, freedom from custom, and a stress on equalitarian notions of citizenship. It has empowered the stranger to feel at home… Lagos has managed to give other ethnic groups a sense of movement to a common morality by which they could interact. Somewhat, this has helped to distinguish Lagosians from people of the same ethnic stock who are not Lagosians. Another way of saying that is that there is indeed a Lagos ethic of citizenship. More than in any other Nigerian conurbation, it has tended to be conferred more by presence than by ancestry.

Chapter One

THE STORY OF LAGOS
EVOLUTION OF A MULTI-ETHNIC GENE POOL

"If Lagos, instead of being a nest for slave-traders, were to become a port for lawful trade, it would become an outlet for the commerce of a large range of country in the interior, and instead of being a den of barbarism, would become a diffusing centre of civilisation."
                    Lord Palmerston, 1849

"It is at best only a half-truth to say that Lagos was bombarded in 1851 because it was a 'notorious slave depot.'"
                    J. F. Ade Ajayi *in Nigeria Magazine*, 1961

"This is a mini-Nigeria. Everyone is in Lagos, every ethnic group. But we have to use the power of that migrant culture to strengthen our position."
                    Governor Babatunde Fashola, interview with the
                    author, August 2008

ORIGINS: OGUNFUNMINIRE, OLOFIN AND THE IDEJO

This is the story of the piecing together of what eventually became one of the biggest and most diverse conurbations in Africa. The sources of the phenomenon that became Lagos are rooted in oral tradition, rendered more complex by the interweaving of two different traditions, from Lagos itself and from Benin. Among the many different versions of the origins of Lagos, local historians of the city and traditional accounts have it that the original inhabitants are the descendants of Ogunfunminire, a hunter from Ile-Ife in the heart of the homeland of the Yoruba people, who having settled in Isheri, moved to rule from a fishing village on the mainland at Ebute Metta (which means "three wharves"), one of many such villages the Yoruba-speaking Awori people found near the coast, as far as forty miles north of what is now Lagos. He acquired the title of Olofin. The timing of this event is hard to place, but it was probably at some point in the sixteenth century.

The twelve descendants of Olofin later became known as the Idejo, the "white cap" chiefs who still hold important authority in Lagos and are still said to be custodians of the city's oral history, although their main authority came, and still comes, from ownership of land. Because the mainland was subjected to warring kingdoms, one of the Idejo, Aromire, went first to the island of Iddo and then to the comparatively greater security of what is now Lagos Island, and established a fishing camp and later a pepper farm, although there are even conflicting stories of the origins of this farm. The Idejo all eventually established themselves on and around what are now Lagos and Victoria Islands, and apart from still possessing substantial land titles maintain a vital role in traditional institutions.

THE FIRST PORTUGUESE CONTACT

From external evidence we know that Lagos lagoon featured in early Portuguese maps of the late fifteenth century, but there was no settlement marked. In 1485 a visitor, Duarte Pacheco Pereira (quoted notably by the great scholar of the Brazil slave trade Pierre Verger) observed that "there is no trade in this country nor anything from which one can make a profit." In other words it was a low priority from European traders' point of view. According to Agiri and Barnes, "the Portuguese were sufficiently interested in trade in this area to have established themselves in the Ijada quarter of Ijebu Ode," but documents are silent on the subject of the island that later became Lagos. They also went further along the coast to Forcados, from where they established their celebrated relations with Benin in the sixteenth century. On later maps of the period there also appeared *agua de curamo* or *lago de curamo*, apparently named after the fishing village on the creek of that name, a name still given to the small lagoon near Bar Beach called Kuramo Waters, fronting onto Kuramo Beach. The first European map reference to Eko (still the preferred local name for Lagos) appears to have been on the work of a number of mid-seventeenth-century Dutch cartographers who refer to "Ichoo."

The present Oba (King) of Lagos, Akiolu I, told the author that the first building of the Iga Idunganran (Palace of the Pepper Quarter) was constructed by Oba Ashipa on the site of Aromire's pepper farm in the seventeenth century, and a courtyard that was part of it is still physically there, even if many of the buildings are essentially Portuguese-inspired constructions from the late eighteenth century and the first part of the nineteenth. The palace was extensively reconstructed in the late 1950s—the modern extension containing the offices of the Oba, his throne and his reception hall were opened at the time of independence in October 1960.

THE BENIN IMPRINT AND "EKO"

The kingdom of Benin in its heyday, between the fifteenth and eighteenth centuries, was one of the greatest and most developed empires that West Africa has seen. Oral tradition recounts that in the latter part of the sixteenth century, in the reign of King Orhogba (probably c.1550-78), the island and settlement of what became Lagos Island were occupied by Benin forces and a military camp was built there. The name Eko, traditionally ascribed to the island from the seventeenth century onwards, comes, so some authorities say, from the Bini word for "encampment," derived from the settlement already there. Odia Ofeimun, in *Lagos of the Poets*, insists convincingly more than once that it is in fact Bini for "meeting place," although that could have a military connotation.

Another version, quoted by Dele Cole, suggests it was an adaptation of *oko* ("farm" in Yoruba), a name given by Awori fishermen to the island. Both versions may well have historical foundation. Benin at the time was in expansionist mode and outmaneuvering its neighbor to the west, the Yoruba state of Ijebu, it was pushing through to the frontier of Dahomey at Allada, setting up staging posts on the way, of which Eko was one of the more significant. Not for the first time the island in the lagoon was subject to pressures from wider forces on the mainland.

The German surgeon Andreas Ulsheimer's account of his 1603 visit on a Dutch merchant ship gives an interesting and historically vital portrait of the town of Lagos although he does not use the name; it confirms the presence of a camp of Benin soldiers on the island—he describes a well-fortified military town inhabited by "none but soldiers and four military commanders, who behave in a very stately manner."

The formal bid by the Benin Kingdom to make it into an outpost came later, however, probably in the first part of the seventeenth century (there are some serious arguments over exact dating). As the story goes, one Awori warrior called Ashipa was selected to take the body of a Bini war leader, Asheri, back to Benin for burial, and so impressed the Oba of Benin that he was sent back as the first recognizable ruler (some say in 1603, though others put it a bit later, and J. B. Losi even suggests it was at the end of the seventeenth century). After him there came Ado, who further consolidated the foundations of the Obaship, although it was eventually assimilated by the descendants of Olofin, who as the "white-capped" land-owning Idejo constituted a true oligarchy, and whose writ on the ground was more effective than that of the notional tributary of Benin. The ownership of land was a powerful force.

The Benin imprint led to other categories of chiefs introduced in the reign of Ado's son Gabaro (once dated as having been in the latter part of the seventeenth century but now, it seems, put by some historians in the early eighteenth). These were the Akarigbere (the elders and principal advisers); the Abagbon, the military leaders headed by the Ashogbon, the chief of staff; and the Ogolade, chiefs versed in traditional medicine, described by the late history professor of the University of Lagos, A. B. Aderibigbe, who has written much of the history of Lagos, as "collectively responsible for the well-being of the community." In spite of these essentially Bini introductions, land remained securely in the hands of the Awori Idejo, who retain considerable powers to this day, while the other categories have become more purely ceremonial as part of the culture of the Oba's court. The rulers of Lagos in the first instance were known as "Eleko," a title officially maintained for many years; "Oba," which has become more generally accepted, is simply a word for king in both Yoruba and Bini languages. The coronation ceremonies of the Oba of Lagos still have many analogies with those of the Oba of Benin.

AKINSEMOYIN AND THE COMING OF THE PORTUGUESE
When Akinsemoyin (see Chapter 8 for profile) succeeded his brother—probably in the mid-eighteenth century—there seems to have been a major change in the nature of kingship in Lagos, although according to some accounts he may only have ruled for fifteen years. This was partly because at some point in his reign a deal was done with the Portuguese, which contributed in important ways to wealth creation in the town and helped alter the balance of power between it and the Benin monarchy. Aderibigbe says that that the formerly strong ties of the royal house with Benin became gradually attenuated at this time. He writes:

> True, in times of constitutional crisis appeals to the political and spiritual sanctions of the Oba of Benin continued to be invoked; but with

the relative decline in the might of the ruler of this once powerful African kingdom, and the growing wealth and power of its vassal, the annual payment of tribute became not only intermittent but a much more intolerable duty perfunctorily carried out.

Certainly, in the second half of the eighteenth century the Portuguese presence in the city became increasingly significant. The slave trade on the west coast of Africa had previously been concentrated on other well-known centers from Gorée in the far west, via Elmina and other forts on the Gold Coast, to Ouidah, which waxed on the supply of slaves available as a consequence of the wars engaged in by the aggressive kingdom of Dahomey, at its zenith in the eighteenth century. The maritime-inclined Portuguese had been, in Hugh Thomas' expression, one of the main "managers" of the Atlantic trade from its inception, although by the eighteenth century the British had taken pride of place.

The equatorial island of São Tomé in particular had for two centuries been one of the main pivots of the Portuguese trade. Towards the end of the eighteenth century there was a switch of focus to Lagos, partly because of the same question of availability of supply, but also because it had become a more notable center of commercial activity, and in Oba Akinsemoyin there was a ruler the Portuguese felt they could do business with. Although he was of Bini lineage descended from Ado, after a century the peculiar cross-cultural nature of Lagos had begun to leave its mark. There has always, however, been a Bini quarter of Isale Eko (the area in the immediate vicinity of the Oba's palace, the Iga Idunganran). As Lagos developed as a slave port in the late eighteenth century, and then opened up to a wider range of trade and influence, the Oba's power as an independent entity became more significant. As Dele Cole says in his book *Traditional and Modern Elites in 19th Century Lagos*: "Foreign trade, rather than the Oba of Benin's conquest, was responsible for the transformation of Lagos from an oligarchy to a kingdom."

The varying Benin and Awori versions of Lagos history are still the subject of argument among historians. It is not, however, that one can positively state that there is a Benin version and an Awori version of early Lagos history—there are merely differences of emphasis. What is certain is that there was from early in the town's history a multi-ethnic crossroads, a melting pot or "gene pool" which attracted more and more ingredients, and that while the unique culture of traditional Lagos is the result of a synthesis of these two original components, many other elements very soon became added. Indeed, the concept of a gene pool is one of the most important defining characteristics of the city. It may sometimes seem to be a quintessentially Yoruba city in terms of its basic culture, but it has always been able to encompass a larger view, perhaps the outstanding example of the legendary inclusiveness of Yoruba culture.

It is generally accepted that it was the Portuguese who gave the city its name of Lagos, but there is hardly any evidence that it entered into current usage until the second half of the eighteenth century, and even then it was not widely used. Although (as recorded above) the traveler Sequeira had first recorded visiting the place in 1472, and Pacheco had dismissed it as being of no interest a few years later, the Portuguese had been a presence elsewhere on the West African coast for some time. This presence was maintained in Angola and São Tomé as well as Bissau and Casamance. In spite of Portugal's loss of sovereignty to Spain from 1580 to 1640 and constant attacks on its imperial pretensions by the stronger British, French and Dutch, Portugal's outposts were maintained, perhaps because of its strong maritime vocation which found expression in an interest in trade, especially the slave trade. The Portuguese found a historic opportunity to establish themselves on the island in the lagoon in the second half of that century after the Akinsemoyin deal.

It is not clear when the name of Lagos came into wide usage, especially as the frequent retrospective and unhistorical use of the name by most people who write of it sometimes adds to the confusion. John Adams, who visited on two occasions between 1786 and 1800, calls it Lagos in his account, which was written in 1826. In some official documents the Portuguese refer to it as Onim, which was probably another Bini name for it, although it never seems to have had wide usage.

Most likely, it had been given its name by the eighteenth-century Portuguese (in the manner of other Europeans finding themselves needing to name outposts in new countries) because of the town of Lagos in southern Portugal, especially as it was a port, similarly named after neighboring stretches of water. The word *lago* in Portuguese means "lake" and so Lagos means "lakes," while strictly speaking the Portuguese word for lagoon is *laguna*.

The Portuguese found that the port, for all its inconveniences, was a new opening for the slave trade—having been excluded from the more popular slaving ports further west along the coast developed by the British, Dutch and French. The Portuguese had also established strong ties with the monarchy. Adams records that Ologun Kutere (1775-1805), who picked up and consolidated what Akinsemoyin had begun in these relations, had received lavish gifts from the Portuguese traders, finding

> articles of trade, and costly presents in a state of dilapidation; namely, rolls of tobacco, boxes of pipes, cases of gin, ankers of brandy, pieces of cloth of Indian and European manufacture, iron bars, earthenware, a beautiful hand-organ, the bellows of which were burst; two elegant chairs of state, having rich crimson damask covers… and two expensive sofas.

The increased wealth which the trade brought to the city permitted what was now a city state to pursue a more active foreign policy, not just in asserting a hold on Badagry, which needed help against Dahomey, but also in the first rudimentary exercises of diplomacy—the sending of missions (Ambassadors of Onim) to both the court in Lisbon and to the Governor of Bahia in Brazil. After Brazil's independence in 1822 there were attempts to establish diplomatic relations between Lagos and Salvador da Bahia on a more permanent basis.

The Early Nineteenth-century Context: The Ending of the Slave Trade and the Yoruba Wars

The Lagos of the late eighteenth century is described by John Adams as having a population of about 5,000 with a small international merchant community living off not just slavery but other forms of trade. Apart from the Portuguese a mixture of peoples from different areas to the north was starting to develop, including the beginnings of a small Muslim community, partly of Hausa and more particularly Nupe origins, which is first recorded in the eighteenth century. Then early in the next century Lagos began to feel the impact of several international developments. First among these was a consequence of the French Revolution, which in 1793 had abolished slavery in France's New World possessions and the start of a campaign against the West African slave trade.

Amidst all the self-congratulatory enthusiasm in 2007 for the bicentenary of the British abolition of the slave trade, it was barely mentioned that the French had done it fourteen years before, and between 1793 and 1797 French naval squadrons swept the west coast of Africa arresting slavers and their ships, including particularly British ones. It only lasted for a decade, before Napoleon re-imposed the slave trade, but it disrupted the west coast slave trade, removing the French slavers from the picture and giving more opportunities for the Lagos market, which also offered a safe haven.

Some scholars suggest that the Portuguese slave trade from Lagos, although beginning in the late eighteenth century, only really took off after about 1820, so in historical terms it was a fairly short-lived experience. Paradoxically the independence of Brazil may well also have given the Portuguese/Brazilian slave trade a boost in this period (slave trading to Brazil and Cuba continued until the 1860s). Although in line with most other European countries the Portuguese officially abolished the slave trade in 1836, it carried on in clandestine form, as it was still profitable, and Lagos, to which the Portuguese had privileged access, became one of the centers of activity. It is said that the Portuguese expression "for English eyes," used in Brazil when engaged in a deception, comes from the slave traders' experience with the Royal Navy anti-slavery squadron.

At the same time, the intensification of the Yoruba wars, following the collapse of Old Oyo (capital of the old Yoruba Empire) in the wake of the jihad of Uthman dan Fodio in what later became Northern Nigeria, increased both the marketing possibilities for slaves to the south, and the sanctuary of towns. The demise of Owu and the destruction of old Egba towns in the 1820s led to a series of wars which meant that for the first time Yoruba people were offering their kinsmen for sale to the slavers, where previously they had only been traders in peoples whose origins were to the north of Yorubaland.

Lastly and most significantly, the abolition of the trade by the British in 1807 brought into being the Royal Navy's West Africa Squadron which put more pressure on Lagos. Abolition also created a situation for the further diversification of the Lagos "gene pool" with the introduction of returned slaves, both the Saros (Sierra Leonean Creoles) and the Brazilians (called both *amaro* and *aguda*). Even before the British intervention in Lagos in 1851 a small population of both Saros and Brazilians had built up in Lagos. Mabogunje says that there were 250 Saros and some 150 Brazilian families. Saros from Freetown had saved money to hire a vessel in 1838 to take them along the coast, and they recognized that Lagos had been their port of embarkation.

The early influx was made easier by the fact that, from the early 1840s onwards, for a number of reasons the British patrols became more active. Oba Kosoko, however, was hostile to the immigrants when he became Oba after 1846 and there was an episode in 1850 when he had a number of Saros killed. The influx only really took off after the British took *de facto* control in 1851, when there was a need to repopulate since half the population had fled with Kosoko from the bombardment, and the missionaries also moved in to establish a presence.

Slavery itself was abolished by Britain between 1833 and 1838 in the West Indies and wherever British writ ran. Important pressure for yet further action by Britain came from the missionaries. It was in 1841 that Thomas Fowell Buxton published his *African Slave Trade: A Remedy* in which he recommended that as well as using the naval blockade plus diplomacy to end the slave trade, the problem could be tackled at source. Inspired by the Lander brothers' Niger expedition of the 1830s, he proposed pioneer sorties in the interior to make treaties with chiefs to show them the possibilities of private capital. Conceived from a missionary point of view, this idea came at the same time as a new burst of missionary activity which accompanied a push to expand and, ultimately, to colonize.

BEHIND THE BRITISH INTERVENTION: THE ROLE OF PALMERSTON

This is where the context both of events and personalities becomes important. In the first half of the nineteenth century, especially after the peace of 1815, Britain enjoyed an unprecedented freedom of action in foreign policy because of its unrivaled domination of the seas. As the Victorian period began, there were increasing signs that two of the characteristics of that era were converging in pursuit of the utilitarian notion, popularized by Bentham and Adam Smith, of gaining benefit from doing good. These ideas fed the element of moral superiority around the anti-slavery movement, which also enveloped the pursuit of free trade, in both of which the role of the Royal Navy was paramount. The increasing demand for palm oil, for both sanitary and industrial purposes, pointed to an ideal alternative to slaves. The more vigorous prosecution of the battle against the slave trade in the 1840s also coincided with the campaign by free-traders against the Corn Laws, repealed in 1846 in a political convulsion that caused the fall of the government of Robert Peel.

The influence of personalities comes into play significantly here, for the change in Westminster and the return of the Whigs in 1846 saw the return as Foreign Secretary of Sir William Henry Temple, Lord Palmerston, who was to play a crucial determining role in the history of Lagos, and in the eventual British takeover. But who was he? Palmerston had made his mark as a robust and independent-minded Foreign Secretary throughout the 1830s, but these successes had been mainly in European and Middle Eastern politics. His tendency to act on impulse meant that he and his foreign policy never had an easy ride, and his view of foreign affairs had many critics and opponents, but he always had a measure of popular support. This was seen above all in the Don Pacifico affair of 1850 (in which a gunboat was sent to the Aegean in support of a British citizen of Gibraltarian extraction). In a famous five-hour speech in the House of Commons in which Palmerston proclaimed the right of any British citizen anywhere in the world to be protected by the strong arm of British government, using the dictum *Civis Romanus sum*, he managed to survive impeachment. But he had also intervened the year before in the affair of British citizens attacked in Rio Nunez (further westwards along the West African coast).

While Palmerston was in interventionist mode and enjoying populist success, the pressures to do something about Lagos were increasing. The "missionary party" based in Abeokuta (capital of the Egba Yoruba state) mounted a particularly effective lobby, bringing the eminent churchman Samuel Ajayi Crowther (a returned slave from Oyo who came back to near to his homeland: see Chapter 8) to London. While he was there, Palmerston and Prime Minister Russell arranged for Crowther to meet Queen Victoria and Prince Albert, to argue the case for intervening in Lagos.

All the records suggest that in the takeover of Lagos it was Palmerston who was the prime mover. Although others on the ground such as Beecroft, who had been made the first and only consul for the Bights of Benin and Biafra in 1849 (perhaps with a pro-active move in mind), and Commander H.W. Bruce of the Royal Navy West Africa Squadron implemented the policy, it is clear they felt they had cover from Palmerston.

Left: Lord Palmerston: "a crucial determining role in the history of Lagos"

Below: Bishop Samuel Ajayi Crowther: "an increasingly uneasy conflict with the missionaries"

In response to messages from Beecroft and Bruce in February 1851 recommending the use of force to bring Lagos to heel, it was Palmerston who sent two vital dispatches.

The first dispatch authorized the signing of an abolitionist treaty with the ruler of Lagos; the second said that it should be represented to the same ruler that "the British Government is resolved to bring to an end the African Slave Trade, and has the means and power to do so." The dispatch gained in menace as it continued, insisting that Kosoko should be told that "Great Britain is a strong power both by sea and by land, that her friendship is worth having, and that her displeasure it is well to avoid." If he refused this advice and the signing of an anti-slave trade treaty he should be reminded, in language redolent of classic Palmerstonian gunboat diplomacy, that "Lagos is near to the sea, and that on that sea are the ships and cannon of England; and also to bear in mind that he does not hold his authority without a competitor, and that the chiefs of the African tribes do not always retain their authority to the end of their lives."

Palmerston always linked the ending of the slave trade indissolubly with promoting commerce, and indeed with free trade, the golden principle of the age for the British in their period of supremacy. In a minute to the Foreign Office in December 1850, he wrote that his like-minded supporters,

> wishing most earnestly that civilization may be extended in Africa, being convinced that commerce is the best pioneer for civilization, and being satisfied that there is room enough in... Africa for the commerce of all the civilized nations of the rest of the world, would see with pleasure every advance of commerce in Africa, provided that such commerce was not was not founded on monopoly and was not conducted upon an exclusive system.

This was a plausible stating of the case, but it was ultimately the disguised language of imperial domination. Robinson and Gallagher in *Africa and the Victorians* explain Palmerston's policy thus: "Free trade was the necessary condition for improving Africa. To apply this policy properly, Palmerston saw the need to set up bases from which order, trade and the useful arts could radiate through Africa." It may have seemed hardly necessary that these bases should be annexed, as the policy had been successfully applied without conquest by "the Palmerstonians" elsewhere (China, Turkey, Morocco); on several occasions he had proposed that the big slaving port of Whydah to the west be turned into another Lagos, under the same kind of remote control.

Armed with Palmerston's endorsement, Consul Beecroft and the Royal Navy combined to stage the deposition of Kosoko and the installation of Akitoye. The first attempt in November 1851 was bungled, in part because of a serious under-estimation of Kosoko's defenses and capacity for resistance, but the second bid, which began on Boxing Day, eventually succeeded by superior fire-power and, according to Consul Beecroft, the destruction of half of Lagos. Kosoko and many of his supporters fled to Epe, so the town occupied was a partly deserted ruin (for a full account of this episode, which was effectively the beginning of the British takeover of the area that became Nigeria, see Chapter 6). It was a triumph of force of arms (and for British domestic opinion a blow against the slave trade) but it was not a victory to the long-term credit of the British, even if it changed history forever. Robert S. Smith in *The Lagos Consulate 1856-1861* says judiciously: "the defence of Lagos in November and December 1851 was one of the most determined attempts by Africans to resist the conquest of their continent by the European invaders of the 19ᵗʰ century." The Lagos Consulate was formally established in 1852, and an anti-slavery treaty signed with Akitoye.

1851-61: FROM THE CONSULATE TO THE TREATY OF CESSION

Ironically, Palmerston himself had been forced to resign in mid-December 1851 over his unwise recognition of the coup d'état of Napoleon III in Paris, so when the completion of the overthrow of Kosoko took place at the end of that month "Lord Pumice Stone" was no longer in office. When the news of the event reached London two months later, Earl Granville, who was briefly Palmerston's successor at the Foreign Office, rebuked Beecroft weakly for exceeding his instructions: "if the chief of Lagos refused to abandon the slave trade, you were to remind him of British power, but not directed to immediately begin hostilities". But the die had been cast. As on many other occasions, the *fait accompli* prevailed.

Looking at Britain's sometimes stealthy, sometimes blatant, imperial adventures, it should not go unremarked that 1851, the year which ended with the exercise in gunboat diplomacy in Lagos, was also the year of the Great Exhibition, a seminal moment of Victorian self-confidence putting on display all the wonders of the Industrial Revolution and new inventions such as railways, gas lighting and sanitation (including the newly popularized water-closet, a major feature at the Great Exhibition), all there to be exported to a waiting world. The power of trade in the Victorian psyche is a more convincing historical explanation of the events of 1851, however much it was dressed up in the moral fervor of eliminating the slave trade. The respected Nigerian historian Professor Ade-Ajayi has some very terse comments on British motives, questioning both official and unofficial British interpretations, which have proved remarkably durable in putting the event entirely in the context of suppression of the slave trade:

> The anxiety of Britain to intervene in Lagos was not just the philanthropic desire to destroy the slave trading activities of the Portuguese and Brazilians there, but also the economic desire to control the trade of Lagos from which they had hitherto been excluded and from where they hoped to exploit the resources of the vast country stretching to and beyond the Niger.

In the cold light of history there is a certain inevitability in the way Britain progressed from the 1851 bombardment (which restored a deposed ruler by external force of arms just as surely and brutally as in the twentieth century the French deposed the infamous Emperor Bokassa and replaced him with the virtual puppet David Dacko in the Central African Republic) to the signing of the Treaty of Cession in 1861. The logic of power was remorselessly at work despite reluctance among bureaucrats in London to make new commitments. In its intervention Britain had cracked the power of Kosoko, a much more authoritative ruler (see profile in Chapter 6) than either Akitoye or his son Dosunmu (spelt Docemo at the time, an alternative spelling that endures), who succeeded on Akitoye's death in 1853; this simply meant storing up trouble unless they moved in more effectively. Robinson and Gallagher write:

> With its slave trade gone, and its rulers over-awed by Palmerston's gunboats, the independence of Lagos existed on paper only; and when in

1861 it was decided to annex the port, the Foreign Office decided that the change would be slight since "the Consul has for some years been the ruler of the place". Britain had yet another possession on the west coast. The Colonial Office was disgusted—"Lagos is a deadly gift from the Foreign Office," wrote one of its advisers... All the same, on Palmerstonian principles the move was right.

The twists and turns of the intervening ten years, under a series of resident consuls, are told in great detail with an expert marshaling of evidence in Smith's *The Lagos Consulate 1851-1861*. He highlights the increasing need to intervene in local politics, which meant facing reality and coming to some kind of accommodation with Kosoko and some of his powerful allies in their alternative base in Epe, especially as they were using their position there to divert the valuable palm oil trade from Ijebu away from Lagos to the two ports that came under Kosoko's control at Lekki and Palma—also still being used by him and his entourage for the export of slaves.

Moreover, the mere act of installing a consul undermined the Oba's position, and there were many policy disagreements. From his very weakness he had had to concede important stretches of land along the south side of the island to both merchants and missionaries. Ade-Ajayi tells us that by 1861 Lagos had "virtually become a protectorate." At the same time, to make sure that the bridgehead established for Britain after the intervention was not reversed, and that others did not step in—notably the French who were increasingly active in Porto Novo along the other end of the lagoon—the demands from Britain for consolidation, especially from the missionary party, began to grow.

The pro-annexation lobby was fortunate in that the British Prime Minister by this time was none other than the same Lord Palmerston who had encouraged the original "gunboat diplomacy" ten years earlier. Although this was still in the period of the title of John Hargreaves' excellent book *Prelude to the Partition of West Africa*, the interactions of European diplomacy were already having their effect. Palmerston was particularly concerned that Lagos, having been drawn into the British sphere of influence, should not be lost to France. This was especially true at a time when he was planning increased British investment in trade on the Niger, notably after McGregor Laird's ground-breaking expedition of 1857. The activities of the Marseille-based trader Victor Régis the Elder (Régis Aîné), was also of concern to the Palmerstonians. Régis had close links with Kosoko, and was established in Lekki and Palma after Kosoko's exile to Epe, still apparently trading slaves as well as palm oil.

The actual pretext for compelling Oba Dosunmu (Docemo) to sign the Treaty of Cession was the threat posed to Lagos by the war in 1860 between the new power of Ibadan and Ijaye in alliance with Abeokuta and Ijebu. This conflict posed a threat to the commercial position of Lagos, and the British were concerned at the increased risk of instability. Professor Ade-Ajayi says that it was "an important factor" in Palmerston's decision. The first move was made by Bedingfield on the *Prometheus* on 20 July 1861, and after some skirmishing and demonstrations of power Oba Dosunmu (Docemo) and his chiefs put their marks on the Treaty of Cession on 6 August (see also "1861: the Crunch" in Chapter 6). Thus in the space of less than three weeks, the remains of the independence of Lagos had been signed away.

The town of Lagos in 1851 had already also began to attract a group of mainly European merchants (a motley international crew) eroding the Portuguese/Brazilian supremacy; they were principally involved in slaving, although as that practice became excluded they switched to the lucrative trade in palm oil produced in the Yoruba hinterland. It was also believed that the hinterland had great potential for cotton growing, for which the mills of Lancashire had permanent demand.

Just as Eric Williams, in *Capitalism and Slavery*, argued that the abolition from 1807 onwards only came about because the infamous trading in slaves to the Caribbean had lost its vitality as Britain was switching from a mercantilist to an industrial economy, many academics now argue that in West Africa the pressure to expand trade in other commodities, above all palm oil, whose suppliers would also provide a market for the products of new industries, brought additional incentives for pursuing the abolition of the slave trade. It had certainly been in the mind of Lord Palmerston when he sought to pursue proactive policies in West Africa, within which Lagos was just a stepping-stone.

The term "palm-oil ruffians" was applied more to the buccaneering characters who plied their trade in the Niger Delta, but the crude entrepreneurs were also known in Lagos. They were not so different from the slavers who frequented the place before 1851, and in many cases were the same people, the ones whom Sir Richard Burton, the Victorian traveler and eccentric, had seen as having in those "merry days… nothing to do but sleep or smoke, with an occasional champagne tiffin on the beach" and who had become "condemned by hard times to such grovelling work as selling palm oil." The Church Missionary Society's Hinderer was glad to have the consul as a neighbor rather than a "noisy palm oil merchant".

In 1861, although the slave trade was officially no more, Burton writes of mysterious individuals who landed from his boat:

> They are dark, but European or Brazilian; they speak Portuguese, travel under aliases—today Soarez, tomorrow Pieri—and they herd together. One claims to have been a lieutenant in some royal navy. They have visited England to lay in a further stock of money for the next cargo of 'casimir noir', and with a view to medical assistance. They are worn out by excessive devotions at the shrine of Venus, and they seem to live chiefly on tobacco smoke. Part of their game is to supply naval officers with champagne and excellent cigars; to ask them to dinner, and to offer equality with them, as if both were of the same trade.

The two-stage British annexation of 1851-61 was a great climacteric moment of confusion and turbulence in the history of the city. What was happening, in slow motion, was a shameless piece of colonial appropriation, even if the highest motives were claimed and believed. Akitoye had in fact been a slaver too, as Scala and others have pointed out, but for the British it was enough that he was ready to renounce slavery in order to get his job back. The churchmen also used him for their own purposes without respecting him. Whatever one may think of the morality of the operation, it shook things up irreversibly.

The annexation also added to the complexity of the city, and not only because of the influx of the British, of whom in the early years there were never very many, as there was an unfortunate propensity among the consuls to die off, which was why the consulate building was described by Burton as "the iron coffin." Consul Benjamin Campbell (1853-58) was one of the longer stayers, but he too died on the job. The arrival of the British meant the establishment of different clearly defined quarters, with the colonials and the merchants located along the Marina, which was one of the earliest streets they constructed.

SIERRA LEONEANS AND BRAZILIANS: SAROS AND AMAROS

The Sierra Leoneans or Saros (mainly people freed from slave ships and re-settled in Freetown, and their descendants) particularly entered Lagos on the back of the missionaries' activities, some of which had been based in Abeokuta, capital of the Egba kingdom, which had initially been more receptive to Christianity—Lagos being seen by the missionaries as a sink of iniquity because of the slavers. Indeed, Saros were among the foremost in advocating a British takeover of Lagos. A few had already made their way there: many were among those liberated by navy patrols and taken to Freetown who then chose to make their way back to their place of origin.

The head of the Saro community, "Daddy" William Akilade Savage, was granted by Akitoye the district of Olowogbowo at the far west of the island, near to the port area, which had been virtually destroyed in the British bombardment, with its residents fleeing with Kosoko to Epe. The Oba also recognized the Sierra Leone Association, which Glover later said "in the days of Consul Campbell ruled both the King and Lagos," although Glover himself was not so close to the Saros.

Apart from providing the missionaries with congregations as well as assistants, catechists and others like Ajayi Crowther who eventually became church leaders, the educated and literate Saros were also the mainstay of the administration. Robert Smith notes one Adeduju as the first local (i.e. non-Saro) Lagosian convert to the Church Missionary Society, but conversion was a slow process as the Yoruba pantheon had, and still has, a remarkable resilience and hold on the spiritual imagination.

The last two decades of the nineteenth century saw the Lagos Saros come into their own, as the principal adjuncts of the still not very numerous British because of their leading role in education, the church and the professions, and their aspirations to be part of the upper echelon of society. The many Johnsons and Williamses, the Coles, the Cokers and the Macaulays were having their moment in the sun, reinforced by the continued ties maintained with Freetown. During this period many of them went back to Freetown to go to Fourah Bay College for higher education, which, unbelievably, was only introduced in Lagos in the 1930s with the first medical school and Yaba College. Those who could afford it also found education in Britain, again following the example of Freetown.

The Brazilians ("Amaros" or "Agudas") were not so education-oriented, nor were they encouraged to be, but many were skilled craftsmen and artisans concentrated in the area behind the Marina, notably Odun-lami, Kakawa and Bamgbose Streets, Campos Square and Igbosere Road. From very early on, this area was known as Portuguese Town, or Oke Popo. Sometimes the terms "Portuguese" and "Brazilian" were interchangeable. There were also some returnees from Cuba who gravitated to the same area, and there was a little Brazilian quarter at Queen Street, Yaba, but they were mostly concentrated on Lagos Island.

They were not like the Saro "recaptives" or "interceptees" from the Middle Passage, but they were still victims of the Portuguese trade from Lagos in the early nineteenth century, so many knew where they had come from and their African names. They had their own practices and customs, including exuberant festivals like the Caretta, practiced to this day, and enjoyed culinary delights such as Frechon, a dish with fish and rice and black beans with coconut milk eaten on Good Friday. They were also at the origin of the thriving Roman Catholic community which developed in the city, whose more relaxed approach sometimes caused tensions with some of the more austere Church Missionary Society militants.

There were a surprising number of Brazilian Muslims, who had re-mained of the faith even when transported to Brazil. Some early returnees had been forcibly repatriated following the Muslim slave uprising in the 1830s that had been known as the "jailed jihad." Others converted on their return as a way of gaining greater respect in traditional society. Indeed, Islam won the adherence of the great majority of indigenous Lagosians, especially when Kosoko's people returned from Epe in the 1860s, settling around Oke Suna in Isale Eko. Islam was considered much more in tune with the local way of life than Christianity, in spite of the strong syncretist element in Brazilian Catholicism.

THE GROWING GENE POOL

There is still the perennial question of "who are the Lagosians?" We have already looked at the Awori-Benin duality, and the Saro-Amaro influx, but the identity question involves the Yoruba nature of Lagos, including the city's vitally important melting-pot overlay originating from different parts of Yorubaland. Most notably they were Egba, but the Ijebu factor was also always a strong element in Lagos. Even now, probably over eighty per cent of the population of Lagos remains Yoruba.

The strong nexus between the Egba and Saro communities in Lagos was partly due to the fact that important members of the Saro community had known of their Egba origin. They played an important role in the group of missionaries established in Abeokuta, where they entered in the early 1840s via Badagry because of the highly unreceptive nature of the slaving center of Lagos. For historical reasons the Egbas had been more receptive to Christians (Burton mocks Charles Kingsley's reference in his novel *Westward Ho!* to "Christian Abeokuta"). The missionaries, both European and Saro, desperately wanted the British to intervene—a classic illustration of the extent to which evangelization supported imperial expansion at this time.

The Egba enthusiasm for the British waned rapidly. Glover's sympathies for Ibadan and his shelling of the Egbas in Abeokuta in 1867 led to a movement to Lagos, and the settlement of Christianized Egbas in Ebute Metta and the founding of St. Jude's Church there. This reinforced the already strong Egba-Lagos nexus.

From the 1860s onwards the Egbas became one of the main points of resistance to British encroachment. After the development of the Southern Nigeria Protectorate from the 1890s the obstacle of Egba separatism and independence of spirit meant that the brutal conquest of Abeokuta in 1914 by Governor-General Lugard and the crushing of the subsequent rising in 1918, clinically described in Harry Gailey Jr.'s book *Lugard and the Abeokuta Rising*, hurt even more deeply. Apart from the Egba presence in Lagos Oyo, other Yoruba states—Ibadan, Ife and Ijesha and in particular Ijebu—all had pockets of settlers in Isale Eko.

There was also an important Nupe element in cosmopolitan Lagos, which came in part because in the early nineteenth century the ancient Nupe kingdom by the Niger some hundreds of miles inland (described lovingly in Siegfried Nadel's 1961 study *Black Byzantium*) was caught up in both Dan Fodio's conquest and the spill-over of the Yoruba wars. There were almost certainly Nupes among the mercenaries known as "Glover's Hausa" whom he took to Lagos with him after moving from Baikie's ill-fated 1857 Niger expedition overland to Lagos (see profile of Glover in Chapter 8). Many Nupes were slaves who had risen in their masters' households, such as the remarkable Oshodi Tapa (see profile in Chapter 8), or had bought their way out.

There is considerable evidence, however, that there were Hausas (a term often used as a generic name for people from all that part of the interior lying north of Yorubaland) present in Lagos as early as the eighteenth century, often for military or policing purposes, but also as preachers and kola nut merchants as well as herdsmen bringing their cattle, a sight that can still be seen. The Nupes, although different from the Hausas, had a very distinctive Lagos connection that still survives. Even now in Epetedo (the area of Isale Eko inhabited by those who returned with Kosoko from Epe in 1862, including Oshodi Tapa himself) there is an annual Nupe festival.

CITY OF RELIGIONS

Perhaps the most significant example of the true and remarkable diversity of Lagos is the peaceful coexistence of great religions. The most fundamental phenomenon is the traditional, vibrant belief in the Yoruba pantheon which goes way back into the deep history of the Yoruba people and has its own beliefs and practices such as masquerades and festivals, and the complex system of divination known as Ifa. In Lagos there remain Ifa festivals such as the one held in Ebute Metta in July, one among many. The Oba of Lagos is still a central figure in the city's traditional culture. This was witnessed in a most powerful way at the 2003 coronation of Oba

Eyo masqueraders

Akiolu I. The attachment to the traditional that lies at the heart of the city's culture is not immediately apparent to outsiders and visitors. It can be seen in the perpetuation of the Eyo ceremony held on the occasion of the death of an Oba or other prominent Lagosians, which has now, to the regret of some purists, been expunged of some of its more unusual and harsher aspects in the interests of making it a powerful tourist attraction.

One of the most important results of the British takeover of Lagos was the final arrival of Christianity. From 1840 onwards there had been a rise in the impulse to proselytize in Europe, and teams of missionaries went from Britain and Germany in particular. The early Victorian British, both of the Anglican Church Missionary Society and from the Wesleyans, took part of the growing evangelical movement. Some had been inspired by the Fowell Buxton pamphlet already mentioned and, already having footholds in Freetown and the Gold Coast as well as Calabar, targeted the notorious "slave coast" with an eye on the hardest nut to crack, Lagos.

With the establishment of the Consulate in 1852, the missionaries were invited in, beginning with the CMS. They established the first Anglican Church, St. Paul's Breadfruit Street, which began as a bamboo shed on the site where slaves were tied to the breadfruit trees, but acquired a contiguous site in 1859 where a church was built in 1880. Apart from Christ's Church on the Marina, it was the most significant Lagos church, although by 1890 there six parish churches had been built. The present magnificent wedding cake of Christ Church Cathedral was erected in the 1920s. The Wesleyans (Methodists) also came at the same time and built a chapel further down the Marina, putting up a church in Olowogbowo in the 1880s. At the same time an essential part of the evangelizing mission was the establishment of schools, and so there was first of all the CMS Grammar School (1859) followed by the Methodist Boys School (1879), the Catholic St. Gregory's College (1886) and the Baptist Academy (1891).

There have been many critics of the high-handed and insensitive approach of the missionaries to the societies they targeted, but of the impact of their work through the promotion of literacy there can be no doubt. It bore fruit in the generation that flourished towards the end of the century, which sought to establish itself as the next social layer after the British, and proved to be an essential foundation for modernity. However, as the sense of empire grew in Britain, so also did alienation in its new African outposts. As Leo Spitzer has written of the Creoles of Sierra Leone, whose sentiments were reflected among the Saros in Lagos, "When British deeds and attitudes towards educated Africans became more negative as the century progressed, educated Creoles deviated from the starry-eyed idealisation of Britain and her aims. They began to feel betrayed, scorned."

The difficult subject of Saro relations with the colonial British will be treated in greater detail in Chapter 2. In the context of Christianity's expansion, it led directly to the growth of African churches. Bishop Crowther, that most dedicated of missionaries and believer in the virtues of the British Empire, came increasingly into uneasy conflict with the CMS. Above all James "Holy" Johnson, vicar of St. Paul's Breadfruit Street for more than twenty years, attacked the increasing racial arrogance of the missionaries (see profiles of Crowther and Johnson in Chapter 6). The secessionist churches of the 1890s, whose most notable monument is Bethel Cathedral of the African Church in Broad Street, were the precursors of more remarkable independent apostolic churches of the early 1920s and 1930s such as the Church of the Lord Aladura and the Cherubim and Seraphim, still to be found among the more recent crop of evangelical churches in Lagos.

There is a remarkably strong population of Muslims in Lagos; indeed, in the early years of the twentieth century there were more Muslims than Christians, the numerical balance only tilting in favor of Christians around 1950. There was a presence from the eighteenth century due in part to the twin phenomena of war and trade, and the community that developed included many Hausas brought in by the British for their security forces. The Muslim population grew substantially in the nineteenth century, paradoxically furthered by the arrival of the British, who encouraged immigration into Lagos. The Muslim presence was actively aided by Governor Glover in the 1860s, especially, as we have seen, after he facilitated the return of Kosoko from Epe.

Burton, writing in 1862, provides a picture of the relatively small Muslim population of Lagos of some 800, noting that they had achieved a political importance and that "those wearing turbans," some of whom were light-skinned, had been among the bravest and most active opponents in the military action of December 1851. He exchanged alms and kola nuts with one of their leaders, Shaykh Ali, who had wandered from

Tripoli and knew Borno, Sokoto and Adamawa, and who wanted Burton to return with him.

An important agent of the spread of Islam in Lagos came through the Shitta-Bey family. They were of Saro descent—Saliu Shitta, a prominent Freetown Muslim scholar who had been the Imam at Fourah Bay, had traveled to Lagos in 1844 in the company of several Sierra Leonean Muslims (the Saros were highly identified with Christianity, but Freetown had its Muslim community) and settled in Badagry, where there had already been a group of Muslim immigrants from Oyo since 1821. In 1852 they moved to Lagos (following the Mewu chieftaincy crisis in Badagry) and settled with other Saro returnees in Olowogbowo. There was already an important community of Muslims in Lagos, both Yoruba and non-Yoruba, especially Hausa and Nupe. Siyan Oyeweso in his book *Prominent Yoruba Muslims* notes a number of leading Saro Muslims in the 1850s, including Muhammed Savage, Amodu Carew and Abdallah Cole. More unusually there were also Brazilian Muslims, who, as noted above, had taken their religion from Nigeria to Brazil.

Saliu Shitta's son Mohammed rose to prominence as a Lagos merchant (see profile in Chapter 6), and was the leading light behind the campaign to secure the building of the city's first mosque in 1894. The title Bey was added to his name by the Sultan of the Ottoman Empire in the same year, and the Shitta-Bey Mosque is still one of the architectural wonders of Lagos. The building, the work of Brazilian masons, has survived and is still an astonishing example of adapted Brazilian architecture, though it is sad that the old Central Mosque, an even more splendid example of the specifically Brazilian style, was demolished in the 1950s.

Muslims, through their own involvement in trade, acquired wealth and, although they had been disadvantaged educationally vis-à-vis the Christian elite, made rapid strides to catch up, especially through the Ansar-ud-Deen movement founded in the 1920s. This sought to found Muslims schools, which also provided Western education. The reformist Ahmadiyya movement, which came to Nigeria around 1910, also attracted many supporters despite its history of problems with other movements. Its motto "hatred for none" and its strong support for education, gave it enduring popularity, and it continues as the Anwar-ul-Islam.

Muslims soon became an increasingly important part of the elite, especially as they were well entrenched in traditional society. Most of the

The Shitta-Bey Mosque in Martins Street

Obas of Lagos have been Muslim, and Islam was always strongly rooted in Isale Eko from well before the British occupation. The Imam of Lagos, a Nupe who had been encouraged by Kosoko, fled with him to Epe. Yoruba families have often had a pragmatic attitude to imported religions, both Islam and Christianity, treating them almost as insurance policies for eternity which exist alongside the still significant traditional religion, even if it is said this has declined in the last thirty years. There were many Muslims among the Lebanese traders who found their way to Lagos and Kano as early as the 1880s, although there were also Maronite Christians. Since the creation of Lagos State in 1967, more Governors have been Muslim than not: both Governors Tinubu and Fashola are Muslim.

THE 1850S TO THE 1890S: THE BRITISH BECOME COLONIAL

Into this cauldron of different elements there came implacably, with the overweening authority of empire, the British. Relatively acceptable at first, there were at the beginning a few colonial officials, as well as the missionaries and businessmen. These included British (notably McCoskry, who arrived in 1853, see Chapter 6) and other Europeans, such as Sandeman, Giambattista Scala (the Sardinian consul who established the first brick kilns in Lagos), Germans including G. L. Gaiser and Diedrichsen, agent for Messrs Oswald of Hamburg, the French firm already cited, Régis Aîné, and one Mme. Pittiluga, "a spinster of Austrian descent." They were established on the shoreline (which later became the Marina), between the mission establishments. Where previously the Portuguese had had the commercial edge, the period from Akinsemoyin to Kosoko had marked the slow beginning of the international dimension of cosmopolitan Lagos, which was still basically trade-focused in spite of the British annexation.

By the 1880s the context had fundamentally changed. Power conflicts in Europe and its growing industrialization meant that attention began to return to the great and still largely untouched continent of Africa. The Berlin Conference of 1884-85 set the scene for the scramble for Africa to take off, although earlier maneuvers had indicated what was likely to happen. Not for nothing did George Taubman Goldie, the adventurer of the Niger Delta, actually go to Berlin to lobby successfully for the River Niger basin to remain a British sphere, against the intrusions of the French. There was a dramatic change of mood leading to the mad end-of-century *Zeitgeist* of theories of racial supremacy that made possible the high noon of serious empire, whereas earlier there had been cautious reluctance to get involved and more tolerance towards African peoples.

In Lagos, when the colony was placed under the authority of Freetown in 1872, there was a kind of pause for stocktaking, as the newly scrambled-together population of immigrants, indigenes and merchants began to find common cause in pressing the British to return authority there, writing petitions even to Lord Derby, the then Foreign Secretary. If the 1870s seemed inconsequential, it was in the next decade, after the seat of colonial government returned to Lagos in 1886 and a Governor was appointed, that the psychological transformation began as the authorities in London, aware of the evolution of matters in the Niger basin, applied a new concentration of effort. At the same time there was another important change from the beginning of the decade in the development of newspapers, fragile and with small circulation, but still a critical focus for a budding public opinion.

The British presence was always very small and, until the turn of the century and the discovery of the causes of malaria transmission, Britons faced constant health problems, so there was a need to entertain and depend on close relations with the local population, both migrant and indigenous, although Governors tended to keep traditional society at arm's length. The example of Glover, who according to R. J. Temple (in the foreword to Lady Glover's life of her husband) "endeared himself to the native population of Lagos," was exceptional.

Both Governors Moloney and Carter enjoyed a degree of popularity, certainly in comparison with some who came later. They oversaw material benefits, but this was also a period of consolidation. And if Carter was an expansionist who brought most of the Yoruba hinterland under British control, there were elements in Lagos that approved his actions, in the interest of freeing trade. That had been one of Glover's purposes, which had even got him into trouble.

It was in the 1890s that the British started coming to Lagos in greater numbers. Joseph Chamberlain's organizing and building up of the Colonial Office was an important factor, but this was also the decade when the British control of the hinterland beyond Lagos became stronger and the shape of what was later to become Nigeria began to emerge, in a combination of treaty and conquest. In part it was due to the push of Goldie's new Royal Niger Company in the Delta and along the Niger, but then came Carter's annexation of Ijebu in 1892, and Lugard's move to Bussa in 1894 and his later epic sweep further north. At the same time the ruthless Benin expedition in 1897, which brutally crushed its independence, had a profound local impact both physically and psychologically. Suddenly a patchwork of arbitrary frontiers crept all over Africa, and the Niger basin was no exception. With the capitulation of Sokoto and Kano (1903) there was a great mass of territory acquired through a ruthless mix of conquest and purported treaties, giving Lagos a huge hinterland just as it was on the brink of making a great heave to be able to service it.

One major issue for successive Governors in Lagos concerned relations with those whom the British unashamedly called "the natives," and some did it better than others. The arrival of larger numbers of Colonial Office officials and the consequent displacement of often more qualified Africans, combined with the rise of racial attitudes, caused a progressive strengthening of nationalist feelings. This had been seen for some time in Christian circles, especially as already noted in circles around "Holy" Johnson at Breadfruit Street, even as the white missionaries demonstrated a parallel increase in attitudes of racial superiority.

These issues are discussed again in Chapter 3, but it is worth here citing Dele Cole, in his *Modern and Traditional Elites in the Politics of Lagos*: "With the expansion of the colonial service, and the resultant increase in whites in Lagos, the need to accept qualified black candidates into the white dominated elite social club was no longer pressing." The resulting disillusionment hit the Saros hardest, as they had been the most anxious to model themselves on the British. The rise of the African churches was paralleled by the development of "nativism," a back-to-the-land movement, but more particularly there was a unifying of the critics of the newly unattractive British rule. In Cole's words:

> By 1910, the old social distinction of Lagos—European, Brazilian, Saro and indigene—had become politically unreal. Instead there were two political divisions in Lagos, white and black. The blacks became a united opposition from 1897-1915, obstructing government policies on principle. The Seditious Offences Ordinance, the municipal rate proposals, the water rate scheme… are merely a few examples in a long list of protests by both sections of the black elite, both traditional and modern, against governmental measures.

Those who were perceived as bringing progress, such as Governors Moloney, Carter and McGregor, earned respect and had their authority accepted by the nascent indigenous political class, while Egerton (1907-12) and above all Lugard (1912-18) had more difficulty. Lagosians judged each British Governor on his actions and those that were found wanting became objects of attack, especially once the newspapers got into their stride. The sensitive issues of land and taxation for water, in particular, came to a head under the authoritarian Egerton. These antipathies became crystallized in the Lugard years, with some dramatic political side-effects (described in the profile of Lugard in Chapter 8).

After the turbulent period under Lugard, Clifford produced a new concordat, but he remained suspicious of political agitation, as seen in the handling of the National Congress of British West Africa movement which flowered briefly in the early 1920s. That collapsed due to internal problems, and the main agenda of Lagos politics became the rows among different tendencies of Lagos Muslims (which had political undertones) and the drawn-out affair of the deposition of the popular Eleko Oba Eshugbayi in favor of a dissident faction of the House of Docemo/Dosunmu in 1925. This was a bitter row, which went on for several years and engaged the nationalist politician Herbert Macaulay and the Nigerian National Democratic Party (NNDP), which he had founded in 1923—interestingly, with strong support from one of the active Muslim groups. The "Eleko affair" was a classically complex Lagos problem in which the colonial government found itself pitted against traditional authority, but it was seen by some as a distraction from nationalism. The seven-year exile of Eleko Eshugbayi ended in his return with the authority of the Obaship reinforced, although he did not live to benefit from it (see profile of the Eleko in Chapter 8).

The impact of the global depression after the boom of the 1920s was conspicuous and led to a new bout of political activity. The emergence of the Lagos (and then Nigerian) Youth Movement (NYM) was overtaken by the emergence of Nnamdi Azikiwe at the end of the 1930s to challenge the long supremacy of Macaulay. They eventually came together when Macaulay took on the role of elder statesman with the formation of the National Council of Nigeria and the Cameroons (NCNC) in 1946, just before he died.

After the political difficulties under Lugard and Clifford, the later British Governors Sir Donald Cameron (1932-37) and Sir Bernard Bourdillon (1937-43) both found ways of enjoying some kind of relatively positive rapport with the Nigerian people, especially Bourdillon. The fact of having a relaxed progressive in charge at a time of change during the Second World War meant that in the post-war turbulence Sir Arthur Richards had a harder time (see profiles of Bourdillon and Richards in Chapter 8).

The years between the wars were nonetheless a period of rapid development, though there had been major advances from the 1890s: innovations in sewerage, health, electricity (1894), the railway, the tram and above all the opening up of the port in 1924 following the dredging and clearing of the bar through construction of the mole. Following the horrendous epidemic of bubonic plague in the late 1920s a new effort at helping the city to progress was witnessed in the setting up of the Lagos Executive Development Board; this body continued the work of land reclamation which had been a continuous process almost since the arrival of the British.

The Modern Melting-pot

Thus the city was changing and growing in the inter-war period, facilitated by the development of rail and later road transport. Lagos became the microcosm of a whole country, attracting Nigerian "strangers" and notably the Igbos, whom demographic pressure pushed out to all commercial points of colonial Nigeria; they were first brought to Lagos by the railway for which they were a particularly influential workforce. The already-mentioned Hausas were from an early date involved in commodity trading (cattle and kola nuts) but they had been encouraged to get to Lagos even before the arrival of the British because of army recruitment. There is evidence from even the nineteenth century of a Hausa presence, although the term "Hausa" often became coterminous with "soldier" and then with "Northerner," as we have seen in connection with the Nupes. There is a particular concentration of Hausas, mainly butchers, in Agege.

Almost all the other ethnic groups that have been attracted have their own communities and congeries, all with their own self-help and improvement organizations. Being the federal capital made Lagos a crucible of Nigerian-ness, but being a commercial capital made it a Mecca for all. Peter Enahoro, a celebrated newspaper columnist in the 1960s under the soubriquet of "Peter Pan," wrote in his immortal short book *How to Be a Nigerian* (published in 1966) that "you can never become a true Nigerian until you have passed through the grill, come to Lagos, or at the very least, aspire to come to Lagos."

There was also a heavy non-Nigerian African dimension to the gene pool of the city of Lagos, with a growing population of other West Africans. The Saros and the Brazilians were all used to moving along the coast, but old trade routes were no respecter of colonial frontiers. And as Nigeria became more prosperous so the population swelled, especially after the oil boom of the 1970s. This was particularly true of Ghanaians, whose vast presence was highlighted at the time of the expulsion of aliens in early 1983—maybe 1.5 million left in a mass exodus, even though Ghana's own economy was at that time in crisis (one reason why they had moved out in the first place). The same migratory impulse applied to the Togolese and Dahomeyans/Béninois, often in the domestic service sector. There have also been Cameroonians who have a very special place in Nigeria's population (Anglophone British Southern Cameroons was once administered with Nigeria), deriving partly from colonial history, and, from further afield, the Congolese who have their own community concentrated on Lagos Island.

The latest addition to the Africans of Lagos are the South Africans, many of whom ironically are white Afrikaners, by a turn of the wheel of fortune of history. Post-apartheid South Africa has been able to do good business in Nigeria, from the mobile phones of MTN to the hotel chain Protea and security companies. South Africans can often be observed at the weekends at the pool at the Eko Hotel, but they tend to live in gated communities. From my own experience of living in Lagos from 2001 to 2002, I recall a certain Wayne who had been in the apartheid regime's special services in Angola, and was hating every minute of Nigeria. On the other hand there was the case of Australian-born Adrian Wood who, as CEO of MTN-Nigeria, became temporarily "Nigerianized."

Then there are the rest, who give Lagos a uniquely cosmopolitan feel—the French and other Europeans, the Lebanese/Syrians, the Cypriots, other Arabs, the Indians and Pakistanis, the Chinese and even Japanese, Iranians and Turks. Some came in with the embassies which have now mostly gone to Abuja, but often leaving commercial consulates. Others came as entrepreneurs, occasionally going into the restaurant business such as the important group of Hong Kong Chinese, although they also expanded into other industries. Alongside the considerable presence of those from the Peoples' Republic, they constitute an important feature of contemporary Lagos.

Is there any evidence of particular groups in particular areas? This was certainly the case in the nineteenth century, in Isale Eko and Lagos Island as a whole. When it came to separateness for Europeans, for a time British administrators of a more racist type encouraged segregation, especially in the planning of Ikoyi and GRA (Government Residential Area) Ikeja and particularly in the early twentieth century. There is, however, a natural tendency to merge and mingle in Lagos that has operated against too much segregation, so that it is much less evident than the sort of townships to be found in east and southern Africa, reaching its apogee in apartheid South Africa. There is still a certain class dichotomy, or perhaps it is just a case of split perceptions, between Island and Mainland (reiterated in subsequent chapters), but on the whole the "citiness" militates against intolerance, except when a mob mentality prevails, which alas is not unknown in Lagos.

THE STATUS OF LAGOS: CROWN COLONY TO STATE

The administrative status of Lagos, from its early vagaries, became settled in 1886 into that of a Crown Colony. It was divided into Lagos and Colony districts, together coterminous with what eventually became Lagos State. In the 1880s it was absorbed de facto into the developing protectorates of Yorubaland, falling effectively under three different groups of officials. In 1906 it was formally merged into the new Protectorate of Southern Nigeria, losing its treasured separate identity but retaining its colony status. From 1914, when the two protectorates of the north and the south were merged as a federation, it housed the federal capital (despite a proposal by Lugard in 1916 to move this to Kaduna or Zungeru in the north) at the same time as placing Lagos itself under administration of the southern provinces and running it from Yaba. None of this happened, as although technically Lagos came under the Southern Provinces, it was a reshuffling of titles. When, after the First World War, the Lagos Executive Council merged with the Nigerian Exco (created in 1914), Lagos was given a city council, which progressively became more and more elective (it was granted a mayor in 1953), and lasted even (for a short while) after the territory became a State in 1967. After 1906, until the post-Second World War constitution-making, all Nigeria was known as the "Colony and Protectorate," an oblique reference to the continued different status of Lagos.

The status of Lagos only became a major issue again in the early 1950s, when for two years after 1951 the whole area was transferred to the newly created Western Region. Then, after much discussion in which the city was treated as a political football, the 1953 Macpherson Constitution resulted in Lagos proper (but not the wider "Colony" area that included Epe, Ikorodu, Ikeja and Badagry) becoming federal territory with a Minister for Lagos Affairs—to the annoyance of Chief Obafemi Awolowo, Premier of the Western Region, who had been faced with an alliance of the Northern and Eastern Regions (under the political parties dominant in each one) to keep Lagos separate. The federal territory status continued after independence, while the four other districts remained in the Western Region. Agitation for a separate state in Lagos had been mounting since the mid-1950s, and had attracted a great deal of political support until finally in 1967, when Nigeria was in the middle of a full-scale crisis of survival, Lagos State was created as part of the new twelve-state structure enacted by General Gowon. This was the most important development in the city's post-colonial history. Although the early years of founding a State administration had its difficulties, the fact of statehood has been a major factor in its present flowering.

The Action Group (AG), one of the leading parties in the transition to independence under its leader Awolowo, had secured hold of Lagos from the previously dominant NCNC mentioned above (renamed the National Council of Nigerian Citizens) of Nnamdi Azikiwe (of whom more later) in its city council elections in the early 1950s, having made a powerful pitch both to the Muslim community and to the market women. It had relentlessly held political control even when the party was plunged into crisis, although ironically it had originally preferred the solution of Lagos joining the Western Region. Indeed, the excision from the West in 1953 had been supported by the Northern and Eastern parties as a way of undercutting the AG, and Chief Awolowo had been very angry at the loss. But the creation of Lagos State in 1967 had the Chief's approval, and the first elections after state creation, held in 1979, brought a huge majority to Awolowo's new party, the Unity Party of Nigeria (UPN), using his continued highly effective party organization. There was a natural majority for one political tendency that has continued to this day under a succession of differently named parties (the Social Democratic Party, the Action for Democracy, the Action Congress and now the Action Congress of Nigeria).

Being the capital thwarted completely the ideas circulating in some quarters during pre-independence years that Lagos should actually become an independent City State. Its long years as federal capital ensured its primacy at the center of the theater of politics until the major move to Abuja in the early 1990s. The revival of development in Lagos in the boom years of the early twenty-first century has also led to revival of the possibility of a special status for Lagos (if not actually the dream of becoming a City State) depending on its growing and increasingly successful financial autonomy as developed under the civilian Governors Tinubu and Fashola (see Chapter 8).

THE RISE AND FALL OF POLITICS: THE MOVE TO ABUJA

From the time that nationalist politics became an important force in the 1940s, Lagos became a major theatre of national political events, both in the fifteen years before independence and in the turbulent post-independence years, even if the civil war did not affect the city directly (one episode the author experienced directly is recounted in Chapter 6).

It all changed, however, after 1976, when the decision was made by the short-lived Murtala Mohammed administration to move the federal capital to Abuja, a project substantially achieved by the early 1990s. Murtala's assassination was one of Lagos' most traumatic moments, and it helped convince the military that the decision to move to Abuja was the right one, although little was done in the next three years when Nigeria was effectively ruled by the duumvirate of Olusegun Obasanjo as president and Shehu Yar'Adua as his number two. The Shagari regime (1979-83), possibly because it was a more Northern-influenced administration, started making the move, but it was under the military President Babangida (1985-93) that decisive steps were taken, especially after events played a decisive role. A critical moment impelling the move to Abuja was Major Orkar's attempted coup of April 1990 against Babangida led by the Brigade of Guards from Bonny Camp, a uniquely Lagos event (see Chapter 6).

This precipitated the acceleration of the move of the capital decided fourteen years before, which had been proceeding in a leisurely, even sporadic, way. The change was a major psychological moment in Lagos history, affecting the mindset of its inhabitants and leaving many buildings as simply repositories of former glories, in some cases shells like the now privatized Federal Secretariat, and the increasingly tacky parade ground in Tafawa Balewa Square, the racecourse in colonial times, which by independence had fallen into disuse. The new arena had a brief moment of splendor after it was built in the 1970s but after 1982 independence was never celebrated there again: it is now always at Eagle Square in Abuja. The square is now given over to small shops and offices.

Chapter Two

THE TOPOGRAPHY OF LAGOS
ISLAND AND MAINLAND

"Lagos is a marvellous manifestation of the perversity of man coupled with the perversity of nature."
> Mary Kingsley, *West African Studies*, 1899

"Lagos is Eastern in its feeling that sheer naked human life, mere existence, bubbles and pullulates with the frightening fecundity of bacteria."
> Elspeth Huxley, *Four Guineas*, 1954

"Once upon a time, when men were still in romance with nature, the lagoon nourished the social, commercial and even political being of the city and people of Lagos."
> Jahman Anikulapo, from "Collapsing Borders: Tinubu
> Square as a Metaphor for a Multi-cultural Society,"
> lecture given to the Goethe Institut, Lagos, 2005

"Two names the City has, two souls,
One native and inexpressibly deep,
The other a rapid baptism from a pale altar;
The two sometimes kiss and sometimes quarrel."
> From *Eko* by Niyi Osundare

THE AMBIVALENT ROLE OF THE "BAR": BARRIER AND ENTRY POINT

Describing the topography of the city is essential to understanding it: the strange way in which Lagos is laid out in a tangled dichotomy between land and water is an essential part of its soul. What is needed is a "social topography" which dwells on the haphazard way in which the city "just grew," dictated by the imperatives of nature, politics, commerce and plain circumstance. No one would have planned to build an enormous city on the basis of such an unusual configuration of lagoon and island. The sheltered parts of the shoreline were conducive to fishing villages, but in an era

35

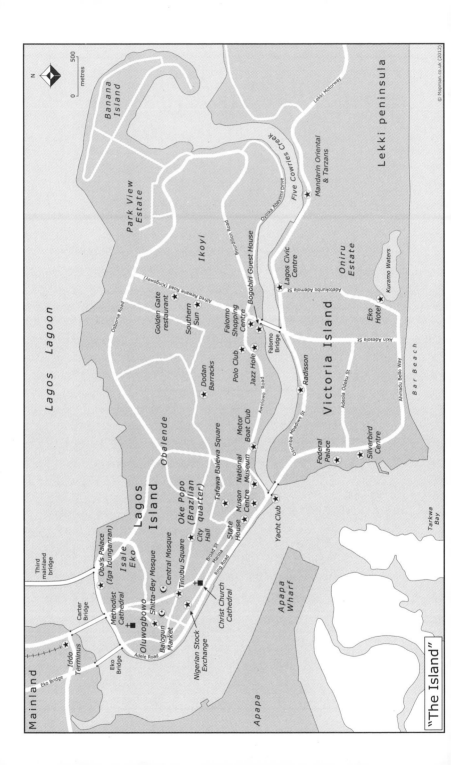

"The Island"

© Mapman.co.uk (2012)

of "water power" the island represented greater security. At the same time, access to the deep-water anchorage that lies between what is now Lagos Island and Apapa was rendered perilous by the "bar," a sandbank across the entry to the lagoon from the Atlantic Ocean that made all navigation perilous, especially for larger ships.

A look at the map shows the straight Atlantic shore along the line of the 6th parallel that stretches along what Akin Mabogunje, writing in *Nigeria Magazine*, called "150 miles of featureless un-indented coastline" from Porto Novo in the west to way beyond Palma in the east. It is the one break in this shoreline (just near what became Lagos) "where ships can steam into calm waters to load and unload cargoes away from the great unrelenting surges of the surf." The gap by Lighthouse Point with the shifting and treacherous sand bar, with its shallow water (never more than 14 feet until 1914), permitted entry by smaller ships to the long octopus-like wriggling lagoon, and one of the finest deep water harbors on the West Coast.

No wonder, in an age when water-borne traffic was everything, that this harbor became a hub and a fulcrum for trade and thus for political attention, in spite of the notorious bar. This was always there, always an obstacle, making access a risky business. Ocean vessels were forced to anchor for safety far out to sea, while the smaller vessels, the cutters and tenders, had to wait for the showing of a white flag before it was considered safe to risk crossing the bar. Even then it was hazardous, as there was a concentration of sharks by the bar, ready to snatch any survivors.

Some saw the barrier that was the bar as helping the security of the lagoon and above all the settlement of Eko/Lagos. In the last analysis, however, it was not necessarily a protection, for, as we will see, when the crisis came in the mid-nineteenth century, it was not so difficult for the British to send a gunboat and change the course of history.

Even at the end of the fifteenth century the Portuguese were aware of the problem of the bar, one reason why they shunned the place. It was mentioned in Barbot's *Description of Guinea* in the early eighteenth century, and it became an increasingly potent symbol of the peculiarity of the city, and in some ways the vexatious Atlantic currents still haunt the future of the megalopolis, as was witnessed in the ocean surges that swept across low-lying Victoria Island in the 1990s and later, before Lagos State embarked on its "permanent solution." It was the bar that originally gave its name to Bar Beach (see Chapter 10).

John Adams, in the early nineteenth century, noted the dangers of the bar. He found a

> town built on a bank or island, which appears to have been raised from the Cradoo [Ikorodu] Lake by the eddies, after the sea and periodical rains had broken down the boundary which separated it from the ocean… the necessaries of life are there extremely abundant and cheap, and are brought chiefly from the country or northern margin of Cradoo Lake, which communicates with Jaboo [Ijebu], a very fertile kingdom, and inhabited by an agricultural and manufacturing kingdom.

He produced one of the more concise descriptions of life, including some gruesome details, from the early visitors to what was already known as Lagos.

R. S. Smith, in *The Lagos Consulate 1851-61*, writes that the "European traders of the 18th century and perhaps earlier hired Fanti canoemen from the Gold Coast to communicate with the shore as the local people were unwilling to venture over the surf." The bar, he says, "equally deterred European exploration," quoting Heyman, a Dutch trading official, who wrote in 1716 that "the river is shut off by heavens high breakers, and the land is therefore unapproachable." It seems that the bar was especially dangerous at ebb tide when the waters "poured through the narrow gap with the weight of the lagoon behind them."

All through the nineteenth century the dangerous unpredictability of the bar, with its high loss of life, was the first topic of comment by visitors. The anti-slavers had for some time known that the inaccessibility of Lagos and the secretive nature of the lagoons had been one of the reasons the Portuguese had started to concentrate on the slaving potential of the place. At the end of the century, the celebrated traveller Mary Kingsley found it so trying that when she visited Lagos briefly she wrote of little else than the annoying nature of "the bar." And once the problem was cracked in the early twentieth century, it unlocked the port city's huge economic potential.

BURTON'S LAGOS

Sir Richard Burton visited Lagos in 1862, just after the British had taken over the city, and some ten years after the first bombardment of 1851.

Always willing to make a recommendation, he wrote in *Wanderings in West Africa from Liverpool to Fernando Po* that "no one seems to visit Lagos for the first time without proposing a breakwater."

There was, however, more than the bar for the discerning observer, as can be seen in his long descriptive section on Lagos. Although he only had one day there, he did not hide some of his negative impressions. He wrote: "The site of the town is detestable... the first aspect is as if a hole had been hollowed out in the original mangrove forest that skirts the waters..." But although he made it clear he did not think much of what he found, his powers of description are sufficiently good for the reader to have a few glimpses of the spirit of the city to come. Burton offers a succinct portrait of the nascent town:

> The thin line of European buildings that occupy the best sites, fronting the water, are, first the French comptoir, prettily surrounded with gardens; then a large pretentious building, lately raised by M. Carrena, a Sardinian merchant—it is said to be already decaying; then the Wesleyan mission house...
>
> The streets only want straightening, widening, draining and cleaning. There are irregular buildings—intended for market places and called, I suppose squares—into which the narrow lanes abut; they are dotted with giant heaps of muck or mixes, and in hot weather wooden patterns are required. The houses, not the factories, are of switch or puddle clay, built in courses, and fished out of the river...

E. D. MOREL'S LAGOS

Again the bar features in the 1911 book by the Edwardian journalist and reformer E. D. Morel, *Nigeria: Its People and Its Problems*, in which the construction of the mole that helped create the port of Lagos is cited in context. Morel also provides an objective and vivid snapshot of Lagos in that year, contrasting the "unenviable existence," as it had been in the 1870s, of the Governor and his staff ("maintaining themselves from hand to mouth and swept by disease") with the more positive ambience of the city in 1911:

> Today Lagos is a picturesque, congested town of some 80,000 inhabitants, boasting many fine public buildings and official and European

and native merchants' residences, churches, wharves, a hospital, a tramway, a bacteriological institute, a marine engineering establishment, to say nothing of cold storage and electric light plant, hotels, a racecourse, and other appartenances of advanced civilisation.

He notes:

> ...every variety of dress in the busy streets, from the voluminous robes of the turbaned Mohammedan to the latest tailoring monstrosities of western Europe. The Yoruba lady with a Bond Street hat and hobble skirt; her sister in the infinitely more graceful enfolding cloths of blue or terracotta, with the bandanna kerchief for headgear; opulent resident native merchants or Government clerks in ordinary English costume... a cosmopolitan crowd which includes Sierra Leonean, Cape Coast and Accra men, attracted by the many prospects of labour an ever increasing commercial and industrial activity offers to carpenters, mechanics, traders assistants and the like... A certain kind of prosperity is writ large over the place, but there is good reason to believe that economic pressure in its different forms, none more acutely felt than the ascending price of foodstuffs, is beginning to bear hardly upon the poorest classes, and the political and social atmosphere of the town is not altogether healthy.

Morel writes of work continuing on the construction of the two moles, combined with harbor and channel dredging. This was to permit the beginning of the proper development of the port in Apapa, to link with the railway which had been advancing inland from Lagos from about the turn of the century, eventually to reach Jebba and later Kaduna and Kano. He prognosticates gloomily on how, if the railway traffic increases as expected, "the already crowded and circumscribed area of Lagos can possibly prove equal to the demands on it" (how many times must that warning have been issued!). Doubting that it can play the role of "a West African Bombay" he suggests it is "only by the expenditure of millions which, spread all over the protectorate would have results of much greater fruitfulness, that Lagos can be converted into a harbour worthy of its name."

Morel becomes positively poetic standing looking at the works at the extremity of the eastern mole, watching

…the greedy, muddy-coloured sea absorbing like some insatiable monster the masses of grey rock hurled, at all times of the day and every day in the week, to appreciate the colossal difficulties of a task which, brought to a successful issue, will always remain an impressive testimony to human perseverance under climatic and other conditions of perennial difficulty. West Africa has certainly never seen anything comparable to it. Nature disputes with man for every inch of vantage. As the work progresses, the sand twists and writhes into ever-changing formations; banks arise and disappear only to again re-form; the foreshore on the outer side of the mole grows and swells and rises weekly, threatening to become level with the wall itself and even to overwhelm it; the scour of the sea scoops into the ocean floor, thus forcing the advancing mole into deep water, which demands a proportionately larger meal of stone…

From Abeokuta, thirty miles away, these innumerable tons of granitic boulders must be brought, dispatched in "boxes" from the newly-opened quarries to Ebute Metta by rail… Every foot advanced requires sixty tons of stone. At the accelerated rate of progress now ensured the eastern mole will be finished in four years. The labour and organisation required to bring this great work to its present stage—initial steps in West Africa being invariably characterised by endless impediments—have been prodigious. Despite the sombre prognostications one hears in certain quarters, there seems to be no reasonable doubt the bar will yield in time, as the forest has yielded to British genius and pertinacity aided by African muscles…

Morel's dramatic and in many ways intuitively prophetic writing makes one realize how much building the moles and breaking the bar was the key to unlocking the huge wealth which Lagos was capable of generating. Work was begun on the port in 1907 but it was only opened in 1924, although with the building of the moles access to the quays on the Marina of Lagos Island had already become greatly improved, which gave a boost to maritime trade; this was what really defined colonial Lagos from the late nineteenth century onwards, and along with the railway was the key to the expansion of the colonial period. So much of Lagos' development was port development. The whole topography of Lagos was changed by the national railway system begun in the 1890s and the way it dovetailed into the later opening of the port in 1924, which in turn became increasingly dependent on the macadamized roads that followed close on the railway's heels (the impact of all three is described in Chapter 3).

TWO WORLDS: THE ISLAND AND THE MAINLAND

The lagoon (a presence in the city's very name) snakes its way everywhere, from Tin Can Island to Kuramo Waters, original site of the Lago de Kuramo and the Kuramo fishing village. This still survives, and can be observed from the tower-blocks and hotels on the other side of Kuramo Waters—a microcosm of the two Lagoses, although when the superhighway that is due to go along the south side of the Lekki Peninsula is completed the topography of the area will change again, in the same way as when the ghetto of Maroko was destroyed (a happening which greatly moved a number of Nigerian writers and is examined at length in Chapter 4). The intimate chaos of Maroko was replaced with the creation of the Oniru Estate, tailor-made for the new middle classes.

For contemporary Lagos confronts one perpetually with the great psychological socio-cultural divide between "the Island" and "the Mainland." These are two deep "social topography" concepts which dominate even routine discussion of the place, like East Side and West Side in New York, or North London and South London. In addition, what is usually referred to as "the Island" now consists in fact of three main components.

LAGOS ISLAND: ISALE EKO AND THE IGA IDUNGANRAN

Firstly, and centrally, when one talks of "the Island" there looms Lagos Island, the historic and traditional heart of the city, home of the first settlers and the Oba's palace, focused above all on the area of Isale Eko (it means strictly "Eko bottom" but more prosaically "lower settlement") around the palace on the north side of the island. The built-up area grew in size especially when land was reclaimed in areas such as Idumagbo. It also hosts historic and still flourishing markets such as Balogun, Sandgrouse and Jankara, as well as one district to the south of the Iga Idunganran that was traditionally occupied by Binis.

The Oba's palace itself bears little that is left of the seventeenth-century structure, although it still retains the shrine of one of the first Obas, Ashipa, in a locked cupboard, as well as that of the nineteenth-century Oba Akitoye, who was reinstated by the British in 1851. The area around the Oba's palace is still supremely important as the center of traditional

Lagos. The main building, still called the Iga Idunganran (originally Aromire's pepper farm) is surrounded by a number of subordinate palaces belonging to subordinate chiefs, although the land-owning Idejo themselves were spread out into different areas. For example, the Oniru of Iru's walled palace is very visible on Ahmadu Bello Way on Victoria Island (a modern one has now been built further along the highway). One of the Oniru's princes has been Commissioner for Waterfront Development in Lagos State, and has been prominently involved in the reclamation of Bar Beach and the projected Eko Atlantic City (see Chapter 10).

The Iga Idunganran also contains a large number of rooms and spaces, especially the part that was extensively reconstructed in 1960 with offices, throne room and living quarters. In an interview at the time of his coronation in 2003 the Oba said it had 34 entrances and claimed that he knew them all without divulging them. Much of the old sprawling compound was destroyed for the refurbishment, although there still remains one courtyard whose base is much older and a number of buildings in the Portuguese style from the early nineteenth century. Outside the main entrance to the new palace are three British-made cannons from the Royal Navy gunboat *Prometheus*, under the command of Commander Bedingfield, which was lying offshore when the British coerced Oba Dosunmu to sign the Treaty of Cession in 1861.

Alongside Isale Eko lies the Brazilian quarter, around its centre at Campos Square, stretching from Kakawa and Bamgbose Streets to the island's western end, the area of Olowogbowo, home of the Saros (Sierra Leoneans). This was built on the district that had been flattened in the British bombardment of 1851 but rapidly rebuilt, this time particularly with churches such as the famous Wesleyan church (later cathedral), built as long ago as the 1870s, which had become so unsafe by 2005 that it had to be demolished to be rebuilt exactly on the model of the original plan. Both areas still bear some relics of their origins—in the case of the Brazilians their distinctive architecture (see Chapter 3), but much of this has over the years been knocked down.

THE MARINA AND THE BUSINESS DISTRICT

The other main area that was developed early on Lagos Island lies along the southern strip, where once were the rudimentary wharves for the slave ships and the barracoons housing the "exports." It was a strip of land known as the Ehingbeti, which was outside the boundaries of Isale Eko and considered mainly as a place for the disposal of refuse. Aderibigbe records that "in oral tradition" the point was often made that it was unbelievable that the Europeans should want such land as their headquarters, even though the piers they used had been there for some time (originally used by the slave-traders).

Thus this land was ceded after 1851 without too much difficulty by the British-imposed Oba Akitoye to European merchants and missionaries, such as the plots acquired by the thrusting Rev. Gollmer of the Church Missionary Society. His first mission building was an assembled wooden frame building imported from Sierra Leone, known to local Lagosians as *alapako* or "the House of Planks," very nearly on the site of what is still known as "CMS"—even if it is now the most famous bus stop in Lagos. A little further along the Marina was where the first consulate building was erected; it became known as the "iron coffin" because of the high mortality among its diplomatic occupants, due, it was felt to the inappropriate nature of the structure for the tropics.

This was where Consul McCoskry first began to lay out the Marina, including the planting of eucalyptus trees and the installation of gas lamps in 1859. The Marina project was further developed in the 1860s by Governor Glover, who also laid out a parallel street called Broad Street, still one of the main arterials of Lagos Island. After a pause after 1872 (the fallow period in which Lagos was run from the Gold Coast) there were major developments in both buildings and systems, which took place in the 1880s and 1890s. Because of Akitoye's early cession of title to Europeans (and Saros) of nearly all the land along the Marina, it became the center of the city's first European quarter, and for the same reasons it was where the first business quarter was located, in addition to the earliest administrative buildings.

As government grew so did all the businesses attendant on it, suppliers and contract-searchers aware that the interior was being opened up. And the Marina was where they were concentrated. One important facility for the growth of business was the development of a European-style currency economy. From the 1860s onwards British silver coins were progressively introduced, replacing the cowrie shells that had been brought in from the Indian Ocean and were important tender on the West African coast for possibly four hundred years—cowries were very much the currency of the slave trade and were more widespread than brass rods, copper wire or the horseshoe-shaped manillas popular in south-eastern Nigeria. Cowries were particularly favored by the Portuguese who imported them in large quantities and were still very current in 1861, hence the name Five Cowrie Creek, named after the cost of the ferry set up between Onikan and Reclamation Point.

Sir Alan Burns tells us that barter remained for a long time the currency of choice, especially in parts of the interior, despite efforts by the British rulers like Lugard to stop it. Formerly, he says, slaves themselves were used as currency, replaced by cases of gin, in which the wealth of many a powerful chief was invested. Schnapps and brandy were also popular currencies.

Silver US dollars were also in circulation at that time, but the British brought their own coins which they preferred to use. For some years Elder Dempster was the informal manager of the British currency operation. A treasury was set up in 1891, which became the Bank of British West Africa in 1896 and later Standard Bank and in the 1970s First Bank. Local currency notes only officially came in with the setting up of the West African Currency Board in 1912, and then in low denomination notes. Lagos was the first place where cowries, already hit by massive inflation in the nineteenth century, began to be completely phased out, but there were places in the interior where they were in use well into the twentieth century. Bringing institutional structure to the currency helped to provide the basis of a sound and expanding business community. Another step towards this was the establishment of the Lagos Chamber of Commerce in 1899.

The building that became Government House, and then State House after independence, went through a number of transformations; the version most recognized was built in time for Lugard to occupy as Governor-General in 1914. It housed figures such as Clifford, Cameron, Bourdillon and the last Governors-General, Robertson and—after independence—Azikiwe.

To introduce a personal recollection, in 1982 I attended a lavish Independence Day reception on a sunny afternoon in the gardens of the same building, then called State House. It was hosted by President Shehu Shagari (the last time he did it, as in 1983 the ceremonies were held for the first time in Abuja). I was there again for Independence Day in 1986, the last time I ever entered the premises. President Babangida, still fairly new in power, hosted the same Independence Day reception in the much tenser atmosphere associated with military regimes: it was on a hot tropical night, and my main recollection was of shadowy armed presences on the roof of the building (I was told quietly that they were Israeli marksmen).

From 1991 onwards the building passed to the Lagos State government, which has used it for official occasions, while the Chief Secretary's house and office next door, still in the mid-period colonial style but less ostentatious, became a much remodeled (and to some extent vandalized) official residence for the State Governor.

Glover, apart from developing the Marina and Broad Street, also built what he named Victoria Street (now Nnamdi Azikiwe Street), linking Broad Street to the Ebute Ero wharf (the location later of Carter Bridge). Victoria Street was on the site of what had been called the Ehin Ogba, also outside the boundaries of Isale Eko, where corpses of paupers and *abiku* (children who die soon after birth) were buried.

The next ten years saw the coming of late Victorian symbols of progress such as the telegraph (1886), the telephone (1891) and electricity, which came to Lagos before it had been introduced into many parts of London, with electric street lamps beginning to replace the gas lamps that had been considered a wonder when brought in by Glover. The report of Coode and Partners of 1896 made recommendations for a "permanent solution" to the problem of the bar, essential if Lagos was to enter modernity (a phrase echoed 110 years later with Governor Tinubu's "permanent solution" to the problem of ocean surges).

Governor Carter had the vision to push through the railway, the great project of the 1890s, which opened its first stretch to Ibadan as the century turned. The year 1900 saw the opening of the Iddo rail terminus, but also the first version of Carter Bridge (carrying pedestrians and the probably inevitable steam tram—see below), which gave the development of Lagos Island, as the hub of the capital, a tremendous boost.

Sir William McGregor, Governor from 1899 to 1904, introduced notably the blessing of improved sanitation and water supply. Mabogunje says that in

Iddo rail terminus building

McGregor's five years "the island saw more advances in health and sanitary reforms than it had known since the coming of the Europeans." For example, a massive waterworks was built seventeen miles from Lagos on the Ogun river, which introduced piped water and contributed to the eradication of guinea worm. Most significantly for Lagos, McGregor, a distinguished medical doctor, was quick to see the meaning of an even more important discovery, the conclusive linkage of malaria to the *anopheles* mosquito by Sir Ronald Ross in 1897. McGregor embarked on substantial swamp drainage, and land reclamation, alongside the improved refuse disposal arrangements using the new steam tramway (see Chapter 3).

Lagos became the obvious place to develop as the capital of the new Colony and Southern Protectorate inaugurated in 1906, and after 1914 naturally became the main location of the first capital of united Nigeria. The period after 1906 saw an important period of further development on Lagos Island, of buildings still in existence such as the Supreme Court, the Old Secretariat and the Government Printer on Broad Street, and the first Government Secondary School, Kings College, both of which were located by the racecourse, which from the time it was laid out in 1859 was a central feature of British colonial Lagos. And for a time polo was played in the central area of the course until a separate polo club ground was established in south-west Ikoyi in the 1950s.

This period of construction was paralleled in the 1920s, when business was expanding and government confidence was high. The next equivalent period of building in central Lagos was the great boom of the run-up to independence in 1960, when many important public edifices were constructed.

IKOYI: THE MCGREGOR CANAL TO BANANA ISLAND

The second location that forms part of "the Island" is Ikoyi, which was originally established under Governor McGregor as a Government Residential Area (GRA). The separate and almost unpopulated island of Ikoyi (once only home to one or two farms) became linked to the mainland, although still separated by what became known as the McGregor Canal, a few parts of which can still be spotted.

The district's environment has changed over the years as some of the side roads have developed traditional Lagos potholes, and acquired street detritus, while the old large colonial houses have been progressively replaced by ever more lucrative high-rise blocks. Governor Fashola has claimed that it is the State Government's intention to preserve certain historic Ikoyi streets, such as Glover Road and Lugard Avenue, but it has been accepted that the main road that loops round the island (from Bourdillon to Alexander to Gerrard) has gone too far for rehabilitation, and it has been made into a dual carriageways, convenient for motorists but less easy to cross on foot, reducing the suburb's laid-back charm. There are those who feel that Ikoyi has lost much of its old colonial flavor forever, and there are parts that are seriously scruffy. The dual carriageways also give improved access to the development at Banana Island at the far end of Ikoyi, where reclaimed land has opened up further proliferations of high-rise condos as well as a new headquarters for the Ford Foundation.

But there is also south-west Ikoyi, built a little later on, mainly in the 1950s on reclaimed or swampy land, always something of a poor relation to the grand and affluent Ikoyi, and always more racially and socially mixed, with its own distinctive character (see Awolowo Road in Chapter 10).

Victoria Island: The "Elite Slum"

The third component of "the Island" is Victoria Island (VI), once designated as an uninhabited rubbish dump, but which began to be developed at the time of independence as a residential area. Over the next thirty years, however, it was subjected to more random growth, as higgledy-piggledy development on Lagos Island made it more and more unliveable, partly because of traffic but also because of unemployed and often criminal street youths known as "area boys," often referred to elsewhere in this volume. The unintended growth of "VI" as an unintended business district has created what one writer in the *Glendora Review* called the "elite slum." with banks, offices, restaurants and bars all rubbing shoulders with slightly forlorn grand residences of the 1960s and 1970s, built by those who had acquired title to plots and whose land is still very valuable. The worst aspect of unplanned development was the absence of provision for off-street parking, which brought often unpredictable traffic jams, a problem yet to be solved.

In the 1990s such difficulties were at their worst as the roads had deteriorated, in conjunction with an increase in ocean surges from Bar Beach. Some of these problems have progressively been rectified, especially with the resurfacing of the key arterials of Adeola Odeku and Akin Adesola Streets, both of which bisect the important west end of Victoria Island and had been wracked with potholes. Another main connecting link, Ajose Adeogun Street, was voluntarily refurbished by Zenith Bank, whose headquarters was located there. But this act of self-interested philanthropy has not been repeated elsewhere. The famous slum area of Maroko, beyond the eastern end of Victoria Island, whose notorious destruction in 1990 was commemorated by writers (see Chapter 4), has been replaced as if it had never been by the middle-class dwellings of the Oniru Estate. Much of the future of Victoria Island will depend on the Bar Beach reclamation project, due to grow into the ambitious Eko Atlantic City, which will further intensify the arrival of middle-class dwellings, high-rise blocks and shopping malls on the reclaimed land (more fully considered in Chapter 10).

LEKKI: UNRESTRAINED EXPANSION?

Some would include in "the Island" the Lekki Peninsula, the principal but by no means the only scene of the new but always uncontrolled urban spread. It is a large long tract of land, whose geographical relationship to Lagos is a little like that of Long Island to New York, although it is not now cut off by water.

The Lagos State government has a Lekki master plan, along with a series of other master plans. It highlights the transport links, but in relation to the new Lekki port and airport, which are to service the Export Processing Zone in which the Chinese are already heavily involved. Even so, there still seems to have been too much unrestrained expansion, accompanied by an ambitious staking out of as yet unbuilt real estate by well-known political figures. This can be seen as the latest manifestation of the constant and almost feverish boom in property values that has been a feature of Lagos since before independence.

On the one hand, the peninsula has seen middle-class residential development mingled with prominent business locations such as the headquarters of the US oil company Chevron, mostly along the new Lekki Motorway, currently under construction to go all the way to Epe. It is already the site of up-market housing enclaves like the gated community at Victoria Gardens, and is also now the location of the Pan-African University, one of the new privately owned academic establishments that have begun to proliferate in Nigeria as the state education system has declined in the quality of education offered. This incorporates the Lagos Business School, begun in the early 1990s with private-sector support and discreet encouragement from the Opus Dei group of Roman Catholics.

Another harbinger of future trends on Lekki is the appearance of a major new shopping mall, the first of such size in Nigeria, called The Palms—although if this is the best Lagos can offer even with South African support, it is still no match for some of those in South Africa, notably the vast glittering Sandton Mall in northern Johannesburg. Also to be found on the Lekki Peninsula is the terrain of the Nigerian Conservation Foundation, whose guardianship of environmental probity in Lagos, for long a fragile plant, has had some influence on Governor Fashola's green policies.

The other aspect of development in Lekki concerns its tourist potential. There are already a few modest resort developments, but when the infrastructure improves one can imagine a faster expansion of beach-fronting properties and resorts, both eastwards and westwards along the coast. There is some uncertainty as to what ongoing alterations to the mole will do to the shoreline and displacement of currents. Will the surges that so affected Bar Beach be pushed further down the Lekki coast, as some now fear?

Some argue that the Lekki Peninsula cannot be included in the notion of "the Island" because of its history. Lagos chiefs, notably Kosoko who fled Lagos Island after the British slow motion takeover of 1851-61, made Epe their "capital" and used the coastline for continuing the illegal slave trade through Lekki and Palma, both Portuguese slaving points which in the past had had direct trading access to Ijebu. The area was incorporated into the Colony after Kosoko's deal with Glover in 1863, which provided for a general amnesty. Epe, the other wide of the lagoon from Lekki, remained part of the Ijebu kingdom until 1892.

Apart from occasional sorties in the past to the still largely deserted beaches of the Lekki coast, I did not know the Lekki Peninsula, but I was able to organize an educational visit to Lekki Town, which in the first part of the nineteenth century was a Portuguese slaving port, as was Palma, a little further along the coast. The high point of both was the ten years that Oba Kosoko spent in exile in Epe. In Lekki (previously also sometimes called Leckie) I was shown the ruins of the portico of the barracoon, and the pool where the slaves were washed before embarking. It was also at one time apparently used by the French trader Régis Aîné. My guide, who had family connections there, said the name Lekki (which I am told is not known as a Yoruba word) comes from a Portuguese trader called Lequi who was operating there and was buried in a

The remains of the portal of the slave barracoon in Lekki

circular tomb in which he was said to have been interred standing up. (Indeed, I was told a strange story that at some point Portuguese had come and removed his head). Lagos State has now put a plaque to commemorate the trader on the side of the tomb, which lies just in front of the house in which Chief Awolowo stayed for a few weeks after having been arrested for treasonable felony in 1962, recently refurbished as a small museum by the Lagos State government.

THE MAINLAND: ANOTHER MIND CONCEPT

This is a much bigger land space as well as being a mind-concept all on its own. Although there had been an early Awori settlement in the vicinity of Somolu, it was abandoned because of its vulnerability as the inhabitants moved first to Iddo and then to Lagos Island. Ebute Metta was an old Awori fishing village (the name means "three jetties") that had been chosen by Governor Glover as the site for resettling Egba refugees after the "Ifole" (the breaking of houses) in Abeokuta in 1867 (see Chapter 1). Iddo was also one of the oldest historic settlements of the area, dating back, it is said, to Aromire himself. There were other old villages on the mainland such as Ajegunle and Abule Ejo, which all progressively expanded and partially merged in an unplanned ad hoc fashion as the city grew. The present-day suburb of Mushin was a special case of a group of villages that came together in part as a reaction to the colonial presence, as described in Sandra Barnes' vivid book on Mushin, *Patrons and Power.*

After the bubonic plague epidemic of the late 1920s, there were further drainage schemes for the most insanitary areas of both island and mainland. The Lagos Executive Development Board set up in 1931 (as a direct result of the plague crisis) was responsible for some of the earliest planned developments such as Yaba. These were also added to and partly reconstructed in the later colonial period, as was the new model suburb of Surulere, which still bears some of its middle-class ambiance, albeit somewhat faded. In order to make Lagos a federal capital worthy of the name, some of the older inhabitants of Lagos Island were transplanted into new suburbs, which in their early days were smart residential areas of which Surulere is a classic example (for more on Surulere see Chapter 10).

There is also the area which grew up round the port in Apapa almost from the time it was opened in 1924 (see Chapter 3). This was a moment that released a great amount of pent-up economic energy and brought the development of industries, although more substantially in the era after the Second World War. The better parts of Apapa were for business executives rather than diplomats or civil servants, and the area never had the snob value (or the property values) of Ikoyi, but there are still some very well-appointed villas in Marine Road and Creek Road, and surprising luxury behind high walls and ornamental gates in spite of the public squalor found in a main arterial like Wharf Road.

Mabogunje notes that the administrative separation of the federal territory of Lagos proper after 1953 from most of the mainland led to more dysfunctional development as the 1950s were a period of major industrial growth in Ikeja and Apapa and brought in large members of new migrants to the huge, often turbulent districts such as Mushin, Ajegunle, Somolu, Bariga, Idi-Oro and Agege, to name only some. Sandra Barnes' *Patrons and Power*, cited above, is commended by Mabogunje for pointing out that in Mushin, in the absence of a clear overall authority, autonomous associations and even traditional-type authorities were developed, although these had some problems fitting in with the local government authorities. However, new shantytowns grow all the time like shifting sands in the incredible and continuous expansion of the mega-city, and can be found along the Badagry Road, the Agege Motor Road and the Ibadan Expressway. Ikeja, with the area which developed round the airport, was key to the "colonial project," where the industrial estate was matched by the "garden city" of the Government Residential Area. But again the real development of Ikeja came after the Second World War when it became and remained part of the Western Region as intended by Chief Awolowo, the regional Premier, to balance the weight of Lagos, a situation that continued until 1967.

The classiest mainland residential area was indeed GRA Ikeja where large company houses can be found. The Maryland and Palm Grove estates and Antony Village are other examples of attempts to create middle-class enclaves, exploiting the fact that at that time there was plenty of available land on the mainland. Ikeja carried on growing after independence, and the creation of Lagos State after 1967 gave a considerable boost to its expansion, especially as the headquarters of the State—the Governor's office (the Round House) and largely undistinguished administrative buildings—were located in Alausa to the north of Ikeja. The area also benefited from the development of the new international airport, named after the assassinated leader Murtala Muhammed in the 1970s, although it already had a historic position as the location of the first Lagos airport (now the new refurbished domestic terminal known as MM2), originally opened between the wars.

There are many other areas of the mainland that have developed since independence: the further removed suburbs and the semi-elite pockets each with their own subtle distinctions of personality—Ogudu, Ilupeju, Ipebu in the vicinity of Ikeja, or, along the Badagry Road, Festac Town and Amuwo Odofin (see Chapter 10).

The question seems to intrude again and again, however, of what, ultimately, is Lagos—how is it to be defined, and how far do its boundaries extend? There is a basic structure in the main administrative unit of Lagos State, going as far as the old town of Badagry, itself a historic slaving port which became a take-off point for missionaries, and then right up to the borders of the Benin Republic, which might meet strict modern criteria for boundaries. Although Badagry was not originally Yoruba, being part of the area of the Egun (the principal group in Porto Novo), it is said to have acquired more and more Yoruba immigrants.

Development along this highway has been notable, as one would expect with a main international route now being majestically expanded as a ten-lane highway. But the new megalopolis has tended to grow more dramatically northwards, even into Ogun State, towards Ota via the Agege Motor Road and Ikorodu more to the northeast. Likewise the urban spread along Lekki Island towards Epe in the past twenty years has been perhaps the most remarkably rapid of all. Thus there is certainly considerable urban overspill in all directions northwards, westwards and eastwards, which are parts of what might be called the Lagos conurbation.

The Ever-present but Under-used Lagoon

The lagoon began by being more important than the land. History gradually diminished its importance but it never went away. First of all there were a series of fishing villages scattered around the different branches of the lagoon. As we have seen in Chapter 1, when the island was chosen by the Binis in the early seventeenth century as the site for their encampment (*eko*), Isale Eko, the area around the Oba's palace, superseded the jetties of Iddo and Ebute Metta, both ancient and kingly places. The island was also alongside one of the best stretches of deep water on this part of the coast, so its port facilities began to develop despite the problems already - recounted.

As the city has expanded, so land has been almost continuously reclaimed, and continues to be. The shape on successive maps has subtly changed each time there have been reclamations, from Idumagbo to Victoria Island to parts of Ikoyi. But the omnipresent lagoon, restless, switching between odorous and odoriferous, and over the years slowly changing shape, has always been and is still an integral part of the city's life, giving atmosphere, character and inspiration.

To what extent are the creeks and lagoons of Lagos now used for

The lagoon: "an integral part of the city's life"

communications? Although there is a Lagos Water Transport Authority, it has not in the past been particularly well-funded, and while most of the Lagos master plans include references to the potential of water transport, it has been a poor relation. The main visible traffic nowadays consists of yachts and motorboats, both the preserve of the wealthy, and there are clubs for each on the north side of Five Cowrie Creek. Traditionally the lagoons have been the preserve of fishermen from time immemorial, and in the eighteenth and nineteenth centuries the authority of rulers was reinforced by war canoes, a phenomenon much more apparent in the Niger Delta although Oba Kosoko made much of the power of his canoes. From early in the twentieth century there were government ferries, but these are now mainly on franchise—although the Lagos State government is engaged in dredging and is planning new jetties in "strategic locations," realizing that it is a cheap way of moving a workforce around.

Two well-known Lagos brothers both have operations on the south side of the same creek. Fiki (Taofiki) has concentrated on a substantial boat-building and selling side as well as marine supplies from his location just by Falomo Bridge, but his senior brother Ganiyu, much better known as "Tarzan" (from a T-shirt he wore in his youth) has prospered as a ferry operator, notably to the nearest thing Lagos has to a usable and popular beach at Tarkwa Bay (one of the few Lagos beaches where it is reasonably safe for swimming) on the other side of the entrance to the port, round the corner from Lighthouse Point. They were both encouraged into the boating business by their father, who had joined the engineers of the Royal West African Frontier Force in the Second World War, actually working at the army installations at Tarkwa Bay, which meant he was constantly making the journey there. At the end of the war he purchased cheaply an army motor boat, which was where his business as a ferryman took off. "He was the pioneer of motor boats in Lagos," says Fiki.

If Fiki's joint has a small restaurant with a lagoon-side veranda serving fresh fish, Tarzan's base, which is along the Lekki Motorway, has a bigger entertainment venue and thriving internationally patronized restaurant by the ferry, much frequented by the Tarkwa Bay visitors. For a time there was a highly popular Congolese orchestra playing makossa. There is also a small ferry connection to Ikoyi just by Tarzan's joint, which now lies in uneasy juxtaposition to the grand Chinese hotel complex, the Manadrin Oriental, which opened in 2008.

Fiki took me on tour of some of the power cruisers, naming their owners and saying how much they owed him. He showed me the brochure for his Marine Supplies and Boat Club ("where dreams come true"), describing the huge potential for the boating business in a water-bound city like Lagos, that is worth quoting:

> We stock the widest range of boats and seek to deliver a full lifetime experience from the time our clientele walk through the door to getting their chosen craft onto the water. We promote an irresistible lifestyle as more Nigerians are becoming involved with the prestigious "Big boys' toys". Together with the average man on the street, there is the need for functional crafts on limited budgets.

Talking to me on his relaxed terrace overlooking the lagoon, as the boats come and go, he said he favors the fourth mainland bridge linking Lekki and Ikorodu. Neither brother is keen on more bridges linking Victoria Island and Ikoyi because of the way they might impede lagoon traffic. Tarzan in particular looks to a steady growth in traffic, including even car ferries, as development continues apace on the Lekki Peninsula. Both brothers say they are planning a large expansion of their businesses.

BRIDGES AND MOTORWAYS

A network of bridges has long connected the various parts of Lagos, from the original wooden bridge over Five Cowrie Creek in the 1890s and the Carter Bridge first built in 1901, over which the steam tramway passed. Because of the growing popularity of motor transport including bus services in the inter-war years the Carter Bridge was replaced in 1931 with an impressive cast-iron structure that was a real Lagos landmark. When a new all-concrete structure was built in the early 1970s as part of the new ambitious overhead motorway system, the iron bridge was sadly cast off and left rusting by the lagoon like a strange alien shape. Apart from the new Carter Bridge, this period saw the creation of Eko Bridge and Falomo Bridge (the latter linking Ikoyi and Victoria Island). The Third Mainland Bridge, connecting Lagos Island to Yaba, is the most dramatic of the current bridges, sweeping far into the lagoon. It is still perceived by some as an "elite" bridge, linking Ikoyi and Ikeja, or even as a "military" bridge for fast access from island to airport.

Long ago a connection between Lekki and Ikorodu was planned—a project ahead of its time—just as there have been plans on the drawing board for two more bridges linking Lekki and Ikoyi, which in Governor Fashola's rapidly changing city are now being realized. Plans are indeed now well in hand for a Fourth Mainland Bridge from Lekki going straight to Ikorodu, across one of the narrowest parts of the lagoon, which will involve the creation of islands in this shallow part of the lagoon and which will further affect the social topography of the city. Moreover the designs imaginatively incorporate a two-level bridge with a lower tier of shops and markets.

The overhead motorway system was built mainly in the rush to expand concrete surfaces in the late 1960s and early 1970s. In the words of Giles Omezi, a London-based Nigerian architect, this brought about a "social carve-up" of communities, creating new artificial boundaries. He even sees the railway as an "extractive scar" that marked the first creation of such a social divide on the mainland, but the constant push to build more and more roads both on the mainland and on the islands compounded what Omezi sees as anti-community compartmentalization of the city. What is just as striking is the way the railway runs parallel to the Agege Motor Road, one of the earliest routes out of Lagos, as direct as any Roman road. For the same reason the railway revival under Governor Fashola is also compelled to be routed via the Agege straight line.

THE JULIUS BERGER PHENOMENON

You cannot write about roads in Lagos without mention of the redoubtable German construction firm Julius Berger. Although it has existed in Germany since 1895, and is now a subsidiary of Bilfinger Berger—a construction company which has business dealings all over the world from France and Poland to Australia—the Nigerian outlet is the star in their corporate horizon. Berger's first contract was the building of the Eko Bridge in Lagos from a contract awarded in 1965. Although the company went on to construct a whole overhead motorway system in Lagos, it only became incorporated as Julius Berger Nigeria Ltd. in 1970. It was particularly close to the military, who appreciated the support given during the civil war and benefited in kind from the goodwill created.

Gerd Meuer, a veteran German radio journalist who has been covering Nigeria for nearly fifty years, drew my attention to a headline in the

Daily Times of Lagos in the 1970s: "If you have a problem you must Berger it!"—a reference to the company's pragmatic capacity for "overnight solutions." It insisted, he says, on perfect planning and total independence from the Nigerian administration, but it delivered. It was entirely self-sufficient with its own camps, energy and water supply, and prompted admiration when it built the container port at Tin Can Island in eighteen months.

But Julius Berger's *chef d'oeuvre* remains the already cited nineteen-mile Third Mainland Bridge, one of the longest bridges in the world. Berger's success depended on extremely close relations with power and maintaining low-profile discretion around those relations, but ultimately it was the company's reputation for efficient delivery that secured for it many juicy contracts. It had many in the construction of Abuja (where it moved its headquarters in 2001), notably the new stadium. The company would still on occasion pick up a contract in Lagos, like the resurfacing and creation of a dual carriageway of Adeola Odeku on Victoria Island. It was also heavily involved in the development of the Park View Estate in Ikoyi. Anywhere you see a large blue sign with a capital "B," you know that Julius Berger is at work.

Chapter Three

CHANGING SOCIETY AND THE "LOOK" OF THE CITY

"Who would have dreamt that this island, known only as a slave market, would have so rapidly become a flourishing emporium for legitimate trade…"

Memoirs of Giambattista Scala, 1862

"Going from the Lagos mainland to Ikoyi on a Saturday night was like going from a bazaar to a funeral. And the vast Lagos cemetery, which separated the two places, helped to deepen this feeling. For all its luxurious bungalows and flats and its extensive greenery, Ikoyi was like a graveyard."

Chinua Achebe, *No Longer at Ease*, 1960

THE IMPRINT OF CHANGE

Much of the history of Lagos is that of its economy, in the context of political, social and cultural change. Economic transformation is thus one of the most important forces to have had an impact on the city, its society, its landscape as well as its "look," which forms an essential part of the quest for the city's soul. It is always said that architecture is one of the best expressions of the *Zeitgeist*. This dictum can certainly be applied to Lagos, especially in the context of the convulsions of the nineteenth century and the revolution brought about by British colonization, which inevitably had its own impact on the style of buildings, landscape and, indeed, the whole urban environment.

The expansion of the city's political economy in the second half of the nineteenth century led to growing wealth, which in turn brought a range of new aspirations for modernity that followed in the wake of colonization. Modernization also brought, however, an intellectual and spiritual crisis among the new elite, especially in relation to the effect of external influences on their own traditional culture and way of life. This dilemma illustrated the complex relationship of Nigeria with the rest of the world, through the pre-colonial and colonial periods, leading up to the vast extraverted expansion of the post-independence decades, as the country moved into the era of ever more intensive globalization. And all the time Lagos' buildings and other external manifestations reflected these changes.

VICTORIAN LAGOS

M. J. Echeruo's insightful study *Victorian Lagos* uses the writings in Nigeria's early newspapers which burgeoned in the last two decades of the nineteenth century. There had been a precursor in the shape of the short-lived *Anglo-African* produced by the Jamaican Robert Campbell, which had a brief but useful life in the 1860s, but there was a flowering in the early 1880s (see Chapter 4).

Echeruo looks at physical examples of change as observed through the pages of the papers, but always assessing the intellectual and spiritual condition of the city. He returns many times to the colonial impact, which is why "Victorian" figures in the book's title, as it was the Victorian values that the colonialists brought, especially through the activities of the missionaries, which took hold especially through the Saro community. The attempted imposition also produced its own consequences, ironically enough some of them from within the same Saro community that had aimed too high in seeking to be like its British masters, as we have seen in Chapter 1.

The arrival of the British had an impact on the look of Lagos, beginning with the creation of the Marina (with the planting of eucalyptus trees) and Broad Street; the new style of imported buildings in iron, bricks and timber; and such basic Victorian innovations as street lights and drainage, gas and electricity, telegraphs and telephones. The foreigners also brought their own styles, fashions and morals, which many of the locals, especially the Saros, were enthusiastic at adopting until a reaction to such mimicry set in—a reaction well-documented in Echeruo's book where he records that a certain confusion was caused over "what names to adopt, what clothes to wear, and how many wives to marry." Whereas in the late nineteenth century European-style dances and concerts were popular, eventually indigenous musical styles, sometimes in fusion with outside influences, created a genuinely local music.

The Rise of Racism

In the nineteenth century after the arrival of the British there was a much greater willingness on the part of men like Governor John Hawley Glover to encourage and promote suitable and available locals into the administration as they attained education. Some notable examples were Otunba Payne and later the dominant figure of Herbert Macaulay. It was only the more substantial arrival of the personnel of the colonial power that began to block such individuals from running the administration, even as the colonial government started more residential segregation.

Although Governor McGregor, who initiated them, justified these measures on health grounds (see Chapter 2) at a time when the Colonial Office was sending out people in greater numbers, in their application they were openly racial, if not racist. This was the beginning of the creation of "white Ikeja," "white Apapa" and above all "white Ikoyi." There is a case for saying that it was Governor Egerton who saw the pursuit of as much segregation as was possible almost as a duty. Fred Omu, in his illuminating book on the press in Nigeria in this period, calls Egerton the "arch-segregationist." Lugard also found it a natural evolution, especially given his well-known poor view of Lagosians, but it ultimately proved a development that could not last, inimical to the open spirit of the city.

In the 1890s and the early years of the twentieth century racist ideas were at their apogee in Europe, culminating in 1930s Germany. In Lagos such views seem to have been an accompaniment to the ascent in importance of the Colonial Office, as it brought in young and sometimes inexperienced men in larger numbers. Echeruo cites in detail complaints in local newspapers at the privileged conditions of the colonial expatriates and at incomprehensible recruitment decisions, such as bringing out an English bricklayer in 1898 well after many important government buildings had been constructed using Lagosian bricklayers. The colonial officials had a different ethos from those merchants and pioneers of the 1850s and 1860s, and brought attitudes more suffused with the rampant imperialism of the 1890s. They also brought their wives, who at that time were more prone to racial prejudices, as had been seen in British India. Although many of the policies that sought to divide the city along racial lines were introduced under the McGregor Governorship, it was, as has been noted, Egerton who proved really provocative, engaging in such measures as introducing a water rate, which may have seemed logical to the colonial mind, but led to a prolonged series of demonstrations.

Dele Cole discovered "a vivid picture of bustling economic activity in an atmosphere of intense racial hatred" in the writing of the German anthropologist Leo Frobenius (who has often been criticized for espousing dubious racial theories, but in the history of anthropology was still a seminal figure). In his book *Voice of Africa* he wrote of a visit to Lagos in 1911. Frobenius was panicky about the dangers of mob violence ("the white race is running the gravest risk"), but his vivid description of Lagos crowds attending church on a Sunday evening has unusual intensity:

> The people pour in and out of numerous buildings like music-halls, glaring with electric light. They come on bicycles, swagger canes in their hands, cigarettes between their lips and top hats on their heads. They can be seen from the outside sitting in tightly packed crowds, singing for hours together. They display all the outward signs of advanced European civilisation, from patent leather boots to the single eye glass and every other individual wears spectacles or eye glasses of gold. And the ladies! Good Gracious me! The picture hats! The stoles! The frocks of silk! These temples of vanity blazing with illuminations like Variety theatres are Christian churches.

Chinua Achebe writes of how, even in the 1950s, he felt a stranger visiting "white" Ikoyi. He says he was one of the first Nigerians to live there other than stewards and cooks in the "boys' quarters"—the little boxes that were *de rigueur* behind every house built there, some of which have now been refurbished for renting out as one-room bedsits. Achebe's image of the duality of Lagos in his second novel *No Longer at Ease* (1960) is a powerful one: the city reminds his hero Obi Okonkwo of "twin kernels separated by a thin wall in a palm-nut shell. Sometimes one kernel was shiny-black and alive, the other powdery white and dead."

This was an unashamedly European quarter, with fine architecture, including the broad eaves and verandahs from the era before air-conditioning. It was also the location for the colonial institutions like the Ikoyi Club, which specifically stated in its constitution until the 1950s that it was "whites only" and never saw the possibility of Nigerian members. Not that they were particularly salubrious establishments. Sir Alan Burns in his memoir *Colonial Civil Servant* wrote of a predecessor of the Ikoyi Club called the Lagos Club, which in the 1920s was known as the "Gin tank," where "the imbibing of large quantities of hard liquor often led to the frenzied destruction of property."

The Yacht Club founded in 1938, as John and Jill Godwin stress in their history produced for the club's 75th anniversary, never had that kind of constitutional bar. In fact it had virtually no Nigerian members originally because of the high cost of yacht ownership. It was nonetheless said that the post-independence growth of the Motor Boat Club in southwest Ikoyi, not too far from the Yacht Club, attracted a largely Nigerian membership in part because of the "distant" nature of the Yacht Club. The two places still have strongly different ambiances.

A turning point in the official attitude to race relations came with the politically explosive Bristol Hotel incident of February 1947 (see a detailed account of this episode in Chapter 6) which led Governor Richards, probably to his own surprise, to bring an end to racial discrimination in the city. This had for a time been imposed in certain bars and public places apart from the Ikoyi Club, an imposition that proved to be against Lagos' general openness.

The 1950s saw the development of a new kind of elite, especially once political power began to be transferred, which meant that any color bar in the area soon began to disappear. With the rise of nationalism, Lagos was not the sort of place where overt racism could survive. African elites began to move to Ikoyi from the overcrowded Island, but it always kept its superior cachet as the place for the upper crust and was regarded with awe. Cyprian Ekwensi in his novel *Jagua Nana*, published in 1961 just after independence, has his eponymous heroine draw in her breath at the very mention of the place:

> Ikoyi. That was the Government Reservation where the white men and the Africans high up in the civil service lived. Ikoyi, where the streets were straight and smooth, where they played golf on the open sands: a reservation complete with its own police-station, electricity base, motor-boat beaches, a romantic place…

Small wonder that Fela Kuti sang in the 1970s of "Ikoyi mentality" in pointed contrast to "Mushin mentality" (see Chapter 9). Thus the duality of the palm kernel perceived by Achebe survived in a different but equally vivid non-racial form.

THE BRAZILIAN IMPRINT

The Brazilians were not as driven to education as the Saros, and because initially they did not speak English they were not considered as recruits to the administration. They were more skilled as craftsmen and builders, and the particular techniques they brought from Bahia made them much in demand. The impact of Brazilians on architecture has been set out in detail by John Godwin in a paper on the subject: where British colonial building derived more from Rome than Lisbon, the Brazilians brought designs "less inhibited by classical rules." Although there were large expanses of solid walls punctuated by smaller windows, "the plastered surfaces reflect the plastic nature of cement and lime mortar to produce heavily moulded architraves and cornices embellished with features resembling plant forms…"

Ironically Brazilian style was seen at its most spectacular in the mosques, and although the beautiful Central Mosque was knocked down in the 1960s to be replaced with the kind of standard flat-pack mosque found all over the Islamic world, the Shitta-Bay Mosque in Martins Street, built over a ten year period and opened in 1894 (see Chapter 10), has miraculously survived. It used Brazilian masons (directed by the particularly brilliant mason Juan Baptist da Costa) and is still an astonishing example of Brazilian architecture adapted to the service of Islam. Alas, the tradition of craft among Brazilians did not survive the generations. By the 1950s the construction industry in Lagos was conducted by Italian firms such as Cappa d'Alberto, and is now in the hands of a range of other companies, both national and international, including the ubiquitous Julius Berger.

The Brazilians were particularly renowned for building their own fine replicas of the architecture of Salvador de Bahia and Recife of which there are many examples still in Lagos, although some are in a poor state of repair. In *The Torchbearers*, a short book by J. Laotan published in 1910, the achievements of the Brazilian community in its unique and distinctive heyday are lovingly recounted, and some old Brazilian families still treasure their copies of the book.

Godwin praises specially the Vaughan House and the Lumpkin House (painstakingly restored ten years ago with help from the Leventis Foundation). However, the best known Brazilian two-story structure still standing is the Water House in Kakawa Street, commemorated in literature in the novel of the same name by Antonio Olinto, former cultural attaché at the Brazilian Embassy in Lagos in the 1960s. *The Water House* was first published in Portuguese in 1969 with the title *A Casa da Aqua*, and translated into

The Water House

English the next year. Over the years it has become an unusual work of reference. The story centers on a girl from Abeokuta who is taken to Brazil as a slave, earns her freedom and returns to Lagos, but it concerns her family and her descendants and gives a comprehensive portrayal of changing life among the Lagos Brazilians over several decades.

The book also shows how far the Brazilians, particularly those involved in trade, were restlessly moving up and down the coast, especially to Whydah and Porto Novo. Olinto's story tells how they moved across the newly drawn colonial borders with no difficulty, even during the First World War. He still uses a fictional country.

There are also important Brazilian families in Cotonou, Lomé and Accra. The Brazilians in Lomé in particular became politically highlighted by the Olympio regime and its demise in 1963, but Togo was the only country along the coast where "Brazilian-ness" ever became a political issue: it was used ruthlessly by Gnassingbé Eyadéma after his bloody ascent to power.

Although fictional, the story of *The Water House* bears some resemblances to the story of the Da Rocha family: João Esan da Rocha was taken as a slave to Brazil but gained his freedom and returned to Lagos with his wife and child in the 1870s. Entering the Lagos-Bahia trade, he was given land in Kakawa Street where he built the real Water House. His eldest son Candido launched his own business career, and his second son Moyses was one of the earliest Nigerian medical doctors, qualifying in 1913. The family still owns and lives in the Water House, and like many other Brazilians retains contact with the parts of the family that remained in Brazil. The accountant Bode Emanuel tells me that there is a branch of his family, the Manuels, who own a good deal of property in Bahia. Indeed, the old Brazilian families—Fernandez, Pereira, Medeiros, Gomez, da Costa, da

Silva, da Rocha, Pedro, Agusto and many others—still form one of the core elites of old Lagos.

At one point Olinto quotes a character in the novel talking of all that the Brazilians had brought to Lagos. "Old Teresa," a veteran Lagos Brazilian, tells young Mariana, newly returned from Bahia to Lagos in the late nineteenth century, when she asks why locals disrupting Brazilian festivals are referred to as Africans: "We are Brazilians. You have just arrived and don't know what things are like here. We are civilised people, different from those others. It was us who taught the people here joinery, we taught them how to build big houses, and churches, we brought cassava, cashews, cocoa, dried meat…"

The Brazilian contribution to the buildings of Lagos is obvious and visible, and they also found themselves prominent in trade. They may well have contributed to the nineteenth-century spread of cassava in Nigeria, where it is one of the staple crops today. There is some uncertainty about the claim that they brought cocoa, as historians generally believe that cocoa was smuggled to Nigeria in 1874 from the highly protected Spanish plantations on Fernando Po. The cocoa bean was said to have been brought to Nigeria by a Delta trader called Chief Squiss Ibanango, who set up the first cocoa growing area in Opobo, from whence it spread westwards. This was four years before the celebrated Tetteh Quarshie, in a much better-publicized act of enlightened smuggling, took it to the Gold Coast and began commercial plantations there, although missionaries had been experimenting with it in the 1850s. West Africa eventually became the most productive cocoa-growing area in the world.

Cocoa was originally a Mexican plant, and its processed form had become popular in Europe as early as the seventeenth century, but the plants only appeared in West Africa in the nineteenth century. The Portuguese established cocoa plantations in São Tomé and Príncipe in the 1820s, so it is conceivable that the Brazilians may have taken it to Lagos, but this remains obscure. They certainly brought cashew nuts, originally native to northeastern Brazil and propagated in different parts of Portugal's overseas empire. It is on the record that cocoa was grown late in the century in the Agege Botanic Garden which replaced the original one set up by Governor Moloney in Ebute Metta, removed when the railway was built. This was prior to the substantial expansion of cocoa growing in the early twentieth century in what became Western Nigeria.

Breadfruit was almost certainly brought to Lagos by the Portuguese. Although the British were assiduous in spreading breadfruit throughout their empire from the time it was found in the Pacific in the eighteenth century, it predated their arrival in Lagos. It came to be associated with slavery as it offered cheap and plentiful food for slaves, and was taken by the British to the Caribbean, where it is found in profusion. The early nineteenth-century slavers (whether Portuguese, Brazilians or other) brought breadfruit trees to Lagos, and the trees in central Lagos were associated with the barracoons. It was said in the second part of the nineteenth century one could still see marks on the trees from where the slaves were tied.

RAILWAY TRAINS AND MOTOR CARS

British colonial and imperial expansion always had a central role for railways. The Victorian psyche contained a fascination with railways as harbingers of new technology, the true symbols of the scientific progress central to the nineteenth century, but they were also the means to economic progress and early anchors of globalization. Thus once the British found themselves established in the lands of the Niger Delta which were to become Nigeria, a railway was essential to bring the produce that would make the country expand. And the railway was bound to begin in Lagos, even if Port Harcourt was on its way to being an alternative pole of development.

The railway was begun in 1895 from the new terminal in Iddo and was in Ibadan by 1900, advancing northwards. Within the Lagos area it proceeded in a straight line north-northwest to Agege, a line which soon afterwards brought the construction of the Agege Motor Road. The terminal predated the Carter Bridge, actually constructed for the tramway. The first footbridge was at Five Cowrie Creek in the 1890s. The bridge there for motor transport was only built in 1931.

By the 1920s there was a rail network stretching far into the north to Kaura Namoda on the Niger border, with a spur from the central junction of Kafanchan down to Port Harcourt as an alternative outlet to the sea. A further extension was built to Maiduguri in the far northeast in 1964, which was probably the high point of the railway system in Nigeria, but the central nexus ran from Lagos to the north. This national railway system changed the whole character of Lagos because of the way it connected the capital with the hinterland, facilitating movement of people and goods. It was the means by which major development including a few nascent industries came to Lagos, especially in the 1920s, and by which migrant populations flooded to the capital. The railway helped to further shape Lagos into a national melting pot as more and more peoples from different parts converged and mixed. It also made its contribution to the look of the city, as the line of rail, parallel to the Agege Motor Road and bisecting the mainland into two separate areas, was itself a magnet for markets and traders.

Alongside the railways, the greatest boost to development had come from the other great engineering project in Lagos in the early years of the century—the building of the two moles from 1908 to 1913, which meant that the notorious bar became a thing of the past and the port of Lagos could be used all the year round. The first mail steamer to enter Lagos port bound for Customs Wharf on Lagos Island was the SS *Akoko* in February 1914. The opening of the 1,500-foot-long Apapa quay in 1926 was an important moment, preceded by the inauguration in 1919 of the coal wharf at Ijora (vital for generating electricity) and followed by the new petroleum jetty at Apapa in 1933.

The development of the port into the "Liverpool of West Africa" was a huge agent of change, not just of economic development but of social transformation. This was not just because of the way it facilitated movement to the interior, which intensified with the building of the road network in the years between the wars. External trade also increased phenomenally (exports from Lagos port grew from £500,000 in 1900 to over £60 million in 1960) and diversified after 1912 from palm oil and kernels to cocoa, groundnuts, cotton, tin and hides and skins. The 1950s saw a further massive expansion of the port at Apapa, but it was in the 1970s, when port congestion in Lagos/Apapa reached intolerable proportions with the huge traffic generated by the oil booms, that a new ultra-modern container port was built at Tin Can Island on the creek south of Apapa/Ajegunle. It was opened in 1978.

THE LAGOS STEAM TRAMWAY

One of the most unusual features of colonial Lagos was the steam tramway. Of all the new-fangled phenomena brought by the colonialists, which must have convinced the inhabitants of Lagos of the inevitability of

progress, this was it. It took passengers
from Iddo Railway Station across Carter
Bridge through the hub and crossroads at
Idumota to Customs Wharf on the
Marina. From there it went along the
length of the Marina, to cross over the
creek ending at Dejection Point, where

The steam railway

there was a jetty. This was believed to have been named because it originally housed slave barracoons. It is now the site of the Bonny Camp.

The steam tramway only lasted just over thirty years, from 1902 to
1933, although the night-soil trains that moved along it in the early hours
of the morning continued a little while longer. It was killed off by the
motor car, first introduced in the early 1900s, which made great strides as
more main roads became tarred in the 1920s, but the steam railway
remained and remains the model for those who would like to see some
form of overland rail reintroduced to help solve Lagos' present immense
problems with mass transit. As immortalized in Neville Miller's book, the
steam railway was a remarkable pioneering venture for its time, which
must have been sorely regretted when it closed down, and could have been
the basis for a much earlier development of mass transit had it survived.

The Airports
Airport development has been a key feature in the identity of modern
Lagos. When I first went to Nigeria in 1964, I made it to Lagos after a
stopover in Kano and found an extremely modest affair of single-story
shacks. But air was already becoming the main way of moving in and out
of the country, and Nigerians became among the most inveterate travelers
in the world, acquiring the reputation of having more baggage than any
others.

With the oil-fuelled post-war boom in the 1970s traffic increased
vastly, and a new international airport, also in Ikeja, was decided on by the
Gowon administration. It was opened later in the decade in March 1979,
and given the name of the assassinated leader Murtala Muhammed (the
name now being sometimes curtailed to MMA). The terminal building,
thought to be a great wonder when first opened, succumbed in the con-
strained 1980s to the twin Nigerian disease of lack of maintenance and
bureaucratic corruption.

The besetting sins of the airport in its worst phase were memorably captured in a four-part documentary "Lagos Airport" made by Donu Kogbara, a particularly feisty Nigerian journalist who did not "spare her mouth" when it came to exposing some of the shortcomings of the place. Unfortunately, it is still shown as a Third World horror story by Channel Four in the UK and, I am told, elsewhere internationally, even though conditions have changed dramatically. Improvement came around the time of civilian rule in 1999 when open petty corruption by airport personnel was restrained and facilities like air-conditioning and the moving walkways for access to flights along the airport's wings were resuscitated. Although the walkways do not always work and the air-conditioning is feeble, it is still so much better than it was that people do not complain, except when the baggage chains break down. It is still, as they say, due for a major upgrade. The opening of a more modernistic and sophisticated internal terminal (known as Murtala Muhammed II) on the site of the original airport in the heart of Ikeja has opened up prospects of what airport terminal improvement could be like.

THE POPULATION EXPLOSION

From the 5,000 people recorded by John Adams around 1800, the early nineteenth-century growth of the slave trade meant that by the time the British arrived in 1851 the population of Lagos had grown modestly in fifty years to probably 20,000: as Mabogunje says, "compared with Ibadan, Lagos was a very small town occupying a small part of a small island," and the next fifty years were "more a period of consolidation than growth". The British began recording the population in 1866 when it was 25,083, rising to 37,452 in 1871, an increase of 23.9 per cent, after which growth appeared to slow down, although there were, then as now, wide inaccuracies in census taking. By 1901 it was put at 39,387 (41,847 if Iddo and Ebute Metta were included). From then on, especially with the arrival of the railway and port, the population figures took off, enhanced by the increased coverage of the areas where the population was counted. By 1921 over twenty square miles were counted to include 99,690 individuals, and by 1950 this had more than doubled to over 230,000 in over twenty-seven square miles, taking in substantial areas of the mainland including Apapa and Ikeja.

At independence in 1960 Lagos' population was estimated at over

600,000, but since then there has been increasing divergence between federal census figures and what Lagos itself believes its population to be. UN estimated figures for the "Lagos agglomeration," which is not coterminous with Lagos State, show the city's population increased from over two million in 1970 to 3.3 million in 1975 and nearly 7.5 million in 1990, while the 1991 census, generally said to have been undercounted, put Lagos State's population at 5,725,000. The serious divergence came in 2006 when the census gave the State just over nine million, while the State's parallel census came up with over seventeen million, a huge discrepancy which allows no accommodation (see Chapter 11).

The intensity and rapidity of the growth of Lagos relate in part to the fact that from the early twentieth century onwards it was both the federal capital and the nexus of a commercial complex covering the port, the railways and the airport. In the 1950s and 1960s there was a large expansion of both government and private-sector building. This rapid and unceasing growth changed Lagos in the twenty years after independence from a relatively controllable city into a mega-monster, and even after the federal capital formally departed in December 1991 commercial development, alongside the increasing success of Lagos State, has made the management of expansion and change an even more ferocious challenge.

OFFICIAL BUILDINGS

By independence, Lagos was identifiable particularly by its official buildings, wonderful in their day but now, with the loss of the authority and funding of the federal government, more often than not a little dilapidated. From the early days of British rule there were some prime examples of official colonial architecture, notably State House (built in the 1880s though much reconstructed), with its gardens facing on to the Marina. It housed the Governor, then the Governor-General and then, after the interlude of military rule—when the head of state's residence was for the most part in Dodan barracks—the civilian president from 1979 to 1983. It is now a Lagos State building but is no longer used as a residence (already extensively described in Chapter 2). Among early buildings still surviving, one should also note the Government Printer office in Broad Street put up in 1895, one of the most attractive colonial structures still standing, well deserving of preservation in spite of not being in use at the time of writing.

When the Supreme Court building in Tinubu Square was demolished in the 1950s, the Court was given fine new premises by the side of the racecourse. It was not far from the King's College building of 1910, another piece of distinctive colonial architecture, which its alumni are seeking to refurbish in the wake of its centenary. Another

The old Federal Secretariat building: "the most handsome building of its kind I have yet seen in British Africa," Margery Perham, 1931

fine structure from the inter-war period, the former Federal Secretariat on the Marina, still stands.

Although Lagos Island had continued to expand, especially as land was reclaimed, it was only the approach of independence that led to a major new rash of building, very often of a new kind in which the influences of modernism held full sway as it was felt that there should be buildings appropriate for a newly independent nation. One such was the Federal Parliament, home of the short-lived Westminster model, now occasionally used for meetings by Lagos State. It was described by Elspeth Huxley in her 1954 book *Four Guineas* when the building was very new, as "Festival of Britain crossed with a Beau Geste fort." There was a sculpture of Queen Elizabeth II placed outside it by Nigeria's outstanding sculptor Ben Enwonwu, who died in 1994. His many commissions can be seen around, including the Yoruba deity Shango outside the headquarters of the Power Handling Company of Nigeria (PHCN) on the Marina. According to his son Oliver,

who runs the Enwonwu Foundation from Ben's former lagoon-side house in Ikoyi Crescent, the Queen's bust in storage, but it was brought out for an exhibition in Abuja in 2010 to mark Nigeria's half-century.

One also has to mention the Independence Building, a twenty-story structure in Tafawa Balewa Square built in 1960, housing at that time a number of federal ministries. Its height was awkward when there were power cuts in the age before the universal generator. I recall that when the European Economic Community Commissioner Claude Cheysson was visiting in 1977 and found himself on the twentieth floor in the middle of a cut, he decided to run down all twenty flights, saying it reminded him of descending ski slopes. From being the height of modernity with a glamorous view of the city, which I often visited when I was first in Lagos, it deteriorated to a sad structure that the civil servants were eventually glad to be shot of when they departed to Abuja in the early 1990s. A federal property, it was eventually in 2009 privatized and designated as a World Trade Center to house "core parastatals of the Ministry of Trade and Industry."

The political change signalled by the move to Abuja left its mark on the city. There were a number of former federal landmarks of which some were left in decline, while some were taken over by Lagos State such as the federal parliament building and some of the ministries. The emphasis was more on the fact that the city was now definitely the commercial capital. The more recent Federal Secretariat, a vast megalith on the road into Ikoyi, was built in the 1970s comprising three seven-storey structures where the lifts seldom worked. It was eventually privatized in 2009, which means that with basically sound structures it is being converted to private offices on a prime site. A major landmark, the City Hall in the middle of the business district on Lagos Island, a fine modernistic structure originally built in 1964 to house the Lagos City Council but for years in disrepair after a fire and lack of use, has also been smartly refurbished as a Lagos State public function building.

Lagos is now getting used to its newly reconfigured identity as the commercial capital, which geography and history will never take away from it—a New York, a Sydney or a Rio de Janeiro. But it always was more than anything a trading city, and the story of the business quarter is extraordinary, going back to the trade in slaves and other commodities in the eighteenth century, expanding and adapting in the nineteenth and into the colonial period, which gave its commercial vocation an undeniable boost. Although in the various snapshots we have of the city from the mid-nineteenth century onwards there is an astonishingly mixed cast of international characters (some of them fairly disreputable), the arrival of mission education was the key to the rapid development of an educated elite. Commerce, however, made its own special mark on the look of the city.

COMMERCIAL BUILDINGS

The first commercial buildings, as we have seen, were located on the Marina in the 1850s and slowly developed as trade expanded. The 1920s and 1930s saw fine examples such as department stores, notably the United Africa Company's Kingsway Stores on the Marina, home from home for expatriates and Nigerian elites for a generation. Some of the buildings put up in the 1950s and early 1960s were of an architectural quality yet to be appreciated.

My friend and informant Giles Omezi stresses that the contribution of British architects is badly in need of documentation. Maxwell Fry and Jane Drew pioneered what he calls "Anglo-West African modernism." Although best-known for the campus at the University of Ibadan, there is a fine example of their work in the Senate building on the campus of Unilag (the University of Lagos). The Nigerian academic Ola Uduku says this modernist period was "unique and short-lived." She praises particularly the "tropical modernism" of James Cubitt's Elder Dempster building on the Marina, which was completed in the 1960s just as the pre-eminence of the shipping line was coming to an end—the line ceased to exist in 1974.

Both Omezi and Uduku praise Century House on the corner of Broad Street and Tinubu Square, built by the British architects John and Jill Godwin, and the imaginative work of more recent Nigerian architects such as Olumuyiwa and Alex Ekwueme. Uduku also draws particular attention to Alan Vaughan-Richards' "exploratory and localised" approach to the production of Nigerian architecture, notably his highly original 1964 Ola-Oluwakitan Cottage in Ikeja, a model for a host of remarkable modern locality-related private residences built over the years, private treasures of the city of the imagination and templates for what Lagos could and can be. The evolution of architectural styles in Lagos is brilliantly documented in the book *Building Lagos* by Vaughan-Richards and Akinsemoyin, produced at the time of FESTAC in 1977, which is hard to obtain and deserves reprinting, if only for its fantastic line drawings of Lagos buildings. I am told that this has now been done by the Lagos State government.

For the first half of the twentieth century, between the arrival of steam and the growth of air travel, Elder Dempster was the leader in both freight and passenger transport, and its building was intended as a symbol of the line's major role in Nigeria's contacts with the outside world. As Uduku notes, MV *Aureol*, its flagship mail boat, which "took missionaries and government functionaries to British West Africa in the last days of 'empire' and also the newly returning elite from their educational sojourns abroad," ended its life as a leisure facility for workers in Dubai. The shipping office's position built on the shoreline of the Lagos Marina "ensured its incorporation into the Lagos skyline as the first view of the city as the first view of the city by passengers and ships coming into the Lagos lagoon." She makes the point that its distinctive sculpted funnel atop the building symbolized the company's self-perceived (if soon to be ended) dominance. The building soon became overshadowed by bigger buildings, and was distanced from the lagoon by motorways, but it is still an architectural gem, last heard of as the home of a property company.

At John Godwin's eightieth birthday celebration at the Lagos Yacht Club in 2008, his son Anthony said his parents had been "doing sustainable architecture long before anybody had thought of the word." They were providing "tropical architecture in the modern movement style." He added, "When all of the gas guzzlers and glass buildings have gone, students will rediscover how to build appropriately in this climate." There was also a tribute at the event from Demas Nwoko, the tall and white-bearded artist/architect whose buildings, it is said, took the Godwins' ideas and added a cultural dimension.

In the 1970s and 1980s new building in the center of Lagos became more dramatic and aspirational, as seen especially in new high-rise construction on the Marina such as the First Bank, Union Bank and Nigerian Stock Exchange buildings, the beginning of the myth of the African Manhattan. An early example was the building of Nigerian Telecommunications (NITEL), damaged in a fire in 1983—an event seen at the time as symbolizing the blockages represented by Nigeria's parastatals. This was before Nigerian telephony was revolutionized from the 1990s onwards by the arrival of mobile phones, beginning in Lagos and spreading through the country so that by the end of 2010 there were over seventy million such phones, some ten million of which were in Lagos, reducing landlines almost to obsolescence.

And then there were the hotels: although there were certain lodging houses from early in the century—and Morel mentions hotels in 1911—most overseas visitors lodged in rest-houses (both government and company) or, like Mary Kingsley, stayed with officials or traders. The era of hotels proper began after the Second World War with a number of legendary hotels on the mainland like the Ambassadors or the Empire, and on Lagos Island the Domo on Campbell Street. These did not figure, however, in the hotels listed in the *Nigeria Handbook of Commerce and Industry* for 1952, which included the Bristol Hotel in Martins Street, the Grand Hotel and the Olympic Hotel in Broad Street and the Savoy Hotel in Balogun Square (near the still thriving Balogun Market).

Apart from the Bristol, none of these survived into the 1960s. The Bristol was an old hotel of some standing that was reconstructed in the late 1950s on the corner of Broad Street and Martins Street. A modernistic tower block with plenty of the black mosaic fashionable at the time, it was for a while a great social meeting-place in what was then the authentic business center of the city, concentrated on the western end of Broad Street. I stayed there on my first visit in 1964, when it was still an establishment of reputation, and thought nothing of walking along Broad Street to go to the *Daily Times* office that was maybe ten minutes away.

The two hotels built for independence in 1960 deserve particular note. The Federal Palace, in particular, housed the most important invited guests for the independence celebrations and led to an important opening up of the hitherto neglected Victoria Island. The Ikoyi Hotel on the borders between south-west Ikoyi and Ikoyi proper was another contemporary landmark. Despite the oil boom there were only three new additions at that time to the top-of-the-market Lagos hotel community: the Suites extension to the Federal Palace, built in time for FESTAC in 1977; the Durbar Hotel on the edge of Festac Town; and the Eko Hotel by the side of Kuramo Waters on Victoria Island, which was opened in time for the First International Trade Fair held later in 1977. There were also more unpretentious hotels on the mainland: the Mainland Hotel in Iddo, the Airport Hotel in Ikeja and the Excelsior in Apapa.

A sad tale of the Nigerian hotel business is that of the same Bristol Hotel which, after years as a haven for currency dealers, now appears to be mainly a container depot. For the record, there is a dramatic view of the Hotel Newcastle (with its sign in a quaint late nineteenth-century font) in Ilupeju from the Apapa Expressway, and I personally feel obliged to include the Peoples' Hotel, Ajegunle (see Chapter 10).

The Airport Hotel in Ikeja was built in the 1950s as air travel developed, as were a number of smaller hotels like the Niger Palace in Yaba. The Mainland Hotel was built by the Leventis company (a Greek Cypriot family business well-established in Lagos) at a strategic location in Iddo on the north side of Carter Bridge and was extensively remodeled in the late 1960s. An important new addition came in the 1980s in the shape of the Sheraton on the Airport Road in Ikeja, which was long considered the best hotel in the capital before becoming slightly tattered while remaining highly priced.

In general, it has been a commonplace that Lagos has been starved of good hotels, an unusual state of affairs that only now is beginning to be rectified. Although a number of improved middle-standard hotels such as the Ambassador in South-West Ikoyi and BJs at the beginning of the Lekki Motorway have a certain clientele, Lagos has been notorious for expensive purportedly five-star hotels, disappointing for a major international city. These have to include the Eko (which passed through various management incarnations) and the Sheraton. Some old Lagosians shed a qualified tear for the flattening of the Ikoyi (so full of memories), now replaced with the South African-managed Southern Sun.

There is also the new outcrop of so-called "boutique" hotels, some beginning to be developed by South African companies such as Protea hotels on Victoria Island, and at Oakwood Park on Lekki Motorway (this one has conference facilities) and the very up-market establishments at Kuramo Waters as well as near the airport. Much cherished by some visitors among the smaller hotels is the Italian guest house Manuela's. Others favor the pioneering Moorhouse (Sofitel), including Nigerians themselves who have caught on to the idea, as seen for example in a guest house called Kakafoni, now closed. The top of the market is now rapidly being expanded with the classy ten-year refurbishment of the Federal Palace, the arrival of the Chinese-managed Mandarin Imperial on the Lekki motorway, the popular lagoon-side Radisson on the north side of Victoria Island and the Intercontinental in the center of Victoria Island.

MERCHANTS AND ENTREPRENEURS: THE LIVERPOOL OF WEST AFRICA?

After the British colonial push of the 1890s, some of the elite including Saros were obliged to go into business because of the poor prospects of government and even the professions, though some had been in business from the beginning. There was always a merchant class going back to the days of the slave trade that slipped easily into palm oil and other commodities.

The trade of Lagos, although inevitably extraverted, was never totally dominated by foreigners (unlike in many of the French territories) despite the favors given to European firms by the colonial government and the arrival of foreign bankers and the introduction little by little of sterling, as a Western-style economy was constructed in the last four decades of the nineteenth century, replacing the cowries that had from the previous century onwards shown a remarkable resilience as a West African currency. The establishment of the West African Currency Board in 1912 (see Chapter 2) formalized the colonial financial economy that had been increasingly operational since the 1860s. At the same time banks began to develop, first foreign-owned, progressively replaced by mainly Nigerian ownership. The Colonial Bank opened in 1917, was taken over by Barclays in 1925 and Nigerianized as the Union Bank in the 1970s.

The *Red Book of West Africa*, a 1923 publication enormously rich in material, contains a number of thumbnail sketches of Nigerian business-men in Lagos and presents a remarkable picture of the business society in the city at the time and the extent to which prominent Nigerians were involved in it. Notable Nigerian figures profiled include particularly Samuel Herbert Pearse, produce merchant and wealthy citizen who lived in the now demolished four-story Elephant House on Broad Street, which the *Red Book* describes as "a home of good foundations, of large elegantly furnished rooms, a house beautiful with its roof garden, and its delightful turret chamber, where to the mind attuned to ideal high above mundane things, a perspective may be greater than that of the busy Nigerian port…" The Elephant House was known for its ballroom on the second floor "with artistic electric light illuminations, which, if the whim should arise, could well be dispensed with for the enjoyment of dancing in the glorious Niger-ian moonlight flooding the big room through its extensive windows. The music of a full orchestra is supplied by a large orchestrion operated by elec-tric power."

Other Nigerians highlighted include J. H. Doherty, general merchant of Alakoro; Ekundayo Phillips, chemist, optician, druggist, patent medi-cine vendor and musician in Faji Market; W. A. Dawodu of Daddy Alaja Street, importer of motor cars, cycles, spare parts and accessories etc. There are also several pages of foreign business with photos of look-alike Europeans (often with moustaches) working for G. B. Ollivant, Paterson Zochonis, British American Tobacco and many others.

As a postscript one should record that the global depression of the 1930s put paid to many Nigerian-owned businesses, while the foreign ones were better able to survive. Toyin Falola and Matthew M. Heaton have recorded in their *History of Nigeria* that the total value of exports, which stood at over £17 million in 1929, had shrunk to £9.7 million by 1938, which they contrast pointedly with the fact that the United Africa Company of Nigeria's profits between 1932 and 1938 never went below nine per cent of total turnover.

THE DREAM OF A MANHATTAN OF AFRICA

The physical history of the city has been one of a rhythm of perpetual slum clearances and redevelopment alongside land reclamation, especially from the 1880s onwards. There was a particular bout after the bubonic plague epidemic in 1928, which, as we have seen, led to the setting up of the Lagos Executive Development Board (LEDB), although the global depression led to a more general decline in development after the boom of the 1920s. The same year saw the beginning of a more coherent approach to development after the infrastructure free-for-all following the expansion of railways, port and roads.

Professor Mabogunje also notes that there was a major and conscious expansion to the mainland in the 1950s in the run-up to independence. The LEDB, in counterpoint to the activities of the Western Region, encouraged the build-up of industries in that period, especially in Apapa around the port where there were manufacturing businesses well before the Ikeja Industrial Estate. The coming of Lagos State combined with the oil boom to drive further development, and in spite of the recession of the 1980s expansion continued relentlessly with a logic of its own, fueled by the perpetual attraction of a metropolis paved with gold and reinforced immensely by the parallel boom in the informal sector which has always been such a singular and dominating feature of the city.

The potential of the narrow strip on the south side of Lagos Island adjacent to the Marina was solidly developed between 1860 and 1960 (and indeed up to the 1980s) as a business district. Economic activity exploded even more dramatically just before and after independence and created a further need for new housing for those who could obtain sites. In the 1950s the LEDB organized a push out to Surulere, the suburb beyond Yaba which started life as a new development for the Nigerian middle classes, while shanties were built up in Mushin and Ajegunle.

Yet the possibilities of Lagos Island were never realized. This was partly due to unavoidable inadequacies in traffic planning to and from the Island, leading to the rise of the famous go-slows, worsening as more and more concrete over-ground expressways encircled Lagos Island. There have been many foreign companies that have left their imprint on the city, such as the United Africa Company (from Kingsway Stores to Mr Bigg's) but none more so than Julius Berger (see Chapter 2). One commentator of my acquaintance has written: "The configuration of the interchanges on the expressways had the effect of bypassing the Island, and were in fact mainly built on landfill clear of contentious land acquisitions," which spelt a kind of death-knell for a sympathetic environment. One of the worst effects of the "Bergerization" of Lagos was on the Marina itself. It was, alas, a frustration of the dream of modernization because it destroyed the unique urban togetherness of central Lagos that had always focused on the Marina. However hard re-beautification might be tried, the early special ambiance of the Marina can never really be recovered.

However, the dream of the Manhattan of Africa was circumscribed by the vested interests of the indigenes which, as the same expert says, "froze potential development sites, and pushed business to the mainland, which was adroitly exploited by the Western Nigeria Development Corporation" when control of areas like Ikeja and Apapa fell under the Western Region in the 1950s. So natural expansion was limited, and on Lagos Island itself there was effectively no development north of Tinubu Square. Historically this was due to the initial granting of land along the Marina to foreigners by Obas Akitoye and Dosunmu in the 1850s, while to the north the land was owned by traditional interests. This highlights once again what a seminal period the ten years of the Lagos Consulate (1851-61) proved to be in so many ways for the eventual look and shape of the city. The foreigners were both merchants and missionaries, but the churches nowadays only have one important foothold left on the Marina.

Thus the would-be Manhattan had a lopsided and incomplete look, which remains to this day symbolic of the city's unrealized dream. By the late 1970s when development on the mainland showed its disadvantages,

The African Manhattan?

the center of business gravity started moving to Victoria Island with all the drawbacks of chaotic lack of planning that we are now witnessing there. Lagos Island suffered further setbacks with the recession of the 1980s and the rise of the influence of the "area boys" whose strength on the Island had a stunting effect on the further development of business there, which not surprisingly sought other outlets.

Over the past few years a project to rehabilitate the business district of Lagos Island has resurfaced; Governor Tinubu (1999-2007) included it as part of his "legacy," as described in an extensive advertorial in *The News* magazine. The Eko Atlantic City project, depending on the recuperation of Bar Beach, is also another of the Tinubu projects for Lagos continued in the Fashola era (see Chapter 10). Although this initially generated a certain amount of disbelief, the transformation of Bar Beach into what now looks like a fortification is a portent of things to come.

The departure of federal institutions also contributed indirectly to the city's physical stand-offs. The result is that "the Island" is now a bizarre and dysfunctional mix of the wilderness of skyscrapers, street markets, old shops and residences, all under pressure from the ubiquitous and extortion-demanding "area boys," a phenomenon recently tamed in the Tinubu-

Fashola era but not eliminated. The business focus dispersed northwards, southwards and eastwards, spilling over eastwards through the refurbished Maroko to Lekki. Yet business chaos is still miraculously excluded by influential residents from the slowly fading but still prestigious Ikoyi, although the sneaking in of British Airways, MTN and the redeveloped Ikoyi Hotel named the Southern Sun (which eventually is to have a shopping mall attached) presages further creeping commercialization, especially as blocks of apartments replace the old low-eaved colonial houses. There is so much money now to be made from redeveloping high value land, especially as the reclamation of land continues in places like Banana Island.

In this context the question of real estate and land ownership becomes a subject in itself. When one starts examining the issue of who owns which property one raises the fundamental issue of the social anthropology of wealth and the way in which the identity of the seriously wealthy of Lagos has changed rapidly, a by-product of the history of oil money and of politics (especially military politics) and the growth of corruption in Nigeria as a whole. This is an area where only the writers can do justice to the social flavor, from Achebe and Soyinka to Kole Omotoso in *Memories of Our Recent Boom* (which although not a Lagos novel is one of the best recreations of the effect of the oil boom on the Nigerian psyche) to the current new crop of novelists who are writing more openly and objectively about Lagos and its unique reality.

ROADS, MARKETS AND MALLS

Two special features of Lagos can be further highlighted—the influence of the motor car, and the distinctive importance of buying and selling. The first motor cars came in the early 1900s and the first bus company was started in 1909. In a few years motor transport had surpassed the railways, especially for passenger traffic, and having put paid to the Lagos steam railway became the dominant factor in transport, especially as macadamized roads expanded in the 1920s. Long distance lorries only came in as competition to the railways when the roads to the north were tarred in the 1940s. In Lagos the motor vehicle was just about manageable up to the 1960s, when congestion began to get seriously out of hand.

The introduction of assembly plants (Mercedes, Volkswagen, Peugeot in the 1950s and 1960s) augmented the vehicle population and encouraged the growth of the motorway and the accompanying jams, among the worst anywhere in the world: Nigeria now has 20 cars per kilometer, while Lagos State has 220 per kilometer—even if the assembly plants in Lagos and Ibadan are now closed and multitudes of vehicles find their way into Nigeria from the Benin Republic. A visit to the enlarged port of Cotonou reveals a massive number of stored containers waiting to go to Nigeria. With the oil boom and the supply of subsidized fuel—which despite pressures to increase prices has continued to this day—the railways went into decline. Opportunities in Lagos for mass rail transit were not taken, although this is now being amended by Governor Fashola's administration.

Markets have been a particular feature of Lagos from very early in its history. If the most notorious was the slave market in the middle of what is now the Marina, there was a produce market in Eko known as Faji, after an eighteenth-century market woman called Madam Faji, a precursor of Madam Tinubu. The area of the market is still known as Faji. Indeed, from the eighteenth century the markets have had a traditional relationship with the Oba. The political significance of market women is also historic, going right back to Madam Faji and above all Madam Tinubu a century later, the symbolic forerunners of all Lagos' hugely powerful trading women.

Their contemporary successor is Hadja Habibatu Mogaji (Iya Oba, or Oba Yeye), nonagenarian veteran President of the Nigerian Association

Hadja Habibatu Mogaji

83

of Market Women and Men. When I arrived to visit her in 2007 on one of the Tuesdays when all the heads of markets in Lagos gather in her compound in Ikeja, she was asleep and I was told that not even the Oba is allowed to wake her up—he removes his headwear in her company, the only person to be so privileged. She has been the confidante of all the main political powers in Lagos since the 1950s from Chief Awolowo onwards, and still engenders enormous respect. After waking up, she received me while taking a footbath and, in the Yoruba language, blessed all my projects including this book. A formal interview was conducted with her secretary, however.

The trading imperative that has always governed Lagos developed into the huge retail operations like the Alaba international market on the Badagry Road, which are pillars of the informal sector, the lifeblood of Lagos. There has been a continuous uphill, almost Sisyphean, battle of governments against street traders going back to the colonial period; it has entered a new phase under the Fashola administration, seen in the way in which the massive congestion at the Oshodi bus stop, on the Apapa expressway, was eased in 2008 by clearing away the traders who had multiplied there. How long the smoother passage will last is anybody's guess, but it demonstrated that modified regulation (which some have deemed an impossible illusion) could be possible.

Local industries also played a role in trading patterns that grew up in the colonial period, especially in the latter part when industrial estates were developed in both Apapa and Ikeja (the latter more a result of the time Ikeja came under the governance of the Western Region in the 1950s). Of particular significance were the food and drink industries such as Nestlé and Cadbury, Nigerian Breweries (connected to Heineken) and Guinness.

Students of the internationalization of Lagos will note changes in the retail sector. Until the Second World War the sector comprised mainly corner shops selling "everything," of a kind that still proliferate in certain commercial streets on Lagos Island, but the post-war boom saw the arrival of the department store. The Bristol Hotel was just across the road from Kingsway Stores, opened by the United Africa Company in 1948 and up to the 1960s the most significant department store in Lagos. (The onetime British Labour MP for Putney, Tony Colman, told me that in 1968, when he was manager of Kingsway Stores while working for UAC he was drafted to play the role of Father Christmas.)

For a time, when there was still some attempt at commercial zoning, all the British-style department stores were concentrated on the Marina— Union Trading Company, A. G. Leventis, G. B. Ollivant and Chellarams. But by the 1970s old-style, largely foreign-owned department stores were out of fashion and were also squeezed, eventually to be replaced with shopping "plazas" and still later "malls," even if the foreign ownership often did not change. It was the era of structural adjustment and the impoverishment of the middle classes (called at the time the "respectable poor"). This period saw the dwindling in scope and influence of the United Africa Company, now UAC Nigeria and Nigerianized, the firm that was once the jewel in the crown of British colonial Lagos, the ninth biggest earner in the whole of the Unilever empire. Some saw its demise almost as asset stripping but its downsizing was a by-product of devaluation and economic changes. For long-term expatriates the end of Kingsway Stores signaled the collapse of a fount of memories and of a certain lifestyle. Yet the passing of Kingsway and similar stores on Lagos Island was, of course, not the beginning of the end of retail activity, only a portent of change.

Then there are the bukkas, the bars, the suya spots. Obalende, a popular quarter on the fringe of Lagos Island and western Ikoyi, was at one time noted for its Hausa population, which accounts for the reputation it still has for the best suya (spice-coated meat, mainly beef, which is largely supplied from northern Nigeria) in Lagos, obtainable at its fabled motor park. Obalende, it is said, is also to be cleaned up as it is notorious for having had some of the filthiest storm drains in Lagos. There was a legendary bukka in Moloney Street, still widely known as "Ghana High" as it stood by the building used to house the offices of the Ghana diplomatic mission (it still houses a consulate).

Modern Lagos also has a prolific number of fast-food joints, particularly popular with the young, from Mr Bigg's to Tantalisers: these places may appear increasingly romantic as one explores their unusual brandings: Sweet Sensation, Temptation and, lurking in Festac Town next to a modest branch of the Intercontinental Bank, the exotically named Thriller. It is still hard to offer any explanation for the success of Mr Bigg's except that it was the first in Nigeria, having been launched in the 1980s, and has a fairly successful formula of mixing local foods with Western cuisine—but then all Nigerian fast-food chains do the same, apparently using Mr Bigg's as a model. The irony is that Mr Bigg's helped give new life to UAC Nigeria.

The fast-food chains now compete for the custom of the rising new middle classes that have emerged from the business community (IT specialists, bankers, accountants), in search of the trappings of consumerism and modernity. In 2001 an imported fast-food business from South Africa named Chicken Licken twinned with a pizza parlor called St Elmos, but the operation seemingly did not really appeal even to the upwardly mobile Lagos palate; the name, fairly meaningless to Lagosians, was changed to Chicken Republic and seemed to do better. Nando's, the popular Mozambique-originating South African fast food chain (specializing in spicy chicken with peri-peri sauce), although present for some years in other African countries including Ghana, came late to Nigeria and by 2009 had two outlets in Lagos, in the Palms Mall and on Ajose Adeogun Street on Victoria Island, although more are expected. Finally, in a breakthrough in 2011 for global franchises, Kentucky Fried Chicken opened several outlets. McDonalds never came at all because, it was said, Nigeria had the wrong size potatoes for making their French fries—although other outlets seem perfectly able to do so. The resistance of Nigeria to certain brands, at least in respect of fast food, is a refreshing mark of individualism. Even now, one will never find in Nigeria any Starbucks preaching about fair trade coffee.

The South African connection began, strictly speaking, after the Mandela revolution of 1994, but it was really only with the return to civilian rule in Nigeria in 1999 that it flourished. The collaboration has been most successful in the mobile phone business, especially with one of the pioneers, MTN Nigeria, and has also made inroads into the hospitality industry, the security sector and advertising. It was only in 2009 that the South African drinks multinational SAB Miller, purveyor of Castle Beer, which had long been eyeing Nigeria's resilient beer market, finally penetrated the united front created by Nigeria's two beer giants, whose international personas are Heineken and Guinness—and only by acquiring a couple of state breweries. Other investments, including media and entertainment businesses, have had variable results, some of the problems because of cultural adaptation. Nigeria is too big a market, however, for South African business to ignore.

South Africans have also been involved in the promotion of shopping malls (Michela Wrong has written of what she calls Africa's "plaza fantasy"). In Nigeria the main South African investment so far has been in The Palms on the Lekki Peninsula, host to the supermarket Shoprite, which has been reported as planning to open fifty outlets by 2012. Initially there were a number of smaller malls like the much loved but disorganized Mega Plaza on Victoria Island (burnt down in 2005 and rebuilt with not much change in 2006) or the constantly expanding supermarket Park and Shop. These are the symbol of the new middle classes, even if they are still nowhere near as flashy as their South African models. It is somehow emblematic that Wole Soyinka sets his play *Beatification of an Area Boy*, an ironic exploration of poverty and change published in 1995, in front of a shopping mall.

Lagos is also a city of society and socialites—weddings and funerals, naming ceremonies, even birthdays are outstanding events in the calendar involving huge resources, time and prestige. On the other hand, one of the most significant sociological developments of the last thirty years has been the rise of the evangelical churches. The best ways to make money in Nigeria, I was told in 2001, were "currency speculation and religion." The growth of evangelical churches was symptomatic of the depression years in the 1980s, but despite recovery the churches have expanded unabated and are now more than ever a determining factor in both social and political terms, paralleled by the longer and steadier growth of Islam.

This phenomenon has also been well covered in contemporary Nigerian literature, for example in the novel *The Interpreters* and the two *Brother Jero* plays by Soyinka, or (touched on) in Okey Ndibe's *Arrows of Rain* as well as the writings of Ben Okri and Helon Habila (see Chapter 4). There are others who have written more academic treatises on the subject such as Professor J. D. Y. Peel in his seminal work on the Aladura churches and Ruth Marshall's 2009 book on the rise of the Pentecostal churches in Nigeria.

Another activity that has some of the marks of a religion in Nigeria (indeed in Africa as a whole) is sport, above all football. This was introduced as a matter of inevitability by the British colonial power and grew in popularity, especially in the year between the two world wars. In recent years there has been a growing obsession with England's Premier League at the expense of Nigeria's own football teams. There are Lagos Man U, Chelsea and Arsenal supporters' clubs, often derived from converted area boys' (or *boyz*) associations. Cricket, polo and rugby have been more minority interests, kept alive by the children of rich Nigerians who have been to British public schools.

Chapter Four

A TRUE CITY OF THE IMAGINATION
LAGOS IN LITERATURE

"The city is indeed a city of literature."
> Odia Ofeimun in *Lagos: A City at Work*, 2005

"You can be good or bad in Lagos."
> Helon Habila in *Sense of the City; Lagos,* essay written
> for the BBC, 2004

"Lagos has, by the early years of the 21st century, become established as
one of the world's pre-eminent fictionalised cities."
> Chris Dunton, "Entropy and Energy; Lagos as a City of
> Words," essay for writers' conference in Lagos, 2005

If, when confronted with Lagos, one does not try to understand that there
is a deep and complex cultural richness in this city that spawns a multi-
plicity of creativities, one is probably likely to write it off as a squalid,
crime-ridden hell-hole. It has, in fact, given birth to all kinds of literature
from novels to journalism, just as it has been the cradle of unique and
unforgettable music and musicians, while artists and photographers have
also sought inspiration from the energy and visual impact of the city. But
there is more to it than that: there is a brooding spirit of rebellion and
contention that often infuriated the colonial rulers, who recoiled in horror
and distaste and often made the most terrible utterances about the inhabitants that can now be worn as a true badge of honor. For example Sir
Frederick Lugard, in 1916, wrote to Flora Lugard that, "the people of
Lagos are the lowest, most seditious and disloyal, the most prompted by
purely self-seeking money activities of any people I have ever met," which,
coming from one such as him, is a commendation, the best report card the
people of Lagos could have had. This spirit of cantankerous defiance runs
deep in the reality of a true "city of the imagination," coming from the
complicated terrain between brutality and exhilaration, a terrain familiar
to all Lagosians who know their city.

THE FIRST NIGERIAN WRITING

The first known printed writing we have about Lagos is inevitably almost all European, beginning with Ulsheimer in 1603, then ranging from John Adams in the eighteenth century to official documents of the mid-nineteenth century as set out in R. S. Smith's book *The Lagos Consulate* and the memoirs of Gianbattista Scala, the Sardinian consul in the 1850s. We have already referred to the early colonial writers such as Richard Burton, Mary Kingsley, Lady Glover, E. D. Morel, Leo Frobenius (the German scholar) and, while he was Governor-General between 1912 and 1918, Frederick Lugard. There were also other colonial servants who wrote, and the two *West Africa* magazines—one published 1900-03 (with a large contribution from Morel) and then the more substantial one published from 1917, were essentially British productions. There have been other more recent accounts by visitors, mostly European, such as Elspeth Huxley and John Gunther, both discerning but not above falling for stereotypes, and by the perpetual stream of visiting journalists and guide book writers, many of whom have some difficulty rising above their own prejudices. But this chapter is devoted to the idea that the best and most illuminating purveyors of words about Nigeria are the Nigerians themselves.

When did Nigerians begin writing in print? There are those who would argue that the ex-slave Olaudah Equiano, whose origins were very probably Igbo, was the first writer from what is now Nigeria in a European language (in the late eighteenth century), but Lagos did not figure in his harrowing itinerary. And there were some among the early Sierra Leoneans who knew their Nigerian origins and who committed themselves to paper. Most notable was Bishop Crowther, who had been released from a slave ship in 1822. But it was in the time of the missionaries that the literature of the city really began. Crowther in particular had correspondence, petitions to the Church Missionary Society and other documents as well as his famous letter to Lord Palmerston urging him to intervene against the slave trade. One should also mention James "Holy" Johnson, the nationalist cleric who defended African rights in church (the Anglican Church) and state. He is not to be confused with another Johnson, Samuel Johnson, also born in Freetown, who wrote the remarkable *History of the Yorubas*, a classic amongst early writing in English by Africans (it was included in a list of one hundred best books by Africans compiled in 2000). The manuscript of his book, written in 1897, was lost, and the definitive work was completed after his death in 1901 by his brother Obadiah, working on notes that Samuel had left, and it was only published in 1921. Otunba Payne's *Almanac* was also a notable exercise in writing over many years at the end of the nineteenth century.

THE BURGEONING OF THE NEWSPAPERS

Almost as soon as the missionaries and their Sierra Leonean acolytes arrived, newspapers began in the 1860s with the short-lived *Anglo-African* of Jamaican immigrant Robert Campbell, who had originally been to Lagos in the 1850s as part of an ill-fated American settlement project in Abeokuta. A Yoruba-language paper, *Iwe Irohin*, was produced in Abeokuta by missionaries from 1859 to 1867. But it was the 1880s that saw the first real flowering of newspapers, even if their lives were precarious and the readership at that time was very small. M. J. Echeruo's 1977 study *Victorian Lagos* is entirely based on them. The papers benefited from the enthusiasm with which the missionaries had plunged into the teaching of the English language.

There was an epic period in the early years of the twentieth century in which Lagos newspapers were the spearhead of the embryonic nationalist movement, dominated for years by Herbert Macaulay, who was himself the proprietor of the often over-exuberant *Lagos Daily News*. Perhaps the most memorable phase was that of the particularly bitter and dramatic confrontation of Lagos journalists with Lugard over censorship during the First World War (see Chapter 6). But although polemical journalism continued to be an important and in some respects typically Lagosian feature of political life, there seems to have been very little adventuring into fiction (except in that uniquely Nigerian creation, Onitsha market literature, which had tremendous popularity in Lagos and often covered Lagos subject matter) until the middle of the century.

The craft of journalism, however, already very well-established, took a new turn in the late 1930s with Azikiwe's celebrated 1937 launch of the *West African Pilot* newspaper (see profiles of both Macaulay and Azikiwe in Chapter 6), which served as a model for other publications that spoke to the rising tide of nationalism which developed during and after the Second World War. This political effervescence in the 1940s had a major influence on newspaper development, above all focused on Lagos, which has remained the media capital of Nigeria despite the political move to

Abuja. Most major daily newspapers and TV and radio stations have pre-ferred to keep their headquarters in Lagos. Even the sadly short-lived high-quality publication *Next* initially chose to locate its headquarters in Igbosere Road in the heart of Lagos Island.

THE FICTION WRITERS: THE FIRST GENERATION

The nationalist impetus to literature and especially fiction in the 1950s (encouraged but certainly not conceived by British publishers) was not a specifically Lagos phenomenon. The writing of Amos Tutuola, one of the first Nigerian writers to be published internationally, was rural Yoruba fantasy-picturesque that, although brilliant, did not really relate to the big city, and the products of the Mbari club, with its organ, the unforgettable literary magazine *Black Orpheus*, were really born in pre- and post-inde-pendence Ibadan. However, there are the gems of Cyprian Ekwensi's 1950s novels like *People of the City* and *Jagua Nana* as well as *Jagua Nana's Daugh-ter*, all of which took evident relish in using the city setting. If Ekwensi sometimes gets on a moral high horse about the wickedness of the city, one suspects that is for form—he enjoys his subject matter too much to be pious for long. Chinua Achebe's second novel, *No Longer at Ease* (1960), is set partly in Lagos, as is his later, often underrated political satire *Man of the People*. T. M. Aluko's satirical political novels *Kinsman and Foreman* and *Conduct Unbecoming* also have Lagos settings. Ekwensi was probably the first writer who hymned the city in the way it deserved. For example, in his novel *Iska* he even included a poem praising "The Girls of Lagos":

> The city is a girl walking
> > walking at dawn
> handbag over arm,
> > heels down and hungry
> Walking at noon
> > hunger in the vitals
> Walking at dusk
> bracelets all aglitter
> > heels high and flattering…

Many of the first-generation novels depicted Lagos as an unattractive sink of corruption—this is particularly true of *No Longer at Ease*, whose sympathetic hero is caught in the toils of his situation as a minor civil servant in the big city, and his fall from grace is counterpointed with the purity of a return to the village. Achebe, in truth, unlike Ekwensi, does not write of Lagos with any enthusiasm. In *No Longer at Ease* the president of the Umuofia Progressive Union, Lagos branch (a proto-typical Igbo town union), tells the hero Obi Okonkwo: "I have lived in this Lagos for fifteen years. I came here on August the sixth, nineteen hundred and forty-one. Lagos is a bad place for young men. If you follow its sweetness you will perish."

The feeling that Lagos is also a place that is particularly unsafe for girls is one of the messages of Flora Nwapa's book of short stories from 1971, *This is Lagos*. The story of that title begins with the line, "They say that Lagos men do not just chase women, they snatch them," and the mantra of the title (a self-explanatory exclamation, perennially popular, that covers a multitude of situations) occurs a third of the way through the tale where Mama Eze tells her daughter Soha: "This is Lagos. Lagos is different from home. Lagos is big. You must be careful here. You are a mere child. Lagos men are too deep for you. Don't think you are clever. You are not. You can never be cleverer than a Lagos man."

KEN SARO-WIWA

"ALALI. What have I to complain about? Haven't I trekked every day from Shomolu to the island for three months? Don't I know all the wretched signboards, all the bus numbers, and…

BASI. And you think that's great? Have you slept under Carter Bridge? Or in the rubbish dumps of Isolo where men who have lost their sense of smell and scavenge right in the dump, waiting for lorries bearing the waste of rich and poor alike? Have you been thrown out by your land-lady for non-payment of rent? Have you taken refuge in the back of a truck and woken up to find yourself one hundred kilometres away without money for the return journey?

ALALI. No.

BASI. Have you been banned for life from every Ministry, every company office in town? Are your very footsteps recognised by every messenger in every office?

ALALI. No.

BASI. I've been through all that and more. For ten good years, Alali, I roamed this city. The streets of Lagos and I are friends. I know their names, they recognise my footsteps."

From *The Transistor Radio*, a short play originally written in 1964 by Ken Saro-Wiwa when he was a student of drama at the University of Ibadan.

Even with the writing of subsequent generations one feels the same sense of distance from the artificial life of the city. This is so in the novels of Chimamanda Ngozi Adichie, as well as to a lesser extent in Sefi Atta's *Everything Good Will Come*. One of the first writers after Ekwensi to really grasp the feeling of Lagos was Ken Saro-Wiwa, better known as the Ogoni political activist brutally executed under Sani Abacha in 1995, and now remembered as a martyr for the continually rumbling cause of the peoples of the Niger Delta.

Saro-Wiwa, although not really a Lagos boy, had much of the cocky obstreperousness associated with the city. He was probably one of the first to cast a harshly penetrating eye on the subject of poverty. If he treats it as comedy, it is against a background of pain and squalor. The above quotation is as graphic a description of the aspirational poverty of Lagos inhabitants as any other in Nigerian fiction. His book of short stories *Basi and Company* (based on the hugely popular series on Nigerian TV in the early 1980s in which the various adventures of Basi in the city are recounted) returns to the subject again and again, even if its hero would probably call it "wealth creation" rather than "poverty alleviation." A *New York Times* correspondent wrote that the TV series "struck a chord because it lampoons Nigeria's get-rich-quick mentality."

The heart-wrenching poverty of the city has been an obvious obsession of foreign writers visiting Lagos. Some of them write well and movingly— an unprepared visit to a Lagos slum can be a grim induction—from John Gunther in the 1950s to George Packer in the *New Yorker* in 2008. A visit to the slums of Lagos is almost a foreign journalists' cliché, a kind of blooding that nevertheless tends to miss out on the essential spirit of the place. Of late, however, there has been a tendency to look for the more obviously life-enhancing, following the trend of the infectiously up-beat Oscar-winning film *Slumdog Millionaire* about the Indian mega-city of Mumbai, highly similar to Lagos. Some of the bleak external perceptions of Lagos have in the past seemed particularly at cross-purposes with the perennial optimism of Nigerians, none of whom has portrayed or lived out the unbreakable Nigerian spirit better than Saro-Wiwa.

At the end of *The Transistor Radio* this spirit is encapsulated when Saro-Wiwa has Basi telling Alali: "Lagos is the place for you, man. With a job, without a job, this is a place of hope. The future lies here, man. I tell you, we'll make it here, suddenly, without warning. And then our lives will be transformed. This room will become a palace, we'll own planes..." And when Alali announces that he is going where he will be neither a fake nor a fraud, Basi, who Saro-Wiwa himself acknowledges is based on the trickster figure familiar to West African folklore, declaims, "Goodbye, then. I'm here for keeps; for the excitement and pleasure, for the sheer joy of mingling with people, for hope. There may be hunger, but after the hunger, there are the bright lights, money and music, and who said we couldn't have part of it?" At which point a voice booms outside the setting, Basi's hovel in Lagos: "Nigerpools! Nigerpools! Win a million naira on Nigerpools!" And then Basi, mesmerized by the thought of easy money, goes off to "the Island" and Alali follows. Whether they make it or not is immaterial—indeed they probably do not. For the record, *The Transistor Radio* also appears as one tale in *Basi and Company*, but it does not include the dramatically cynical ending quoted above.

SOYINKA: THE CITY AS MASQUERADE

The Nobel Prize winning author Wole Soyinka is a case apart. Although his canvases are so broad that he is difficult to pigeon-hole, he is not primarily a Lagos writer, and he does not have the anti-urban bias of some of his contemporaries. One feels even so that he recognizes the theatrical atmosphere of the city, the prevalent feeling of masquerade. More importantly, some of his work captures the spirit of the urban struggle, especially the haunting 1965 play *The Road*, which although it could be set anywhere in Nigeria contains the existential dissociation that hangs over so much of Lagos, where the violent roads and their reckless vehicles are such a dominant part of life, while the action in "the Aksident Store" could apply to any motorway *bukka* in or around the metropolis.

Soyinka's first novel *The Interpreters* (1964) captures much of the same feeling, although it is only secondarily a Lagos novel since an important section of the action takes place on the Ibadan University campus. It has certain emblematic Lagos scenes such as two competing funerals and an attempted lynching of a thief, as well as one of the characters' involvement with an apostolic church, now increasingly a part of the Lagos scene. The novel has the familiar feel of the new educated urban elite enjoying an effortless superiority, but also displays a sensitivity to the contradictions of the city. One bizarre episode illustrates both Soyinka's fascination with the proximity of death and his propensity for taking to task his fellow Nigerians, if not as corrosively as his cousin Fela Kuti (see Chapter 9). A principal character, Sagoe, after coming on a funeral procession, follows a battered car with a coffin sticking "disgustingly" out of its boot ("it was the greatest farce ever enacted before death"), towards the cemetery in Ikoyi:

> He fell in step, almost without thinking, with the odd man at the rear, and they moved down Moloney Bridge Street towards the short bridge, a symbolic bridge because of its situation between the living and the dead. And among the dead he included the suburban settlement of Ikoyi where both the white remnants and the new black *oyinbos* lived in colonial vacuity.

If Soyinka feels the ambiguity of the city, Chris Dunton, an academic literary critic now based in Lesotho, probes further into the literary excitement the city engenders. Dunton wrote in 2005 an essay cited above which puts more focus on the organic nature of the city, especially as expressed in literature. But the ambiguity is still inescapable. He draws particular attention to Gabriel Okara's pioneering novel *The Voice* (1964), which has a strange section on "Sologa" (an anagram of "Lagos-o") going beyond earlier fictionalized records of opportunities (real or illusory) to sustain "the portraiture of the city as an organism bewilderingly diverse, to the outsider at least inchoate… where every strength might on closer inspection might prove to be a weakness." Dunton's use of the phrase "city of words" is a key pointer to the power of Lagos as an inspiration for literature. It helps us to understand the poet Odia Ofeimun's excitement at the appeal of the city, through its "citiness," to the imagination.

URBAN PROTOTYPES AND THE NEXT GENERATION OF
WRITERS: OKRI, HABILA, ABANI

The underside of the city, which takes comic form in Saro-Wiwa, also finds its place in some of the descriptions of ordinary life in Lagos in Ben Okri's 1991 novel *The Famished Road*. Although the book does not refer specifically to Lagos, some critics such as Ofeimun believe the setting has to be that of the city, although Professor Robert Fraser, something of an Okriologist, told me he felt the ambiance more recalled the towns of the former Mid-Western State, especially Warri. Others feel that the settings are unnamed because they are meant to be universal. In Okri's earlier books of short stories there are several Lagos episodes. In *Incidents at the Shrine* the story "Congestion in the City" provides a version of the 1976 assassination of Murtala Muhammed, which features as one of the historical moments of the city (see Chapter 6). The later *Dangerous Love* has a much more specific setting in what he calls "the miasma of Lagos life," a fitting backdrop for the novel's existential desperation. For example, there is a fictitious art gallery in Yaba called "the Ebony" where, at a private viewing, "textbook theories on the derivations and healthiness of modern African art were flung about like mind traps." There are other classic Lagos backdrops: the now-disappeared Ikoyi Park, the Alaba International Market and the Ajegunle ghetto.

The gloomily fatalistic but enduring urban prototype characters also come into the more Lagos-specific 1990s Soyinka play *The Beatification of an Area Boy*. The latest works of writers such as such as Helon Habila, whose first Caine Prize-winning short story collection *Prison Diaries* (and its successor-doppelganger renamed *Waiting for an Angel*) are also very Lagos-oriented. He sets one story in the fictional Morgan Street (which he also calls "Poverty Street" to symbolize all the pent-up frustration and ambition). In 2004, shortly after he won the Caine Prize for short story writing from Africa, Habila set out for the BBC in two pages what he called "Sense of the City: Lagos," writing, "Beneath the depiction of that chaos, beneath that fearful presentation, there is also a sense that if you come to Lagos, the songs seem to say, you just have to be strong, you have to stand on your own two feet, you have to lose your innocence, you have to learn so much, you have to be wise. Lagos actually makes you grow very, very fast."

Within this paradigm one must also include Chris Abani's 2004

GraceLand, the story of the hard life of a Nigerian Elvis Presley imper-
sonator called Elvis Oke; it is essentially a novel set in deep Lagos in the
year 1983, evocative of the ghettos. Part of the action takes place seven
years before in the Igbo town of Afikpo, but this feeds into the recogniz-
ably Lagos theme of the individual overwhelmed by the intensity of the
city and finding salvation only through escape, in this case to the United
States. Abani's volume of poems *Kalakuta Republic* (2001) distilling some
of his harrowing experiences in the notorious Kirikiri jail, is an outstanding example of this bleaker sort of literature.

Abani was a political prisoner several times between 1985 and 1991
(not only in Kirikiri); once, when he was only eighteen, his novel *Masters
of the Board*, about a neo-Nazi takeover of Nigeria, was mistakenly taken
by officialdom as a blueprint for the failed 1985 coup of General Mamman
Vatsa, himself a soldier-poet. The second prison term was for participat-
ing in a "guerrilla theatre group," and lastly he was detained for a play
called *Song of a Broken Flute*, which brought him eighteen months of
incarceration on "death row." Released in 1991, he moved out of Nigeria
first to London and then to the US, where he is now a professor in California. In *Kalakuta Republic* Abani tells of a fellow prisoner who teaches a
soldier to read with the aid of Enid Blyton and Biggles, and of debates on
the relative merits of Zola and Balzac with Lt. Emile Elejegba, who also
believed that Plato and Aristotle stole from Yoruba mythology: "he hated
Kirikiri and its brutality but was posted here, demoted, as punishment for
his refusal to lead a troop into Ogoniland to murder fellow compatriots."

BAR BEACH AND MAROKO

Nigerian writers have shown a fascination with Bar Beach on Victoria
Island, which used to be one of the most atmospheric places of the city and
a much-frequented popular beach that features in the memory of many
people. From the 1970s onwards, when it became the notorious venue for
executing coup plotters and armed robbers, it was an increasingly desolate
and surreal location that haunted the imagination of creative Nigerians. It
can be seen portrayed in the evocative pictures of white-robed Cherubim
and Seraphim included by the Jamaican photographer Armet Francis in his
book *The Dark Triangle*, and as potently in Ola Balogun's underrated film
Money Power. It is there as part of the dramatic action in Soyinka's play *The
Trials of Brother Jero* and its sequel *Jero's Metamorphosis*. Bar Beach has also

Cherubim and Seraphim on Bar Beach (Armet Francis 1977)

been symbolically portrayed as an emblem of despair; Okey Ndibe's desolate novel of post-independence disillusionment *Arrows of Rain* (2000) begins with a body being washed up on Bar Beach. In its barely concealed bitterness it is reminiscent of the first novels of the Ghanaian writer Ayi Kwei Armah such as the 1968 *The Beautyful Ones Are not Yet Born*, and it is fed by the corrosive contempt for the military that characterizes much of the Nigerian fiction of the period of military rule, blending into the "guerrilla journalism" of the same epoch.

Chris Dunton has highlighted and praised this group of novelists and the way they were writing about Lagos. There is a clear broadening of subject matter, sometimes with long historical span, sometimes with a dominant theme. Dunton cites as Lagos novels Maik Nwosu's *Invisible Chapters* and *Alpha Song*, and Sefi Atta's *Everything Good Will Come*, as well as *GraceLand*. These works neither glamorize the city nor portray it as a monster, but are more concerned with showing its multifaceted reality.

Nwosu's portrait of Maroko in *Invisible Chapters* (2001) shows once again the relationship of literature to political developments, and the story of the destruction of Maroko is a vivid and tragic one. Maroko, a lagoon-side ghetto lying between the up-market Victoria Island and the up-and-coming suburbs of the Lekki Peninsula, was undoubtedly illegal, insanitary and an eyesore, especially to the middle classes, but it still had that sense of community found in shantytowns that is hard to recreate in new-build low-cost housing. Its destruction was a very emotional story that captured the imagination of writers because of the pathos of its drama.

Soyinka does it very well in *The Beatification of an Area Boy*, the most Lagos-oriented of all his works. The author describes the play as a "Lagosian kaleidoscope" and gives it the ironic setting of a collection of Lagos characters gathered in the street outside a shopping mall, that symbol of the new middle class. Towards the end, the unnamed Military Officer who has just cleared migrants out of Maroko says: "Oh, they surely got what was coming to them. They had to go. I mean even in their own interest. That place was unhealthy for human habitation..." Then the irony is pursued when Minstrel sings:

Maroko o. What a ruckus
Over a wretched shanty town.
It was stinking
It was sinking
We were rescued or we would drown.

Soyinka's play is one of the first to give a literary shape to that most Lagosian of figures, the "area boy." As far as I am aware, this is an expression only found in Lagos, which had innocuous origins as a description of boys from the neighborhood. Such youths were even present (though not called area boys) in the colonial period, but a sure sign that the modern area boy has come to stay is when the social anthropologists start examining him. Simon Heap's outstanding paper from 2000 on colonial juvenile delinquency traces the problem back to the 1920s in the context of rivalry between Saros and Brazilians, especially during festivals such as Egungun; there were the Campos Square boys, the Lafiaji boys, the Shomolu boys and the Mushin boys. The problem became more dangerous in the 1930s when thieving "Jaguda boys" were wont to run riot. Using mainly newspaper reports, Heap particularly examines the case of the Boma boys of the 1940s (found especially in the port area of Apapa) who took their name from similar miscreants in Sierra Leone, and a group called the Cowboys. Yet there is no record of the term "area boys" being used before the 1990s, when the issue was intensified by the rise of local vigilantism and the growing problem of drug addiction. A further consecration came with a Nollywood film (see Chapter 5) called *Area Boys*, but the issues of gangs and delinquency seems to have been brought under some degree of control, in a manner of speaking, by the mobilization policies of the Lagos State governments of Tinubu and Fashola (see Chapter 8).

LAGOS OF THE POETS

The reference work of choice on poetry about Lagos has to be the brilliant *Lagos of the Poets*, edited by Odia Ofeimun and originally published in 2009. This is a remarkable and painstakingly amassed compilation that shows the extent to which the rough dross of the city can provide inspiration in words to so many, from the older generation icons like Azikiwe and Osadebay to more recent writers who have felt moved by Lagos to express themselves in verse as well as serried ranks of young creative talent bursting to be heard. The poems on display range from Niyi Osundare's moving four-part sequence "Eko" to J. P. Clark's "Maroko" and "Victoria Island." The long poem "Eko" (once again) by Femi Fatoba explores the identity of the city, and what Lagos is or is not, over eighteen pages. I quote at random:

> Lagos is like crabs
> In a basket
> Each stepping in the other
> Each pulling the other down
> In order to get up.
> That is how Lagos is.
> Tough is Lagos.
> Difficult is Lagos.

There are also Ogaga Ifowodo's memorable verses built around a beggar's curse: "God Punish You Lord Lugard. Na you bring this English come Nigeria!" (showing once more how the image of Lugard has become diabolically branded on the Nigerian subconscious) and a host of poems about individual locations from Ajegunle to Allen Avenue, Ikeja. Lastly, here you will find Odia's own nine poems, including his self-defining work "Eko: My City by the Lagoon."

Civil War, Oil Boom, Military Rule

In surveying fifty years of writing—poetry, fiction and non-fiction—one cannot escape the shadow of the Nigerian Civil War (1967-70), on which there is a full and currently expanding body of fiction, from Achebe's *Girls at War*, written in the 1970s, to Chimamanda Ngozi Adichie's affecting novel *Half of a Yellow Sun* (although the Lagos scenes are subordinate to the main action in the Biafran war). These novels deal little with Lagos, which mostly escaped the direct impact of the war, experiencing only its side effects. Chimamanda's own confessed ambiguity about Lagos, somewhat similar to that expressed earlier by Achebe, contrasts with the more sympathetic attitudes of Ekwensi or even Sefi Atta.

The impact of the oil boom of the 1970s was accompanied by a worsening of the political class' corruption—seen already in some of the independence generation novels cited above like Achebe's *Man of the People*. Oil and its side effects only made things worse. Surprisingly few novels other than Kole Omotoso's excellent and moving 1982 *Memories of Our Recent Boom* treat directly the more difficult subject of the curse of oil money and its destructive impact on society and human relationships. But none of its action specifically takes in Lagos.

What have writers said about the military rule, which dominated Nigerian politics for more than thirty years? There is a lot of non-fiction on the war, some of it by participants from Obasanjo to Ojukwu, and of course much of Soyinka's work, both dramatic and polemical, is politically directed against the military. Achebe's post-war fiction, from the short stories in *Girls at War* to the under-appreciated *Anthills of the Savannah*, is often about aspects of military rule.

However, for a picture of Lagos in particular under military rule I would prefer to go to Okey Ndibe's already cited *Arrows of Rain*, essentially set in the city itself. It has the feel of Lagos, from the set-piece scene at the beginning in which a body is washed up on Bar Beach to the round of night-clubs and parties, as well as newspaper offices and the inside of prison. Festus Iyayi's novels, especially *Violence* (1979) and *Heroes* (1986), are cries of pain about the oppression of military rule, but are set outside Lagos. The much later Caine Prize-winning short stories from *Waiting for an Angel* by Helon Habila treat Lagos very much as a theater to play out dramas about military rule.

The second-generation writers specifically illustrate the way in which, from the buoyancy of the early years to the despondency of the post-boom disillusion, there was a major change in Nigerian fiction. It was especially hard to avoid being political—both Achebe and Soyinka found their sensibilities fundamentally affected by the turbulences of politics. For example, Soyinka's early humorous levity found in *Dance of the Forests* and *The Lion and the Jewel* evolved into a deeper cynicism from *Kongi's Harvest* onwards, as politics, especially the aberrations of military dictatorship, came to touch him more and more.

THE "TWO CULTURES" SYNDROME

The ambiguity of living in more than one culture is seen, for example, in the Lagos-Brazilian writer Bernadine Evaristo, whose poem-novel *Lara* (1997), even if essentially about the Nigerian British, deals tangentially with life in the Brazilian community of Lagos. Helen Oyeyemi in *Icarus Girl* and Diana Evans in *26a* are also Nigerian-British writers, but neither book is a Lagos novel.

However, in this "two cultures" syndrome there is surely a place for Adewale Maja-Pearce, whose *In my Father's Country* is an attempt to get to grips with his Nigerian ancestry and childhood, having spent his childhood in Tunbridge Wells. His grandfather Solomon Adewale Pearce, a classic example of the early Saro elite, lived to the age of 96, having for years been a Methodist minister. The book includes his obituary from the minutes of a church conference; he was born in Lagos in 1878, and was notable in his attachment to the twin ideals of Christianity and education. "In appreciation of his many and varied services," says the obituary, "he was made a Justice of the Peace, Assessor to the juvenile Court, Fellow of the Royal Geographical Society and Member of the British Empire." The twist in the tale is that Adewale's father (with whom he did not always get on, and whose native country proves almost too much for Adewale to bear, but to which he felt compelled to return), left him a property in his will at his death in 1981. "I hadn't bargained on this. I had assumed I would get nothing. I had broken with him and by extension with his country. My inheritance changed everything. There is no gainsaying bricks and mortar."

Adewale has lived there ever since, almost as if instructed to by his father. I visited him there a few years ago, in a delightfully rambling two-story family house in a quiet cul de sac in Surulere with wooden floors, secret cupboards and a first-floor balcony suitable for imbibing Star beer during those hot, still Lagos evenings.

LAGOS PIDGIN

A side-look at pidgin—"an English-based contact language widely used in Nigeria alongside Standard English and nearly 500 indigenous languages, lexically based on English and a language in its own right with a stable structure, important functions, and potential for further development," according to Dagmar Deuber—as a Lagos phenomenon is also needed. Pidgin has long shown its vitality and adaptability. Saro Wiwa was a slick practitioner of persuasive pidgin fiction, as in *Soja Boy* (not particularly about Lagos) in the 1990s, but he was specializing in it much earlier: pidgin is used in *The Transistor Radio* (quoted at the beginning of this chapter) and in the stories adapted from his television series *Basi and Company*.

Mamman Vatsa, the poet-general executed by President Babangida for coup plotting in 1986, although a Northerner, used the language for one of his slim volumes, *Tori For Geti Bow Leg and other Pidgin Poems*. Newspapers in the past have had columns in pidgin, and it also has importance in song as the linguistic lifeblood and special characteristic of highlife music. The book *Nigerian Pidgin in Lagos: Language Contact Variation and Change in an African Urban Setting* by Dagmar Deuber deals in some detail with the particular nature of Lagos Pidgin, as opposed to that found along the West African coast in places like Douala, or the classic Krio spoken in Sierra Leone. Its intricate scholarship will probably make it inaccessible to the general reader but it is a veritable mine of information. *Babawilly Pidgin Dictionary* on the internet gives one a little more idea of the power of pidgin as a medium of expression, but for that you really need to go to some of the lyrics of Fela. But it is now so deep a part of popular culture that even highly educated members of the elite use it as a means of communication and as an expression of nationalist feeling because it cuts across ethnicity.

This may be the place to put in a word for a semi-pidgin column called "From de Moto' Park." As all West Africans know, a motor park is an all-destination hub from where you can get a "fast Peugeot" to Cotonou or Onitsha, as I used to in my extreme youth. It appeared in a short-lived 1980s newsletter named *West African Hotline*, brainchild of Patrick Smith before he went on to the wilder pastures of *Africa Confidential*. The column was written by John Howe, Fela addict and 1970s throwback, like Smith a "Mushin graduate."

OUTSIDE PERSPECTIVES

I have already touched on those expatriates, largely European or American, who have written about Lagos. Considering the excitement the city generates, there have been very few.

The case of Elspeth Huxley's *Four Guineas* is an interesting one because of her pro-Kenyan settler mindset, which causes her to be often patronizing and insensitive. She is nonetheless a keen and intelligent observer, who at least found West Africa worth writing about. Perhaps unsurprisingly, she is sometimes caustic and disparaging about the Nigerians she met and waxes lyrical about the style and quality of the costumes of the Northerners she sees in the federal parliament. She has the occasional felicitous, indeed poetic, description for which one can forgive much:

> There are still unspoilt beaches, with long Atlantic rollers breaking on the hot white sand. Nothing is pleasanter than to walk there in the evening, away from the heat and noise of the town. The sea is quiet and colourless and the sun sinks flatly into it, red as a Dutch cheese.

There is also John Gunther's *Inside Africa*, everybody's African reference book of the 1950s. Although he found much to commend in Nigeria and has some very positive observations, he found Lagos slums the worst in Africa outside South Africa. Someone took him to look at the cardboard city under Carter Bridge where he found people packed into "catacombs of filth," which by day were shunned even by flies and at nighttime were "dark as Erebus." More recent American journalists such as Blaine Harden who have written compendium books about their reporting experiences on the African continent have usually included a chapter on Nigeria: the most significant US writer on Nigeria in recent times has been Karl Maier, whose *This House Has Fallen* (1999) was often taken as a textbook on the Abacha years and was considered marketable enough for Spectrum Books to bring out a Nigerian edition. His chapter on the Odua Peoples Congress (OPC), a Yoruba protest movement, is a portrait of the tensions of the Abacha period.

Margery Perham in *West African Passage* (published in 1967, but recalling the colonial period) noted to her credit that visitors from settler cities like Nairobi or Cape Town were surprised to find that "a proud assertive people... walked the streets in their bright flowing robes as if Lagos and its suburbs, its markets and its official buildings was entirely their city and subject to no suzerain power." Nigerian journalists writing in the early press expressed a similar kind of pride in their city and its particular flavor. Echeruo writes that these editors and commentators "knew that Lagos was West African or Negro in the sense of being part of the new African phenomenon—a cosmopolitan black community radically differentiated both by its legal status and its cultural and urban characteristics."

Joyce Cary's 1938 novel of Nigeria in the colonial period, *Mister Johnson*, had nothing to do with Lagos. More recently William Boyd's atmospheric *A Good Man in Africa* was very loosely based on the experiences of his father as a medical doctor in Ibadan in the crisis years of the 1960s, but who among expatriate writers has seen the fictional possibilities of Lagos? No one, it seems, until Nigerian writers themselves came along.

Outsiders so rarely seem to grasp this possibility. Nigerians themselves have had to be the main protagonists of writing about the spirit and the soul of Lagos, even if the city, in truth, has an expansive enough spirit for others to enter into it. There are occasional glimpses of this understanding from writers like John de St. Jorre in *The Nigerian Civil War* (1971), though much of the foreign writing on the civil war while it was happening was disappointingly inadequate, especially at the conflict's end. The British journalists in particular after 1970 almost stopped writing about Nigeria, partly because of the difficulty of access: one was told by an official "now we don't need you any mor."

An exception has been the *Financial Times* in London. Of all foreign publications dealing with Africa it has always made a point of providing extensive coverage of Nigeria: pioneered by Bridget Bloom (a legend in her lifetime) and Mark Webster, carrying on to Quentin Peel and Michael Peel (unrelated), Michael Holman and more recently William Wallis not to mention a whole series of other journalists, *FT* writers have contributed to a magisterial series of country reports. Michael Peel's book *A Swampful of Dollars* (2009) writes entertainingly about Lagos life, including areas boys, *okada* bikes and a ride in a *danfo* bus. All too often Western commentators (like George Packer in November 2006 in the *New Yorker* or Channel Four's 2008 documentary on slum life in Lagos) mostly see only overweening poverty contrasting with overbearing wealth and fail to convey the essential excitement.

In 2010 a new phenomenon occurred when Western reporters seemingly suddenly discovered the filmic quality of Lagos—above all, put a microphone and a camera in front of any Lagosian and you will get authentic film. For example a BBC2 three-part documentary on Lagos tried to capture the optimistic entrepreneurship of the city, but was attacked in Nigeria for its sarcastic title *This is Lagos* and for beginning the film with a sequence of scavengers on a rubbish-tip. Jonathan Dimbleby included Lagos in his documentary on an upbeat *African Journey*, and the controversial Louis Theroux, choosing to go down among the area boys, met more than his match in his subject matter.

The French had a spasm of largely uncomprehending discovery of Nigeria in the Biafra period, but it was only later that they came to a greater understanding. Daniel Bach of Bordeaux University has always written on Nigeria with sensitivity and comprehension. In recent years directors of the French Cultural Centre, in the eyes of Nigerians, always had more empathy than the British Council, even if the libraries of the latter won the admiration of many budding writers. The French Cultural Centre tended to play down visiting French musicians, and for a period concentrated on promoting local Nigerian talent in the area of music, such as Seyi Solagbade and his Black Face Band. There was also renewed and more mature interest from French journalists such as Michèle Maringues whose book *Guerrilla Journalism*, based on her experiences of the tribulations of the *samizdat* media in Nigeria in the Abacha years, complemented the more recent book with the same title by Sunday Dare.

THE JOURNALIST AS A HERO IN NIGERIAN FICTION AND NON-FICTION

Lagos is definitely the media heart of Nigeria in spite of the removal of its political heart to Abuja. The daily newspaper *This Day* built an imposing office there but still has its main HQ in Lagos. Journalists are important as bearers of the keys of the city—anyone trying to understand it has to grasp the powerful attraction of the journalist as prophet, a figure outside society depicting its ills, pointing the way.

The playwright Femi Osofisan has suggested that just as the novel encourages the idea of alienation because of its very individualism, the prominence of writers and journalists in Nigerian fiction represents a kind of displacement. "Where are the farmers and doctors?" he asks. Journalists are central, indeed romantic, figures in Lagos fiction. One of the first Nigerian novels to be published internationally, Cyprian Ekwensi's *People of the City* (1954), has a hero, Amusa Sango, who is both musician and journalist working for a newspaper called the *West African Sensation*. From *People of the City* to new generation novels like Ndibe's *Arrows of Rain* and Habila's *Waiting for an Angel* the central figures are journalists—good-hearted cynics who are heroic figures in spite of themselves, more frequently victims than victors.

One of the most remarkable features of the development of Lagos is how newspapers began to function almost as soon as the British appeared. It was another aspect of the arrival of education with the missionaries, both British and Saro. The real pioneer, already mentioned, was Robert Campbell, a missionary of mixed European-Jamaican descent who started a newspaper called the *Anglo-African* as early as 1863, although it only lasted two years. Fred Omu says that the experience was "historically premature."

The missionary impulse had already been seen in the Yoruba newspaper *Iwe Irohin*, founded by Henry Townsend in Abeokuta in 1859, which lasted eight years before coming up against the reaction from Europeans there, especially the missionaries. The real flowering in the 1880s was due to much more than a desire to proselytize: the development of newspapers along the coast in Sierra Leone and Gold Coast had an important influence, but the rise of cultural nationalism at the time also made its mark. The special chemistry of Lagos, fueled by thirty years of Western-style education through the printed word, worked its magic.

From then on, there was always a strong spirit of criticism, even though the newspapers had small circulations—papers were lucky to sell more than a thousand copies per issue; from the time several newspapers began to appear in the 1880s, the will to produce them achieved a remarkable enthusiasm and vibrancy that even now, as Echeruo has shown,

Newspapers: "liveliness and virility"

make fascinating reading. The compulsion to produce newspapers continued up to the independence era, in part because they had from early times been a force to be reckoned with, and successive colonial administrators had difficulty handling them. The greatest challenge came in Lugard's period as Governor-General (1912-18), which was a memorable conflict, a blooding for the budding nationalist movement (see profile of Lugard in Chapter 6).

In *People of the City*, the fictitious newspaper *West African Sensation* appears to be loosely based on the *Daily Times*, which at the time Ekwensi was writing there in the early 1950s was owned by Cecil King's London-based Daily Mirror group, although Ekwensi actually learned his journalism working on Azikiwe's ardently nationalistic *West African Pilot*. In an interesting allusion to foreign ownership the *Sensation*'s editorial controller McMaster is the only European to appear in *People of the City*, and he remains an entirely faceless person. This perhaps does injustice to the mainly forgotten Europeans who once peopled the famous *Daily Times* premises in Kakawa Street, of which I have astonishingly vivid memories, from the smell of the drains in one corner of the courtyard to the buzz in the newsroom which I felt the first time I visited back in 1964. The journalists I first met there like Kunle Animashaun and Angus Okoli, often charged with showing a wide-eyed visitor around, were to me almost legendary figures, who taught me so much of what I still retain about Nigeria.

What Ofeimun describes as the "citiness" of Lagos was captured as much by the journalists writing in the 1960s and 1970s as by the fiction-writers. Above all was the work of the columnist Sam Amuka, who later became publisher of the *Vanguard*, a quintessentially national but Lagos-rooted daily newspaper that has managed to survive the hurly-burly of keeping a newspaper alive with honor in the sometimes extremely difficult media environment of the past thirty years. Amuka is now one of the great elder statesmen of the Nigerian media, uncompromised by all the contaminations of power that sometimes affect media operators. He embodied the romantic appeal of the journalist throughout his life, from the early cynical columnist "Sad Sam" to the senior citizen-publisher, universally known as "Uncle Sam." He wrote despairingly and affectionately of the city, its strangulated traffic and its struggling citizens in a way that has rarely been equaled.

Another giant from that time stands out: Peter Enahoro, one of the best-known of all Nigerian journalists. Although he was later also a publisher, his immortality derives from his witty and penetrating *Daily Times* column of the early 1960s, "Peter Pan." This gave him a pre-eminence that for many years led Nigerian journalists to believe that having a column was the be-all and end-all of their profession. If Peter's writing was not specifically Lagos-oriented, when one reads his book of the same period, *How to Be a Nigerian*, one realizes that his Nigerians are also the true archetypal Lagosians.

In this context the legendary *Lagos Weekend*, published by the *Daily Times* group in its heyday as Nigeria's number one newspaper publishing house, is also worthy of mention. Mere reference to the name conjures up memories of the 1960s and all the innocently salacious reports gleaned from the Police Station on Panti Street, Yaba, as carefully covered by their ace reporter Chinaka Fynecountry. It was briefly revived in 2008 by those trying with little success to refloat the near moribund Times Group, but it was a different product—the old honest crudity, imprinted with an innocent élan, could not be recaptured. But the experiment showed it was an unforgotten brand. The city can still from time to time inspire classic journalism such as Niyi Osundare's "See Lagos and Die" which appeared in *Newswatch* in October 1995.

The collapse over twenty years of the *Daily Times* empire (the once-proud symbol of the independent media in Nigeria) after a majority of its shares was taken over by the government is a tragic part of the passionate story of the media in Lagos. This is not the place to chronicle the rise and fall, but it is still an object lesson in how the dead hand of government ownership can undermine even the most resilient of enterprises (see profile of Alhaji Babatunde Jose in Chapter 6).

Three other distinctive Lagos media houses (not including the highest circulation paper, the *Punch*), all located on the mainland, deserve attention. The *Guardian*, in Rutam House on the Apapa Expressway near the spur to the international airport, was founded by Alex Ibru, one of the well-known Ibru business dynasty from the Delta. The paper was once the cynosure of Nigeria's progressives and intellectuals but is now more solidly perceived as a kind of successor to the *Daily Times* as an establishment paper.

This Day, housed in a new building near the creek in Apapa, is presided over by the nearest thing to a media tycoon in Nigeria, Nduka Obaigbena, and is increasingly given over to staging show business and fashion events, although it is still noted for its good sources in government, making it required reading. *Vanguard* is on the far side of the people's area of Ajegunle by the canal near to Kirikiri jail. It has a distinctive canteen, the Canal, where much-loved septuagenarian Sam Amuka (already described) sometimes holds entertaining court at lunchtime.

There are also a host of stories from the electronic media, even if state TV and radio do not have quite the same glamour as the private media. The international CNBC chain has dedicated programs about Lagos, often business-focused, but also social and environmental in content. The presence in Lagos of federal TV and radio had to end when their once-joint station in Ikoyi, which had delivered occasional dramatically good stories, was obliged to move to Abuja. But even *Business Day*, a twenty-first-century creation (see below) had to have its HQ in Lagos, years after government moved to Abuja. Likewise the much-awaited but all too briefly surviving newspaper *Next*, published by Pulitzer Prize winner Dele Olojede, was headquartered in the heart of old Lagos. Although political stories are mainly generated in Abuja, it would still be inconceivable for any other national publication to be anywhere else than Lagos despite the removal of the center of power to Abuja and the time-honored resentment in the North of the Lagos-based press.

In a way, being separate from the federal capital is the symbol of the independence of Lagos and its media, an expression of the difference from government-dominated Abuja. This was certainly so in the Abacha years. The Lagos media are still always commended for their liveliness and "virility." They distinguished themselves well in the campaign against the proposed third term for President Obasanjo in 2007. No paper dared come out in favor of the project in spite of the reputed complacency that sets in during civilian regimes which led, certainly in the Second Republic of 1979-83, to a reputation for what was called a "brown envelopes" culture in which politicians subverted underpaid journalists with subsidies. The Fourth Republic has seen a certain stasis, but this situation has been galvanized by the development of groundbreaking international internet websites such as Sahara Reporters.

One should also note the development of business media such as Nigeria's first financial daily, the aforementioned *Business Day*. I was personally involved in the development of this publication in its early years in 2001-02. I had to make my way every day on the Apapa Expressway past the spaghetti junction of Mile Two to Amuwo Odofin, a little known and unremarkable area of Lagos between the "jungle" of Ajegunle and the down-at-heel respectability of Festac Town.

When considering the overall impact of the Nigerian media one cannot avoid the popularity of current "shlock" publications like the weekly *City People* and *National Encomium*, notorious for their *National Inquirer*-type exposés of scandals among those "socialites" usually described as the "big boys" and "big girls" of Lagos, Abuja and other cities. The papers, however scurrilous, are surely in their own way documents of Lagos and its people and society, as is *Ovation*, that consecrator of Nigeria's own peculiar form of designer kitsch. In the context of the cult of ostentatious wealth at birthdays, weddings and book launches, it offers a portrait of conspicuous and vulgar riches in its own way as good as that portrayed in any novel by Thackeray or Scott Fitzgerald, and it will surely be used by social anthropologists of the future to illustrate the mores of an era. The Lagos newspaper *Castles* is also a fascinating read for those trying to understand the vagaries of the sometimes alarmingly successful Lagos real estate market. Like some of the "Homes and Property" supplements in London or New York newspapers, it survives through advertising but is also a form of social documentation.

THE GUIDES: "DARK TOURISM" OR MOVING TO NORMALCY?

The 1995 edition of *Lonely Planet* suggested in its section on Nigeria that "the trick to enjoying Nigeria is to avoid Lagos and the sprawling, congested cities of Ibadan, Port Harcourt, Enugu and Onitsha." Of late the same publishers, always trying to be in tune with the *Zeitgeist*, have discovered the city as a vehicle for adventure tourism and have been producing revised estimates, even sending one of their writers to report on the wilder side of Lagos. This, at least, is the beginning of an understanding of the city. The *Rough Guide to West Africa* has also seen a similar evolution.

The quotation from the thirtieth anniversary edition of *Lonely Planet's Africa* volume cited at the beginning of the Introduction ("Lagos is chaos theory made flesh and concrete") is an original attitudinal take, claiming in effect that the visitor eager for an urban adventure might find Lagos "compelling." While in some ways this is an encouraging development, it comes perilously close to a kind of "dark tourism" that is increasingly part of the international tourism scene, which includes not just visiting slave entrepots in Gorée or Elmina but also slums in Calcutta and Mumbai and even, the most macabre, Holocaust tours to Belsen and Auschwitz.

Back in the early 1980s there was a useful and prosaic guide by Innis Meek called *Inside Lagos*, followed by the even less optimistically titled *Survive Lagos* by Elizabeth Cox and Erica Andersen published in 1984. This embattled title seemed to emphasize the concept of living in the city as a permanent combat. Even the more sophisticated *Lagos Easy Access*, which was produced in the late 1990s by three enterprising members of the American Womens' Club, suggested in its title a certain impenetrability, or at least difficult access that had to be mastered by strangers. It has proved an extremely useful and successful venture, especially as the expatriate population of Lagos grew considerably in the first decade of the twenty-first century. A more comprehensive third edition was published in 2007, apparently produced by a committee of 21, and in its way it is a valuable reference book as well as a testimony to how rapidly the city changes. Bradt has also produced an enterprising guide to Nigeria, which takes Lagos much more at face value, even if it seems to be catering particularly for South African visitors.

The nearest to Nigerians creating their own guide is *Time Out's* several editions of "Nigeria for Visitors" and "Lagos for Visitors" which local publishers offered in 2009 as a joint venture with the London publication. The contributors to this guide were for the most part Nigerian, and Lagos receives just treatment, bringing it somehow nearer to normalcy. Governor Fashola's efforts to rationalize an essentially irrational city, in an attempt to bring it into the globalized world, could mean that we will finally see—miraculously—a much-needed, decent, up-to-date street map.

Chapter Five

MUSIC, FILM, ART AND THE HAVENS
IN THE WILDERNESS

"Broad parallels may be drawn between the emergence of jazz in turn of
the century New Orleans and juju [music] in inter-war Lagos."
> Christopher Alan Waterman, Juju: A Social History and
> Ethnography of an African Popular Music, 1990

"Who was I to think art could save anyone in Lagos?"
> Sefi Atta, "Lawless," 2008

"To understand how the video industry works in Lagos you need to go
to Idumota market."
> Pierre Barrot (ed.), *Nollywood: the Video Phenomenon in*
> *Nigeria*, 2009

SAKARA, ASIKO, JUJU AND HIGHLIFE

According to the musicologist John Collins, the roots of West African
popular music, when traditional African music began to fuse with external influences, go back well over a century: "Modernised traditional music
and dance-styles that developed in the nineteenth century demonstrate
the subtlety of the interaction between black and white music... rhythms
that later were incorporated into highlife and juju music." In Nigeria
specifically there were *sakara* and *ashiko* (*asiko*). *Sakara*, a form of praise
song and dance music performed exclusively and patronized primarily by
Yoruba Muslims, was being performed in Lagos in the early years of the
twentieth century by a part-time musician called Bello Tapa, probably a
Nupe migrant. Western imports helped in the evolution of the technology
of drum-making.

Christopher Alan Waterman claims that the origin of the word *sakara*
may be Arabic, but it became assimilated into Yoruba culture and refers to
a drum, a musical genre and a dance style. Its influence became much
broader than its purely Islamic context. It was linked to "patterns of
African Muslim identity. Many Omo Eko (children of Lagos) including

Saro and Amaro (Aguda) were converted to Islam and the Muslim population of Lagos was continually augmented by migrants from the hinterland," so that the *sakara* style was "grounded in the self-image and values of a diverse Yoruba-speaking Muslim population." One of its main practitioners was Abibu Oluwa, popularly known as "the Preacher."

Asiko, says Waterman, was the Christian equivalent of *sakara*, "a local variant of a kind of syncretic street drumming that had developed in the port towns of anglophone West Africa" from Freetown to Takoradi. Sailors, who had more exposure to international influences, facilitated its spread. In Lagos *asiko* also incorporated an adaptation of Brazilian samba styles brought in by the Agudas who came back to Lagos from Brazil in the mid-nineteenth century. It also absorbed progressively "palm-wine music" (palm-wine being the slightly fermented sap of a palm tree). This music, says Collins, "emerged from the low-class seaport dives and palm-wine bars." Crucially, he says, palm-wine drinking became associated with the guitar so that "anyone playing the guitar was considered to be a drunken rascal." Palm-wine music was a potent influence all along the West African coast but in Nigeria it had particular resonance.

The 1920s and 1930s were crucial in musical development in West Africa because of the way in which externally influenced music al forms that had enjoyed a certain elite popularity were increasingly fused with "native" African-dominated music. The popular dance-band orchestras of late nineteenth-century Lagos (described by Echeruo in *Victorian Lagos*) developed with the ballroom dancing introduced by early expatriates, but were taken up as fashionable by Lagos society which sought to emulate European values, dominated at that time by the Saros, some of whom had already been in London.

Another important influence was the brass band, very often associated with the colonial police and military, which had a similar influence on musical forms in places as far afield as Trinidad and New Orleans. Bobby Benson, one of the earliest highlife musicians, recalled that the Calabar Brass Band, which played in Lagos in the 1920s, used to "steam" from one end of Lagos to the other. Local popular music also received a boost from the first phonograph records of West African music, which came in during the 1920s, although mass-produced shellac records for the West African market were a phenomenon of the mid-1930s. Advertisements in *West Africa* magazine (in the 1920s and 1930s they were usually on the blue paper front page) for Zonophone West African Records confirm the growing popularity of local music including many songs in Yoruba. Duro Idujenyo, a musician who once played with Fela Kuti and was still putting on a show at Bogobiri Guest House each Friday night even in 2010, helped bring out a CD of some of these very early UK-recorded tracks, titled "Living is Hard: West African Music in Britain, 1927-1929," which demonstrated the kind of musical experimentation that was taking place.

These were all elements in the mix—incorporating the instruments of the ballroom and brass bands (which themselves eventually faded out)—that generated highlife on the West Coast. This had a strong Latin influence in which the Trinidad calypso played a role, and in Nigeria in particular, calypso was also a key element in the birth of juju music. The 1930s was the decade in which local musical products truly emerged. In the forefront was the mandolin-playing Tunde King, who, says Duro Idujenyo, first coined the word "juju" to describe his own music, as well as the guitarist Ayinde Bakare. Waterman suggests that the etymology of the word may have come from the tambourine, which had come to palm-wine music both from the Salvation Army bands and from the Brazilians. King's drummer Lamidi George would throw his tambourine in the air and the whirling motion it made may have led to a duplication of the term *jù* (meaning "to throw"), as *jùjù* or "throw-throw."

After the imposition of the military curfew at the start of the Second World War in 1939, we are told, King joined the Merchant Marine, retuning to Lagos in 1941. He then disappeared for eleven years, being reported in places like Conakry and Dakar and returning to Lagos only in 1954. He later said that he had left because a rival had nailed a magical object to the dock in Lagos, and he only returned when the nail had disintegrated. In a newspaper interview in 1988 King recalled how it was indeed the sailors who had drawn him into music at the Lagos waterfront:

> In the evenings, the sailors who had just arrived and anchored their ships at the harbour along the Marina, would sit down playing their trombones and trumpets, some of them had guitars and would be playing to entertain themselves. We, who were young then, would gather round them, helping them to fetch their drinks or attending to their other needs.

Waterman describes the chemistry of the fusion that created juju music thus: "These early juju practitioners were cultural brokers par excellence... In their creative response to the vicissitudes of colonisation and urbanisation, they fashioned an expressive code that linked clerks and labourer, immigrants and indigenes, the modern and the traditional, within a rhetorical framework deeply grounded in Yoruba values." He also enlarges on the concept of "Juju-highlife," showing the contrast between the two in terms of social attitudes as much as in the music. Juju musicians were seen as low-class ragamuffins. King, he says, managed to attract the patronage of Western-educated Nigerians through "his creative juxtaposition of aspects of Christian hymnody, Yoruba praise song and pre-existent popular styles."

Music already profoundly reflected the divisions of the period between the "cultural nationalists" such as Herbert Macaulay, who supported juju music, and the "collaborators" who identified with the British administration and preferred the unadulterated Western music of the colonialists, regarding these new forms as "bastardization." We are told by Dele Cole that Macaulay's political party, the Nigerian National Democratic Party (NNDP), made frequent use of the professional drummers' association of Lagos (with an active membership of over a hundred) at party events.

This "separate-but-equal aesthetic" of the period, says Waterman, was the cultural equivalent of the "anti-Creolisation ideology that justified British attempts to exclude literate Africans from positions of administrative responsibility." This is the justification for Waterman's comparison of juju as a form of protest music with the rise of jazz in New Orleans. Thus both juju and eventually its partner music, highlife, came to be important tools in the development of Nigerian nationalism, often flourishing alongside the new political parties that developed in the 1940s.

Afolabi Alaja-Browne, an academic student of juju music, collected a number of King's songs from the 1930s that were never recorded, in which African resentment at British racism was frequent and explicit. Indeed, Waterman reproduces the full Yoruba text of these, with a translation of *Soja Idumota* (Soldier at Idumota) which is a bitter commentary on the erection of the cenotaph on Lagos Island near the Carter Bridge, ending: "It is good, it is good, oppressor, that you do not forget tomorrow" (in other words, retribution will come). Is this a foretaste of the cutting satire of the lyrics of Fela Kuti? Ironically, the cenotaph has now been removed by the Lagos State government. (For a full discussion of Fela Kuti, see Chapter 9.)

THE HEYDAY OF HIGHLIFE

Juju music continued to be a powerful influence from the 1940s onwards and, it has been pointed out, evolved dramatically with the introduction of the talking drum coinciding with electronic amplification. The first electric guitar was brought back to Nigeria in 1947 by Bobby Benson, the highlife musician, and the first juju musician to use one was Ayinde Bakare. The music was also influenced by parallel styles that developed at the time such as *agidigbo*, a street drumming developed by boys' associations which formed the basis of *kokoma*, a juju variant that has its own durability. All local music benefited from the post-war boom and the economic expansion of Lagos combined with the commercial mass reproduction and dissemination that grew in the period. The arrival of radio, especially the launch of the Western Nigerian Broadcasting Service, was also important and was a factor in the immediate post-independence rise of one of the most celebrated of all juju musicians, Isaiah Kehinde (I. K.) Dairo. Through the 1960s he was one of the most popular of all bandleaders, holding his own against the highlife musicians who had reached their heyday in the 1950s, although juju, as a music that appealed to Yoruba nationalism, never really lost out. I. K. Dairo held the torch until the revival of the genre in the 1980s with the lastingly popular King Sunny Ade and Ebenezer Obey.

Meanwhile, highlife, with its characteristic balance between rhythm, percussion and diversified wind instruments, achieved such prestige and cachet that it sometimes seemed, erroneously, to be eclipsing the juju practitioners. It was primarily sung in English and pidgin and sprang from the cosmopolitan culture of the city. The influences of Latin American music, but above all of calypso, added to its modern appeal. Jahman Anikulapo says that it "perhaps remained the most enduring musical form today, due to its hybridisation in content, context and form." Even now there are certain numbers such as Uwaifo's *Joromi*, Benson's *Taxi Driver* and Nico Mbarga's *Sweet Mother* that are deeply imprinted in the popular psyche. The veteran music critic Benson Idonije remarks that the name "highlife" was "a coinage of the poor locals who, seeing expatriates and the educated local kinsmen going into clubs to enjoy the heavy pulsating music would declare, 'see those top citizens—they are going to enjoy the high-life in that club.'"

Although the exact etymology of the name is hard to pin down, it first entered current usage in Ghana in the 1920s, and in a small way made its way along the coast soon afterwards (Waterman says that there was something of a flurry in 1935 around the visit of the Accra-based highlife orchestra, the West African Sugar Babes). But the real impact of highlife was in the post-war years, especially after the visits of E. T. Mensah and his Tempos to Lagos and other parts of Nigeria in the early 1950s, which revolutionized the way many Nigerian musicians thought about their music. John Collins observes that the genre was copied by leading bands such as Victor Olaiya, Bobby Benson and a number of musicians from Eastern Nigeria such as E. C. Arinze and Cardinal Rex Lawson. Victor Uwaifo, one of the most beloved of all highlife bandleaders in the 1960s and 1970s, always fully acknowledged his debt to "E. T."

Comment on current affairs and society was built into the music from early on and became one of its distinguishing features. The influence of calypso had a role here, and the political lyrics which were stronger in Ghanaian highlife made their way to Nigeria. Social commentary really only developed as the music evolved away from classic highlife with the rise of Fela Kuti, even as his own music evolved into Afrobeat.

Several observers recollect that the outbreak of the Nigerian Civil War in 1967 was a serious blow to the popularity of highlife, as many of the bands were from the East and fled back to Biafra. But there was more to it than that. The 1970s and 1980s were dominated by the thumping rhythms of Afrobeat, alongside Fela's cutting lyrics. If juju music at some point seemed threatened in the 1980s by its variant *fuji* music (especially popular among Muslims), and if from the 1990s onwards various Nigerian versions of rap and hip-hop seemed to be sweeping the musical board and dominating the private music radio stations, there is still much lingering affection for highlife today. If you ask who are Nigeria's most popular musicians today, you will be told, as likely as not, the names of rappers such as Tu-Face, D'banj or Weird MC.

The music of the masked saxophonist Lagbaja (his name means "nobody"), who enjoyed great popularity in the early part of the past decade, is an example of the Afrobeat tradition, if with less bitingly satirical lyrics. At his peak he could command a million naira for a performance

Lagbaja: "my name is nobody"

when playing at weddings and other events. Hi Motherlan' club in Ikeja is for the time being closed. The popularity of this style showed how Fela's music became the commanding influence in Nigerian popular music to date, mainly incarnated in the careers of his sons. They have also carved out a place for Nigerian music in what is called world music. This highlights the problems of Nigerian musicians in the face of piracy and in the wider context of the recording business, both international and Nigerian (which inevitably burgeons out of Lagos). It is a debate that has even reached the United Nations Industrial Development Organization which publishes serious papers on the development of creative industries and even on where "the African Nashville" should be located.

Since 1999 there has also been a growth in "Naija music," especially as, so an informant tells me, "all the R&B/rap/hip hop/dancehall is in Lagos-derived pidgin," which means that "Lagos cool" is broadcast far and wide via new technology. "Storm records have managed to become a major brand, despite a situation of endemic piracy." My informant adds that artistes such as D'banj have become "praise singers for politicians... whereas only a minority have retained the music-as-a-weapon consciousness of the Fela tradition."

THE GROWTH OF THE VENUES

This brings us to one of the most defining features of Lagos—where its music is played. From the end of the nineteenth century music was played in a variety of venues, from the colonial halls of the ballroom dancers to the waterfront joints and palm-wine bars on the Marina, as well as in open-air spaces like Campos Square. Students of the history of the nightclub in Lagos have difficulty in finding any from before the Second World War, although, as we have noted, ballroom dancing goes back to the late nineteenth century.

Although we are told by Musiliu Anibaba in his affectionate memoir of his father, *A Lagosian of the 20th Century*, that popular music used to be played in the daytime at the Swing Time Gardens in Campos Square in the 1940s, the earliest nightclubs seem to have been in hotels (see Chapter 3), the main public music spaces until the arrival of proper nightclubs, which were also largely in the open air. A popular early one was the Crystal Garden overlooking Broad Street. One of the first kings of highlife still living, Victor Olaiya, whose family house was on the square, recalls that behind the Crystal Garden was a passage called Phoenix Street, "a hot spot for night crawlers… local people and the white, Portuguese, Lebanese traders and the colonial office workers." Olaiya used to play in hotels around the Tinubu Square area until he moved to the Ambassador Hotel on the mainland in the early 1950s.

Fatai Rolling Dollar, an octogenarian musician still playing, also recalls that in the 1940s, "Tinubu Square was the junction of enjoyment and it continued till daybreak. We used to have Rees Hotel, Koriko Bar near Bristol Hotel and Shaibu Nowoo Hotel where workers ate when they were on break. In the night musicians like myself, Ayinde Bakare, Moses Olaiya played there." One of the first popular highlife clubs was Bobby Benson's Caban Bamboo at the Hotel de Bobby on the Ikorodu Road on the mainland. While the Caban was covered, the main clubs in this period were open to the stars, notably the Kakadu (see below) and the Surulere Night Club, which later achieved greater celebrity as Fela's first Shrine. Slowly, however the open-air venue fell out of fashion, and air-conditioned (sometimes notionally) rooms became more and more popular. Such were the Bagatelle on Broad Street, and the nearby Paon Rouge. The Gondola Club in a large upstairs room alongside the Niger Palace Hotel in Yaba was highly favored. The trend continued through the next decades, boosted by the oil boom and undeterred by the economic hardship of the 1980s and 1990s. It was, above all, the rise of the revived middle classes as Lagos entered the new century, and the coming of age of a whole aspirational younger generation, that gave a lift to Lagos nightlife.

In the 1970s many clubbers had frequented the Lebanese-owned Phoenicia in Martins Street, but the "area boys'" takeover of Lagos Island in the 1980s killed off nightlife there. In the early 1990s there was also Club 38 in Awolowo Road, the haunt of Tunde Kuboye and his late and regretted wife Fran Kuboye, cousin of Fela. Indeed, the Afrobeat king would sometimes show up unexpectedly to play at Club 38. Kuboye is a real Lagos figure, who was earlier wont to play at the Museum Kitchen, a restaurant in the compound of the Nigeria Museum in Onikan. Sir Mervyn Brown, British High Commissioner in Nigeria during the Second Republic when Lagos still had some claim to be enjoying boom years, was a talented classical musician who also was a jazz pianist. Later he was one of the main lobbyists and fundraisers for the setting up of the imposing premises of the Musical Society of Nigeria (MUSON) Centre, also in

Onikan. Kuboye was later for a time one of the regulars at the Nimbus gallery venue (see below). Such cultural meeting-places sometimes come into the restaurant/club category—the most successful recently has been the enterprising Terra Kulture.

A club called Ojez for a time incarnated the spanning of musical generations by hosting "Elders Nights" for highlife veterans such as Victor Olaiya. It moved in 2005 from Yaba to a larger venue in the surrounds of the Nigerian stadium in Surulere, but from early 2009 the evenings were suspended. Like so much in Lagos, nothing seems to last: only change is permanent. Lagbaja, mentioned above, has his own club Motherlan' in Ikeja. The Coliseum Niteshift in Opebi, in spite of a serious fire a few years ago, maintains a high and quasi-political profile (Ghana's ex-president Jerry Rawlings has been a guest). The successor to Fela's original Shrine, which he opened in Pepple Street, Ikeja, in the 1980s, is still enormously successful as the New Afrika Shrine.

There are virtually no open-air clubs in Lagos now. From the 1970s onwards they all became covered over, perhaps to do more stable business in the rainy season, although Nimbus was partly open-air. There is an ephemeral quality about nightclubs, which become too easily victims of fashion, and their passing is regretted only infrequently by their clients. A few of the bars on Victoria Island have a certain longevity such as the somewhat old-fashioned but frequently swinging Thistle Bar. Higher taxation in Lagos State finally even did for Pat's Place, an Irish-managed haunt beloved of expatriates but which still had a certain Nigerian clientele.

So many of those that I knew on Victoria Island, even in 2001-02, are now defunct, existing only as ghostly memories such as the riotous Tribes, Incognito and Tiberius. Even the notorious Whynot (where Liberian hookers were wont to adorn the swimming-pool) has passed into history. One nocturnal tale I like to tell is how Gloria Ibru of the Ibru business family enjoyed nightclub singing so much that she started her own club, again on Victoria Island, called Legato—and again, like many Lagos clubs, regrettably short-lived. But even in its brief period of success it was an unforgettable experience to hear Gloria belting out numbers like the immortal "If you marry taxi driver, I don't care." As already mentioned, this is an informal popular anthem: some say it was originally created in improvisation back in the 1960s by Wole Soyinka in Bobby Benson's Caban Bamboo.

Another development in the years after 2000 was a glitzy bar/club/restaurant on Victoria Island called Saipan. I was told it was a symbol of growing Chinese influence, even if the Chinese who run it are longstanding Lagosians who came years ago from Hong Kong, rather than mainland China's numerous official workers, although the two seem increasingly to merge. There have long been Chinese restaurants in Lagos, but the most prominent symbol of the Chinese presence is a glittering pagoda-like five-story building on Kingsway called the Golden Gate, owned by one of the most prominent members of the Chinese business community in Lagos.

Of late we have also seen the Swe Bar, for the upwardly mobile children of the new boom years. I wrote an article around 2007 (appropriately enough in a publication called *Nigerian Oil and Gas*) describing how all the stockbrokers and bankers in the lounge alongside the dance floor joined spontaneously in singing when R. Kelly's soulful number "I Believe I Can Fly" was played. It seemed to symbolize the aspirations of a new middle-class generation, especially attuned to Nigeria's permanent and indefatigable optimism, which has not been diminished by the credit crunch. The Swe Bar was in the City Mall, which has sprung up next to the Nigeria Museum on a plot that once belonged to the Museum, but the location almost too near to "area boy" country never seemed to be quite right for a shopping mall. The club in the Palms Mall in Lekki is more a model for the future. The international footballer J. J. Okocha also started a club on Victoria Island called Ten (named after the number he wore on his shirt), located over an up-market wine store whose main product was Dom Perignon champagne, another symbol of the previous financial boom. The global downturn does not seem to have had an immediate effect on Lagos nightlife, still less on the traditional *owambe* parties (*owambe* is "put it there" in Yoruba) despite the ever-present transience of urban life. Informants tell me that at the time of writing returnees from the recession in Europe have generated a new growth of clubs, bars and lounges.

THE NIGHT CLUB AS METAPHOR

"Metal on concrete jars my drink lobes."

Wole Soyinka, *The Interpreters*

The unforgettable opening line of Soyinka's novel *The Interpreters* evokes with vivid clarity the old-style open-air Nigerian nightclubs of the 1950s and 1960s. Just as the activities of journalists and the newspapers they work for are a recurrent theme of Nigerian fiction, so all the major novelists have at some point included nightclubs in their work. The All Languages Club lovingly described in *People of the City* is perhaps the first nightclub in Nigerian fiction, but it was the beginning of a genre.

Ekwensi's *Jagua Nana* and *Jagua Nana's Daughter* move easily around this twilight world, somehow in retrospect converting sleaze into epic, although Jagua, despite her romantic sensual soul, is ever the hard-headed woman of the city with a deeply psychological relationship with the club she frequents: "the Tropicana to her was a daily drug, a potent habit-forming brew. Like all the other women who came here, alone or with some man, Jagua was always looking for a ray of hope." Ekwensi provides lyrical, almost ecstatic descriptions of the Tropicana:

> The music was tremendously rhythmic, coming from the bongo drums, and the bandleader, pointing his trumpet skywards blew till the blisters on his lips widened and wiped his lips, and the sax snatched away the solo, distorting it. This was it, Jagua felt…The dancers occupied a tiny floor, unlighted, so that they became silhouetted bodies without faces, so that even the most unathletic man could be drawn out to attempt the improvisations which went by the name of High-life.

There is even a club (possibly in a hotel?) called "the Imperial" that features in *No Longer At Ease*, although it is a somewhat lower-key description as befits Achebe's lack of enthusiasm for such a symbol of the city. The flatly pretentious atmosphere captures superbly the edgy relations of the independence-generation middle classes whose illusions and pretensions Achebe seeks to describe in the novel. But there is no excitement.

Taking the long view, there is a flashback here to the expression "night-strolling generation" that Echeruo discovered in *Victorian Lagos*, even if it

126

is only in the context of newspaper condemnation of prostitution in the 1880s. But the nightclub known as The Owl in Maik Nwosu's *Alpha Song* is one of the most striking in all Nigerian fiction as it is a focus for all the alienation expressed by the novel's hero, as if only in a nightclub can he find existential ease. This is where the role of the nightclub in Nigerian fiction becomes truly emblematic as a kind of symbol of the Nigerian condition, a place of shadowy "managers of the night" who people the novel. There is a touch of the same atmosphere even in the ambivalent "Champagne" nightclub in Jude Dibia's 2005 novel *Walking with Shadows*, the first and only openly gay fiction in Nigeria.

The Kakadu

Any discerning searcher for atmosphere will have discovered the particular charms of a Lagos night out without necessarily being guided by Nigerian writers. For me, the Mecca of Lagos nightlife during the post-independence period was probably the Kakadu in Alagomeji, Yaba. It is still a well-remembered icon among West African open-air nightclubs, the memory of which still deserves eulogy. In both Nigeria and Ghana these old places under the tropical night were the model for provincial clubs all over the region from the Paradise Hotel in Ibadan to the Gay Palace in Makurdi.

Some of the great highlife bands of the day like Osita Osadebe, Roy Chicago, Arinze, and Cardinal Rex Lawson used to play at the Kakadu. Situated at the Yaba end of Herbert Macaulay Street, it later became the Afro-spot where Fela first played when he returned to Lagos in the late 1960s with his orchestra Koolas Lobitos before he moved to the Empire Hotel and then the Surulere Night Club, which later became the first Shrine.

I was taken to the Kakadu in 1965 in the heyday of post-independence flourishing of social life, almost the symbol of an age before crisis and civil war made it more problematic (though by no means dead). Its memory is still so compelling that there is apparently to be a show titled "Kakadu: The Musical." Tunji Lardner Jr., a typical "Lagos boy," part Sierra Leonean and part Igbo, who graduated from being a subversive journalist of the 1980s to a pioneer of civil society in the twenty-first century, recalls that his father Tunji Senior was manager of the Kakadu for all of that crucial period around the time of independence, when he was a small boy whose head barely reached the bar. In Tunji Jr.'s funeral oration for his father in Ibadan in 2000 he stated, memorably, that Baba Kakadu, as he was known, "in creating the club with its bright green neon parrot sign, had at last found his place in the sun. Kakadu became the defining metaphor that brought together all his entrepreneurial skills, his love of music (he played the piano), his love of people, his love of the good life, and above all else a sense of direction. For close to a decade he was in the spotlight of the Lagos social scene, a genuine bon vivant with a constellation of admirers orbiting his charming, raffish and gregarious self."

The civil war in 1967 signaled a "loss of innocence" and the thrill was gone.

CHAPMANS AND GUINNESS

This subject leads naturally to the role of the bar in society, as well as what is consumed there. Pride of place has to go to the time-honored Chapmans: it is not known who the original Chapman was, but it is a red-colored soft-drink found almost entirely in Nigeria, usually served in a large beer mug and concocted from a mix of Fanta and Grenadine with a strong dash of Angostura bitters (purists abhor the addition of blackcurrant, especially if it is Ribena, which changes the color). It has a certain fruit content and ideally a slice of orange on the side of the mug. One story has it that Chapmans was invented in the now defunct Bristol Hotel, but I have found this impossible to confirm.

Another widespread feature of Lagos imbibing habits is the singular popularity of Guinness and sundry non-alcoholic malted drinks. It is said that the necessary expenditure on the mobile phone since 2001 (the market for which had grown to over seventy million ten years later) led to a depression in the drinks market that earlier downturns had never produced because of the limits mobile phones have placed on purchasing power.

This decline even applied briefly to the market for Guinness although it did not last for long as the famous stout has been a Nigerian institution for years, having been first imported to West Africa as long ago as the early nineteenth century. The first Guinness brewery and bottling plant was opened in Ikeja in 1962. It has an enduring popularity that has spread to other African countries, but Nigeria is the core of Guinness' African market to the point that it has already overtaken Ireland in consumption of the dark brown drink, and may soon overtake the UK to become the number one Guinness-drinking country in the world. A few years ago Guinness even sponsored a film called *Critical Assignment* in which an actor called Michael Power portrayed a black James Bond with one or two shots of Lagos interspersed with other African cities from Yaoundé to Johannesburg. Guinness Nigeria spawned a Lagos legend in the shape of Keith Richards, a one-time managing director who was fond of sponsoring pop concerts with Nigerian musicians, and is still one of those occasional white men fully incorporated into Lagos society, another true "Lagos boy."

The return of an expanding and much more diverse expatriate community, combined with the new private sector-driven Nigerian middle class, has led to a growth of more up-market restaurants that help give Lagos more of the flavor of an international capital. Those with long memories recall the feeling of modernity brought by Chinese restaurants of the early 1960s like the Cathay, and the special phenomenon of Antoines (cosmopolitan Lebanese) and the Tabriz (Iranian) in the 1970s, both in the Broad Street neighborhood before blight hit the business district. The changing patterns of eating out have since evolved into more international-style restaurants like La Scala (very up-market Italian in the MUSON Centre from the 1990s), the Villa Medicis and the Mexican-style Bottles (although there is limited scope for Tex-Mex: the Santa Fe, which had picturesque saloon-style wooden swing doors, became the more tropically themed Coconut Grove and then changed again). Expect another reincarnation as this is the way things are in Lagos. By the time this book appears there will be other changes.

THE NOLLYWOOD PHENOMENON

From the 1920s to the 1960s an active cinema culture in Nigeria found full expression in Lagos. When I first visited in 1964 the best-known cinemas were the Sheila in Campbell Street and the Casino in Yaba, which was wrecked by a home-made bomb early in the civil war (miraculously, the building still stands). There are those who ascribe the decline of cinemas to this sad event, but this was probably as much due to television, which first arrived at the moment of independence at the beginning of the 1960s. The advent of the VCR twenty years later effectively put an end to cinemas until they were born again with the rise of a new middle class in the new century. In 2004 the Silverbird multiplex opened on Ahmadu Bello Way on Victoria Island, located in a glossy mini-mall with modern cinemas on the top floor. This was followed by a similar multiplex in the Palms Mall in Lekki. These smaller cinemas, of the kind that have done so well in the developed world, are seriously different from the earlier variety which in some cases were open-air and were much given to showing Indian films, and the pitch is very much to the new middle classes.

A local film industry also never really got properly off the ground perhaps because it never had the kind of government encouragement, aided by French government cultural money, which obtained in many of the countries of Francophone West Africa such as Senegal and Burkina Faso. Adam Apter commented on the inadequate Nigerian entry in FESTAC, although one should also note the long and frustrated journey of the Nigerian *cinéaste* Ola Balogun, who made a series of films in the 1970s and 1980s, the best-known of which was the corruption-focused *Money Power*. Technology eventually came to the aid of Nigerian would-be filmmakers because the continuous expansion of better quality television, satellites technology and the development of first VCRs and then DVD players meant that Nigeria suddenly found itself with a domestic video business that in the twenty-first century took on international proportions. On the one hand, television channels such as OBE and BEN-TV developed in London could be received in Nigeria, and on the other those with satellite dishes could receive some of Nigeria's independent television channels such as AIT, not to mention the improved government service through the Nigerian Television Authority (NTA). The South Africans, through DSTV and a number of sports channels, were particularly successful in capturing the market in Nigeria.

Even more significant in terms of "value added" to the Nigerian economy has been the phenomenon known as Nollywood. This is a generic term applied (in the manner of the Indian film industry) to the remarkable output of locally made video films. Statistics from the international film market indicate that Nigeria now comes third after the US and India, in terms of the value of sales, in the world. Somehow the natural economics of the business and the small scale of operations made possible what had not been hitherto achievable, and it was also a medium that found its own market, which had once been satisfied with first Indian and then Kung Fu films, and also suited the particular creative talents of a new generation.

This market had once found its expression in Onitsha market literature consisting of locally written and produced pamphlets covering a range of genres from political tracts such as *Chief Awolowo and the Bitterness of Politics* to romantic stories such as *Rosemary's Secret*. These were genuinely local products, which the output of Heinemann's African Writers Series, although playing an important role on a different level, never were, indeed never sought to be. Onitsha literature may now be virtually dead, while Heinemann authors like Achebe and others, including even the London-based Buchi Emecheta, are now on the syllabus and taught in hundreds of Nigerian schools. Yet the creative spirit of Onitsha market literature lives on in the amazing output of Nollywood, which is now a major industry based mainly in Lagos and Eastern Nigeria which has developed considerably from its artisanal beginnings some fifteen years ago.

Nollywood has a market throughout Africa as well as in the Western world, and with the realization that something very original is stirring, it is being taken increasingly seriously as an expression of local culture. At the same time the range of subject matter, once limited to crime, sex, the paranormal and horror, is expanding along with potential for funding, and the technical quality of the product is improving. The industry is based mainly in Lagos although there is a parallel Hausa video business of some importance based in Northern cities. Although there is strong input from Eastern Nigeria, it is above all a Lagos phenomenon with many of the settings in mainly middle-class Lagos, though more "mainland" than "island."

And it has become a huge business. From having a few years ago the third largest global film industry (in terms of output) after Hollywood and Bollywood, Nigeria now appears to possess on its doorstep a world industry leader. According to a 2009 report by UNESCO, Nigeria with 872 productions (in video format) has outstripped the US (with 485) in numbers of films made, hard on the heels of India with 1,081 feature-length films. (These figures are from 2006.)

The figures are in fact hard to calculate exactly. The Nigerian Film Board estimates that the true Nigerian production figure is now anything between 1,500 and 2,500 films a year. Likewise the films' earning capacity is mysterious because it is mostly confined to the informal sector, but a figure of $250 million a year is mooted. Moreover, it is a business that has grown of its own volition, assisted in part by the evolution of technology and the ad hoc nature of filmmaking in Nigeria that make it possible to produce films at modest cost without the substantial investment normally needed.

Yet this remarkable flowering of home-grown talent and enterprise is now in crisis partly because of market saturation but also because of pressures to improve quality without destroying the drive, the creative spark and the intuitive ability to read the needs of the market. The international movie business has already tried to co-opt Bollywood, as seen in the success of the Oscar-winning *Slumdog Millionaire*, but for the moment the outside world is still circling round Nollywood. There have been at least ten international documentaries in the last two years including the award-winning Canadian-made *Nollywood Babylon*, which looks at the central video market at Idumota (in a very traditional part of Lagos Island) and scrutinizes the input of evangelical money that has spotted an outlet for Christian proselytizing.

Havens in the Wilderness

Among Nigeria's lonely cultural pioneers, many of whom are based in Lagos, there is sometimes a feeling that they live in a relentlessly philistine country where money is king and culture is something to be pigeon-holed for traditional society and only wheeled out on special occasions. In the morass of getting and spending that is Lagos, islands of cultural activity of different kinds stand out for the way they keep the flag flying against sometimes heavy odds. This concept of cultural ports of call, of secluded havens in the harsh wilderness of the philistine city, grows on you the longer you stay in Lagos. There are, for example, the arts organizations like those run by those tireless pioneers Jahman Anikulapo and Toyin Akinosho who describe themselves as "cultural landscapists" and who established the Committee for Relevant Art (CORA). They are regular organizers of festivals, book fairs, "splashes" and elders' evenings. There is also a more official Centre for Black and African Arts and Civilisation (CBAAC). Official attitudes may be changing: of late the Lagos State government has encouraged its own festivals such as the Lagos Black Heritage Festival.

These ventures use a variety of "havens," small cultural centers such as Bolanle Austen-Peters' Terra Kulture which has its own performance room and theater company (which participated in the UK 2012 Shakespeare festival at the Globe in London) alongside a gallery, library and restaurant. There is also the Cultural Centre in Yaba, run by another Lagos arts pioneer Bisi Silva, who has a strong line in gender and environmental issues. Larger venues are now also available, and where once there was just the historic Glover Hall (which still manages to survive) there is now the lagoon-side Civic Centre built by a banking tycoon at the beginning of the Lekki highway as well as the aforementioned MUSON Centre and its highly eclectic activities—everything from classical concerts to its recent festival with Earl Klugh playing with Lagbaja. All are faced with the limited nature of official cultural policy, affected by so much philistinism and crassness in the past. Chapter 7 discusses some of the examples that occurred during FESTAC, including attempts to censor African intellectuals in the festival's colloquium. This became part of FESTAC's cumulatively negative image over the years, which in turn gave the whole idea of culture a bad name.

Two of Nigeria's most outstanding artists of the independence generation, the late Ben Enwonwu (see Chapter 3) and the brilliantly imaginative Bruce Onabrakpeya (still very much alive), also have their own havens. In the case of Onabrakpeya, now eighty years old and still producing, his studio in Surulere is matched by a small gallery on Victoria Island run by his son Mudiro. He also has an important workshop in the Niger Delta, his own homeland. Enwonwu's house in Ikoyi is full of a marvelous collection of his own works although some can still be seen around Lagos such as the statue of the god Shango outside the electric power headquarters on the Marina. His son Oliver runs from there a foundation bearing his name.

The Association of Galleries of Nigeria organizes an Art Expo (usually in the grounds of the Nigeria Museum). Its president, Frank Okonta, has his own Nkem Gallery in Lekki, and there are a variety of others, some doing quite well, some struggling. There is tremendous pressure from would-be artists, many of whom are extremely talented but rarely get an opportunity to exhibit. From the great mass of them one occasionally floats to the top. There is an increasing body of wealthy Nigerian collectors, and London and New York auction houses have begun to take on board new Nigerian artists, but there is still a great deal to do for people to discover that this could be big business, the kind of Damascene moment that led to the realization that Nollywood is a valuable non-oil export.

Also among these cultural islands are the non-globalized but important book and music shops such as the Jazz Hole (see the section on Awolowo Road in Chapter 7), home of a small publishing operation called Glendora that produces a magazine and is also progenitor of a large,

Bruce Onabrakpeya, *Eketete and Erbeybuye* (Harmon Foundation)

exciting book referred to elsewhere in these pages: *Lagos: A City at Work*. Nigerian publishing has yet to make an international breakthrough; the earlier Ibadan-based publishers such as Spectrum Books now face increasing competition from a new generation of publishers like Farafina, Cassava Republic and Bookcraft, but there is still not much printing in Nigeria. A visit to the annual International Book Fair held at Lagos University (although it had little that was international) exposed the industry's weakness in spite of evidence of a large and solid output.

Yet Nigeria, both new and old, is culturally so rich and possessed of so much native talent that this lack of official recognition is still bewildering, especially when one considers how important in theory culture is in the world-picture of Nigeria's nationalist endeavor. Also epitomized is the incomprehension in official Nigeria of the concept of tourism, and how it could be developed. Lagos State has increasingly ambitious plans for tourist development, but more cautious minds insist that it has to be approached slowly. Badagry has some potential for the African American "slave route" market with Nigeria's first "storey house," and has even attracted an extravagant projected tourism development to include a Michael Jackson Museum (mooted by Marlon, brother of the late "King of Pop"), but Nigeria does not have the basic assets of, for example, the forts in Ghana, which have proved such a successful tourism lure.

Lastly, the already mentioned foreign cultural centers such as the French Cultural Centre, the Goethe Institut, the US Information Centre and the British Council can all count as "havens" in their own sometimes idiosyncratic promotion of Nigerian and African culture alongside their own national cultures.

THE CASE OF NIMBUS

On a more personal note, the idea of cultural havens was truly opened up for me with the brief but stellar life of the Nimbus gallery in Maitama Sule Street in southwest Ikoyi. When I came to Lagos in 2001 to spend two years sampling the undergrowth of the Nigerian capitalist jungle, Nimbus became a home from home that symbolized for me the "best-kept secret in the best-kept secret." Nimbus was the brainchild of Chike Nwagbogu, one of a new breed of Nigerian cultural entrepreneurs with a flair for spotting and mobilizing talent, a true child of the "city of the imagination."

Nimbus, in its five years of existence before being expelled by an uncomprehending landlord, brought together a wealth of talent of both creative artists and musicians, a foretaste of what this kind of venue in Lagos could be. The bar and restaurant (for a time it had delicious dishes prepared by its Togolese chef Victor K) became a meeting-point for intellectuals and literati (and the occasional journalist). It was not too far from my own apartment in Ikoyi, and I would tend to find my way there at weekends, sometimes even daring to perform. So taken was I with the special liberating atmosphere of the place that I wrote an enthusiastically long eulogy titled "the Glory of Nimbus," which to my knowledge still graces the Nimbus website, even though the caravan of reality has passed on.

The spirit of Nimbus remains just over the road in a guesthouse named Bogobiri (after the Hausa kingdom of Gobir). Many of the artworks and artefacts that once graced the Nimbus gallery were brought to Bogobiri, and much of its essence remains there. The guest rooms have works of art on the walls and traditional bedspreads as well as wrought-iron bedsteads locally made in an almost baroque style. It is much favored by foreign visitors seeking a Nigerian cultural experience in a relatively comfortable setting. Bogobiri is often full: one sometimes finds it full of European visitors in search of the authentic.

Chike also for a time tried to set up a more ambitious project called the "Afrika Centre" in an unfinished property at the side of the Falomo bridge (the name is inscribed in mosaic on the side), but this also was disbanded, remaining one of Chike's many "dreams in progress". The building was relegated to that category of long-incomplete structures that can be observed from time to time as a spectral presence in Lagos. It housed a fine statue called "African Male" carved in the hard wood of the iroko tree by the late Ben Osawe, one of a remarkable and under-appreciated breed of Nigerian sculptors, many of whom came from Benin (whose rich centuries-old artistic tradition still serves as an inspiration for some of its children). The statue is still under Chike's guardianship. A revived Nimbus existed for a time just down the road, where Chike invited patrons to meet and engage in the Nigerian habit of "gisting" (approximately translated as gossiping). Lagos being Lagos, where no condition is permanent, this latest Nimbus also disappeared like the lost city of Atlantis or Shangri-la, even while remaining forever as a concept. The idea that gave birth to Nimbus can still be found alive and well, however, in a re-launched and enlarged Bogobiri.

Chike is from a large and talented family from Anambra State. His younger brother Azubike (Azu), who trained as a pharmacist but is now also fully engaged in the art world, has his own African Arts Association, which staged an important exhibition of young painters and photographers in the Lagos Cultural Centre in 2008, eventually taken to Amsterdam. Chike, a former rugby player and British public school product, has extended his acute sense of innovation to sport. He has devised "Lagos rules" hand-and-football played for several years now on Sunday evenings, on Kuramo beach. Artists, students, workers and area boys all participate. It is a unique experience to watch this sporting improvisation as the evening sun goes down over Apapa across the lagoon and a half-light bathes the beach.

THE SLENDER PLANT OF HERITAGE

There is still a prevalent view in Lagos that old is bad, and that history should not stand in the way of progressive development, especially when it can be so immensely profitable. In this context one has to commend the role of the organization called Legacy set up in 1995 by John and Jill Godwin, British architects who have been in Lagos since the 1950s, with substantial support from interested Nigerians. Over the years they have organized walking tours of historic Lagos, especially the Brazilian quarter on Lagos Island, and excursions on Nigerian railways in which they have had a particular interest. One of Legacy's greatest achievements has been the restoration of the fine old Jaekel house, a gem of early colonial architecture on the tranquil tree-lined railway compound in Ebute Metta (Jaekel was for years Chief Superintendent of the Railways). Legacy has also produced with the government a map of Nigeria's antiquities and historic monuments.

John Godwin has been a particular enthusiast for the restoration of Brazilian houses, notably the Water House (on Kakawa Street) with help from the Leventis Foundation (set up by the Leventis trading family). There is still much to be done here; who will ensure the future of the beautiful masonry and carving by Brazilian craftsmen in the Shitta-Bey Mosque in Martins Street and the seriously crumbling Ilojo Bar, the Olaiya house on Tinubu Square? Approaches made by the Lagos State government to Salvador da Bahia in Brazil, especially after the 2008 visit by Governor Fashola, are encouraging, but even at this late stage there are those who

The Jaekel house

make a case for involving UNESCO more decisively in helping to preserve what is left of the unique Brazilian heritage through restoration or even reconstruction. The twinning of Lagos with Bahia, where the authorities have considerable experience of keeping their heritage intact, is a good sign. The building of relations gives an emotional underpinning to the increasingly important south-south trade ties between Brazil and Nigeria.

Those aware of the value of Nigeria's heritage still express concern at the deterioration of official institutions, notably at the National Museum in Onikan. There is also disquiet at the widespread smuggling out of the country of Nigeria's vast reservoir of antiquities, as happened notably at the Ife Museum in 1994, many of which, I am told, have now been returned with international assistance. Such events make requests for the return of colonial loot from the British Museum harder to support. Teju Cole in his highly original, semi-fictional work about Lagos, *Every Day is for the Thief*, provides a trenchantly depressing account of a visit to the National Museum.

> Along the walls there are white cardboard plaques about various kingship ceremonies, as well as one about a German-led archaeological

expedition to Ijebuland in the 1980s. The quality of the print on the plaque is poor, faded from exposure to the sun, and badly mildewed... Again, there is the inescapable feeling that one is looking at a neglected high-school project.

There is some hope that a new project with $4 million from the Ford Foundation to refurbish the National Museum with training for staff will give it a new lease of life, and that it may be able to host the spectacular Kingdom of Ife exhibition shown in 2010 at the British Museum, which still had the capacity to astonish critics with the beauty of Ife's fourteenth-century artefacts. The US interest also involves the new Museum of African Art in New York as well as the British Museum, suggesting that Nigerians can live in hope despite the present reality. Conversely, a cause for discouragement are the sad case histories of the National Theatre (see Chapter 7) curiously paralleled by the now dilapidated National Stadium, also built in the 1970s and of that other over-inflated and inappropriate prestige project from that period, the International Trade Fair site on the Badagry Road, built by the Yugoslav firm Energoprojekt. It never really took off as a trade fair venue and is now principally a spare parts market, although occasional events are organized there.

There are a few cherished protected places, but there has also been a great deal of developers' vandalism: for example, Ikoyi Park on the north-east side of Ikoyi island was a pleasant public green space that for many years was a venue for picnics (see Sefi Atta's *Everything Good Will Come*, where part of the dramatic action is played out at an Ikoyi Park picnic). There are still many Lagosians who privately regret that Ikoyi Park was turned by military fiat in the 1980s into an upmarket estate with town-houses, condos and apartments, although ironically it has proved highly susceptible to flooding because of poor structural drainage. There is now a certain new spirit abroad, a feeling that a "world city" also needs to be good-looking, a view subscribed to by Governor Fashola who has made environment a priority. He is keen, for example, on the protection of trees, vowing to plant a million trees in three years. In the great maelstrom of Lagos environmental improvements are still an uphill struggle, but I understand that he reached his target.

Engraving of European Quarter, Edouard Riou, 1887

Chapter Six

STORIES TO REMEMBER
A SELECTION OF EPISODES IN THE CITY'S HISTORY

"The first fateful step had been taken towards the creation of Nigeria, black Africa's most populous and powerful nation."

> Kristin Mann, writing about 6 August 1861, date of the signing of the Treaty of Cession of Lagos to Britain, in *Slavery and the Birth of an African City: Lagos 1760-1900*, 2007

The various events described in this chapter have in some cases also been covered in Chapter 1 or elsewhere, but have been selected as marking dramatic, in some cases defining, points in the history of Lagos (often reflecting the history of Nigeria itself). The selection may sometimes seem haphazard, and the more recent ones have tended to be chosen because I have been able to use my own eye-witness reporting, so this chapter has a particular subjectivity. It also involves a measure of repetition.

So much could be featured here such as the coming of the railway and the port or the impact of two world wars, which profoundly affected the lives of the people of the city, but the greater themes have been touched on elsewhere. The other arbitrary choice has been the particular prominence given to the ten years from 1851 to 1861, which marked two seminal moments in the history of Lagos. These were the deposition of Kosoko after the British gunboat bombardment of December 1851 and the full annexation of 6 August 1861, embodied in the Treaty of Cession. It was a takeover in two stages with the first one leading inexorably to the other.

THE LAGOS CONSULATE 1851 TO 1861: THE BRITISH TAKEOVER IN SLOW MOTION:

(1) 1851: GUNBOAT DIPLOMACY
The immediate trigger for the 1851 bombardment was the increasingly

difficult position of the British protégé Akitoye, deposed by Kosoko in 1845 and in exile in Badagry. His appeals to the British had become ever more desperate as Kosoko was putting on more pressure in alliance with Porto Novo, while Dahomey was warring with Abeokuta. Akitoye, in alliance with the missionaries, was calling for the British to intervene and Consul Beecroft was recommending intervention to Palmerston, who, as we have seen, had advised that should Kosoko refuse an anti-slave trade treaty once more he should be reminded of British power. Beecroft took Akitoye to Fernando Po for his own security, but he was also the instrument for the planned intervention as he accompanied Beecroft on HMS *Bloodhound*, a paddle steamer which joined up with HMS *Harlequin* off Lagos.

On 20 November 1851 the two vessels received a message from Kosoko not to advance further, and two Brazilian merchants also came with the same message. At a meeting with Kosoko involving Beecroft and three naval officers, the Oba refused to sign an anti-slaving treaty, saying he would have to refer to the Oba of Benin. Additional support was sought from Commander Forbes, the senior officer of the West African Squadron, to whom Beecroft showed Palmerston's crucial dispatch of the previous February as authority for intervention; on 25 November *Bloodhound*, flying a flag of truce, entered the lagoon with 21 armed and manned boats in tow with altogether 306 officers and men. The boat went aground and was fired on by Kosoko's cannon from the shore. Indeed, it seemed that Lagos was much better defended than anticipated. Fortifications with a trench had been built along where the Marina is now, and also on the western side of the Lagos lagoon at what Burton called Takpa Point. The truce flag was hauled down, but a party that went ashore was able only to destroy a few houses, and because their numbers were felt to be inadequate the flotilla retired. Beecroft wrote in justification that "the mud walls and very narrow streets afforded so great an advantage to the enemy who were swarming in vast numbers and proved themselves such good marksmen," giving a vivid impression of the town and its defenders.

Beecroft and Commander Forbes were reprimanded for having attacked Lagos without referring to the commander-in-chief on the coast, Commodore Bruce. Robert Smith attributes the fiasco to a combination of Beecroft's impetuousness and Forbes' inadequate intelligence on the strength of Kosoko's position. However, the setback reinforced determination to intervene, and steps were taken to send a stronger expedition. On

30 November, presumably as a test, a village on the eastern end of the lagoon was attacked and a Portuguese slaver's barracoon was burnt, but it was only on 18 December that formal plans were made to depose Kosoko and replace him with Akitoye, now back in Badagry and still waiting in the wings (there is a probably apocryphal story that at some point he was on board *Bloodhound* disguised in European clothes). His followers were instructed to march along the beach to Lagos and rendezvous with the British party after they had crossed the Bar, although the larger boats (HMS *Sampson* and HMS *Penelope*) were unable to do so. *Bloodhound* had been joined by HMS *Teazer*, a screw steamer, and *Victoria*, the consul's iron galley fitted as a rocket boat, as well as the smaller boats. After ineffective gunfire from Kosoko's forces on 25 December, a concerted advance was made the next day directed at the north end of the island, where the Iga Idunganran (the Oba's palace) was situated. Despite better navigational knowledge, both *Bloodhound* and *Teazer* still went aground and were subjected to heavy fire.

An attempted landing was made on an un-staked part of the beach but was also subject to counter-attack and was forced to retreat. It was only on 27 December that *Teazer*, refloated, joined *Bloodhound* at the north of the island. There they were joined by *Victoria* with her heavy guns able to bombard the island without any landings, and she duly scored a direct hit on Kosoko's powder magazine which exploded with a roar. It was an exercise in what nowadays would be called "shock and awe," and it seems to have worked as large numbers of refugees were seen leaving the island in canoes piled high with household goods. On 28 December all was quiet and a local chief came to inform Beecroft that the town had been evacuated. It had been a question of superior firepower. Smith tells us of the Yoruba names for the engagement: *Ogun Agidingbi* or *Ogun Ahoyaya* (the "booming" or the "boiling" battle). Smith also remarks that casualties in Lagos were unknown, but other historians have not been so shy. Olowogbowo, on the western end of the island, had been burnt and almost flattened, and there were over 500 deaths with many more casualties. In terms of imperial conquest it ranks as a massacre, which ought to be admitted, just like the destruction of the barracoons on the shore where the Marina was subsequently built.

On 29 December Akitoye was landed on the almost deserted island and was able to regain possession of the ruined Iga Idunganran, to be accepted as ruler by the few remaining chiefs. On the last day of 1851 he was visited by a British delegation and subsequently signed a treaty abolishing the slave trade. After the treaty in Lagos, similar treaties abolishing the trade were signed by the British with ten other localities from Dahomey and Porto Novo to Badagry, Abeokuta and Ijebu. This was still a long way from the abolition of the institution of slavery itself, which was another matter altogether as it was still very widespread both in Lagos and in the hinterland. Consul McCoskry, who was often considered to have "gone native," was of the view, quite widely held among the merchants on the coast, that African slavery was a mild institution, "not properly slavery at all."

Kristin Mann, in her magisterial study *Slavery and the Birth of an African City*, records McCoskry as arguing that slaves in Lagos were "treated more like servants than chattels and that they stayed with their owners not through coercion but of their own free will." The British themselves had only finally passed legislation forbidding British subjects in their own possessions to own slaves in 1834, and its final eradication in a place like Lagos was a process that was bound to take time. Indeed, in some forms slavery persisted to the end of the century and beyond. An important section of Mann's book traces the evolution of moves against domestic slavery, especially in the period after the arrival of the British in the second part of the nineteenth century.

(2) 1861: THE CRUNCH

The 1861 intervention was a more peaceable affair, but more dreadfully final in its consequences. The consulate over ten years had known various ups and downs including a rapid succession of consuls, the most important of whom was Benjamin Campbell, who had been obliged to make deals with Kosoko and some of his powerful supporters from their base in Epe. Kosoko had continued to engage in slave trading through the ports of Lekki and Palma, which had been ceded to him in 1854. By 1860-61 the context had changed, especially by the Ijaye war in the hinterland and the increasing menaces from the King of Dahomey, which had added to the instability of the hinterland with a serious effect on trade, especially the rich palm oil trade from Ijebu. The British were also noticing increased activity in the direction of Lagos on the part of the French, which had particularly concerned Palmerston, now Prime Minister and ever-mindful of European politics and its African extensions, particularly after the visit of the French steam frigate *Danae* to Lagos in January 1861. The next decade saw a prolonged power struggle with the French over Porto Novo at the far end of the lagoon, eventually secured by the French.

In March 1861 Palmerston minuted on a report on this French visit: "this strongly confirms the expediency of losing no time in assuming the protectorate of Lagos." At the same time there were recommendations for the formation of a consular guard from Consul McCoskry, to counter the tendency of local chiefs to revert to slave trading. The Colonial Office, which tended to be reluctant to increase its responsibilities, stated in mid-June that it could "only concur" in this case, while complaining about money and troops. Although the instructions were clear enough, it took the prompt and partial action of McCoskry to press the case. The formal instructions were issued on 22 June to contact Commander Bedingfield who brought HMS *Prometheus* across the Bar to moor within gunshot of the Oba's palace. On 30 July Dosunmu came on board and was told a Treaty of Cession needed to be signed in forty-eight hours. There was some prevarication because of reservations on the part of some of the chiefs, and it took a threat to open fire on Lagos and landing marines to occupy key positions in the town on 5 August to force the signature the next day of the Treaty of Cession with which the chiefs had been presented. It was an arrogant exercise of power that, nearly a hundred years later, rankles in traditional Lagos, which even now has lawyers examining the treaty for loopholes.

Otunba Payne, a prominent Lagos citizen of the late nineteenth century (see profile in Chapter 8), provides a glowingly pro-British account of the public reaction (which he had witnessed as a young man) to the cession Treaty in a letter to the editor of the Lagos newspaper *Weekly Record*:

> On the 27th July, HMS Frigate Prometheus of 21 guns commanded by Captain Bedingfield... entered the lagoon and on the 30th, King Docemo went on board in state when he was received with a salute of 13 guns, and the cession of Lagos to the British Crown was then negotiated. [On 6 August] there was a great commotion in the town when at noon King Docemo and chiefs stood by the flag-staff in front of the consulate and went through the ceremony of touching the rope, by

which the British Ensign became unfurled while simultaneously the frigate thundered a royal salute of 21 guns while all the school children of Lagos with the pupils of the Grammar School then present sang the National Anthem. At the first boom of the guns a number of Muhammedans present exclaimed "La ila la"! The scene of commotion and stir which the day produced will ever be remembered by those who were present on the occasion. They were fixed indelibly on the memory.

Two years later, the events of September 1863 (later referred to as "the excitement of September 13") were an indication that the treaty had been exacted by force. Echeruo notes that the new newspaper the *Anglo-African* of 12 September recorded that Docemo denied ceding Lagos to the British Crown: "The remark 'Mo ofi ilu med torreh' ('I have not made a present of my town'), the ex-King does not deny having said... Did I not in the government house... refuse to sign? Did I not refuse on board the Prometheus? At my palace did I not also refuse to sign?"

Lt.-Governor Glover issued a statement that this was defiance of the supremacy of the queen and that all loyal subjects of her majesty should be sworn in the next day as special constables for the protection of life and property. Parts of the town were shelled (conjuring up bad memories of December 1851) before Docemo surrendered and lost his pension. To add insult to injury, he was fined £50 "to defray the expense of the steam tugs... the employment of which was rendered necessary in consequence of the trouble he had induced." Echeruo remarks that Lagos opinion, judging by letters to the *Anglo-African*, was sharply divided: some looked back on the days before cession when under "the late Consul Campbell of happy memory... black men patrolled the whole town while the European English merchants quietly enjoyed their repose."

The Baiting of Lord Lugard

There are many episodes in the story of Sir Frederick Lugard's relationship with Nigeria that are engraved on the nation's history, from the taming of the North to "the mistake of 1914" and the crushing of Abeokuta (see profile in Chapter 8). For Lagos, however, the most piquant moment was the 1916 trial of James Bright Davies.

The records show how Lagos politicians and journalists made the governor-general's life hell, even if they were only pinpricks in the grand

Sir Frederick Lugard (right)

Lugardian scheme of things in which the Northern way, even the Northern idea of Nigeria, was what mattered. The drama came to a head in 1916. As early as 1913 he had complained in a letter to his wife of the "scurrilous local yellow press" that enjoyed "monstrous freedom." Despite the self-censorship that had been "patriotically" adopted by the editors themselves because of the First World War, there was one editor, the elderly James Bright Davies of the *Times of Nigeria*, who remained a thorn in Lugard's side. He was, says Fred Omu, "one of the great figures of the early nationalist movement in West Africa" with the kudos of having been the first newspaperman to go to jail in Nigeria. Born in Sierra Leone in 1848 to parents of Igbo origin, he was fired from public service in Ghana for "clandestine journalism" and moved to the administration in Nigeria, actually working under Lugard as transport clerk in Jebba. On retirement in 1906 he moved to journalism in Lagos. He chafed under the restraint of British colonial rule and brought Lugard's iron fist down on himself because of two editorials. The first, in December 1915, attacked British policy in Nigeria as "rancorous negrophobism," and a second article was a frontal objection to British rule, as this stirring extract shows: "The people of Nigeria, and of Lagos in particular, will take courage from [the] fact that someday or other, whether distant or near, their own relief from the iron and cruel rule of their own administration is sure to come and we shall be freed from the galling yoke of its iniquitous measures and laws."

Bright Davies was put on trial charged with attempting to bring the government into hatred and contempt and to exciting disaffection, and was fined £100. He was required to enter into a recognizance with two sureties for £100 each and to be of good behaviour for twelve months. Before that time expired he was held to have failed to show good behavior when in August 1916 he wrote an attack on exploitative British merchants, suggesting that some in Lagos might prefer German rule. Although aged 68, he was sentenced to six months jail, in the words of Omu, "to the great delight of Lugard." Davies was released early after appeals from fellow editors Kitoye Ajasa and Thomas Jackson.

In 1917 Lugard pursued his obsession with criticism by introducing permanent censorship; he repealed the Newspaper Ordinance of 1903, which produced a petition from the unrepentant Davies, and much greater criticism from the political class, though this was bound to be inhibited until the end of the war. But, as Omu says, "The eve of Lugard's departure from Nigeria coincided with the emergence of the new generation of newspapermen. Relieved from political restraint by the end of hostilities and determined to settle old scores with the Governor-General, they pounded him with abuse and thus served notice of what unpopular successors could expect."

THE PRINCE OF WALES' VISIT, 1925

Although hard to describe it as a defining moment, the visit to Nigeria of Edward Prince of Wales in 1925 (as part of a West African tour) included a stop-over in Lagos. The account of the visit in a souvenir volume written by St. John Adcock and published "for the Prince of Wales" by Hodder and Stoughton in 1926 wrote of the Lagos segment of the tour thus:

Although on his first arrival the bill of health in Lagos had made a slight change of programme necessary [earlier described as "a slight outbreak of plague and smallpox"], the Prince of Wales, reluctant to disappoint the Lagosians and to miss seeing the capital of Nigeria, had hoped to visit it on his way back, and, due precautions having been taken in the interval, happily this was found possible... On April 22nd, his Royal Highness laid the foundation stone of the Cathedral of Lagos, and was presented by Bishop Melville Jones with a silver trowel of African workmanship; an eloquent address being afterwards delivered by a native divine, Assistant-Bishop Oluwole. In the afternoon the Prince witnessed a march-past of many thousands of schoolchildren, including regiments of Girl Guides and Boy Scouts, from the local Christian missions...

The account also recorded a message given to the correspondent of *The Times* from Governor Sir Hugh Clifford, who said that he had lived for more than forty years among the people of the tropics and had heard "an immense volume and variety of organised tumult," but he had never heard "in tropical lands, so obviously spontaneous, so completely unorganised an outpouring of popular enthusiasm as that which greeted the Prince, as he passed up the lagoon... to the improvised landing place on Iddo island."

DRAMA AT THE BRISTOL HOTEL, 1947

What came to be known as the Bristol Hotel Incident was something of a *cause célèbre* at the time, playing an important role in suppressing the racial prejudice that had accompanied British colonization. In February 1947 Ivor Cummings, an eminently respectable Sierra Leonean working for the Colonial Office, was refused admission by the hotel's Greek manager, who said that he should have been informed in advance that Cummings "was an African." This highlighted the issue of discrimination that existed in some hotels and bars in Lagos and led to uproar and a violent demonstration at the Bristol. Indignation was strongest in Azikiwe's press, notably the *West African Pilot*, and the furore caused Governor Richards—who, we are told in the *British Documents on the End of Empire*, was "initially unmoved by the incident"—to feel obliged to make a ground-breaking statement to the Legislative Council that "the government would not countenance discrimination of based on race and colour."

This statement was followed by a circular outlining government policy distributed to all establishments, which apparently led to the desegregation of the Ikoyi Club and other places, after which the situation eased (although it took time for some to visibly change). Sir Thomas Lloyd, a Whitehall mandarin, had a discussion with Cummings at which the latter described Nigeria as the least enlightened West African territory as far as race relations were concerned. He mentioned specifically the "European Club in Ikoyi" as not even admitting Africans as guests for a single meal, and the whites-only European Hospital. Lloyd's comment was that "this unfortunate incident must be regarded as having served its purpose."

THE BOOING OF THE NORTHERNERS, 1953

A celebrated incident that went down in contemporary Nigerian history took place outside the parliament building on the Racecourse in Lagos on 31 March 1953. This was the day on which Anthony Enahoro, a leading Action Group member of the legislature, tabled a resolution calling for self-government in 1956 to be a "primary objective." It was contested by the leader of the Northern People's Congress (NPC), Alhaji Ahmadu Bello, Sardauna of Sokoto, articulating the Northern view that the pace towards independence should be less hasty and that the 1956 date be substituted with "as soon as practicable." It led to a turbulent debate and was the occasion on which the Sardauna made what he said was "the shortest speech he had ever made" including the immortal line, "The mistake of 1914 has come to light and I wish to go no further."

The debate ended with the National Council of Nigeria and the Cameroons (NCNC) and AG members walking out in protest, and when the Northern members, conspicuous in their robes, emerged, they were subjected to what the Sardauna calls in his autobiography "the screams and insults of the large crowd of Lagos thugs." Many of the Northerners had never been to Lagos before and were deeply wounded by unceremonious treatment, not just the abuse in the streets but also the anti-Northern sentiment expressed in the local newspapers. The Sardauna also records that on the train going north that evening they were surrounded by booing demonstrators at each stop. Six weeks later riots broke out in Kano which involved a "purge" of Southern residents of the Sabon Gari (strangers' quarter).

Pauline Baker observes that "the treatment received by Northern representatives... did as much to shape their attitudes on the Lagos question and to deepen the split between the north and south as did the ideological differences separating the major parties." The constitutional conference of 1953 created the federal territory and put the rest of the former Colony into the Western Region (see Chapter 3). Although this only lasted fourteen years and had been achieved through an alliance of North and West, there was an element of revenge in Northern attitudes, whose practical manifestation was the insistence on the Minister of Lagos Affairs position being held by a Northerner. But the affair undermined the Macpherson Constitution of that year, and probably helped Nigeria to move closer to independence in the next round of constitution-making in 1958-59.

INDEPENDENCE DAY (AND NIGHT), OCTOBER 1960

Midnight between 30 September and 1 October 1960 was one of those poignant moments that Nigerians who were there will have remembered for the rest of their lives. It was at this moment at the Racecourse (later Tafawa Balewa Square) that the representative of Queen Elizabeth, her cousin Princess Alexandra, lowered the Union Jack and raised the green and white flag of the federation.

There is a very touching account that captures the innocence of the occasion written in *Nigeria Magazine* in 1961 by the writer Cyprian Ekwensi. "From all parts of the world messages of goodwill were flowing in by the hour, and suddenly it was apparent that a transformation had taken place—visibly and invisibly. Nigeria had become important in a new way."

One question was whether it would rain. "The sky was cloudy, but not too cloudy to black out the golds and blues, the greens and scarlets that beamed down decoratively from Carter Bridge, and Cowrie Creek Bridges, and Victoria Street [now Nnamdi Azikiwe Street], from which all the petty traders had been cleared, now a new widened street with new shops and a more modern look…"

Ekwensi noted that the Electricity Corporation of Nigeria (later succeeded by the notorious Nigerian Electric Power Authority, NEPA) was working overtime with the slogan "The Lights in Lagos Must Not Fail," and that "the decorations on the Marina were perhaps the most amusing, especially at night when the lights in the harbour were lit up and the comic decorations of parrots, crownbirds, camels and other Nigerian animals winked at passing motorists." He estimates that the Nigeria Museum at Onikan was attracting 30,000 visitors a day and the new bridge to Victoria Island was carrying twenty times as many people to the exhibition site by the newly-built Federal Palace Hotel. Also to be seen was the new Independence Square with its fountain by the Racecourse. But Princess Alexandra was the center of attention, "driving round the Square in an open land-rover, so close she could have stretched out her gloved hand and touched the people—women especially who called her endearing names like *abeke*, in appreciation of her beauty…" She remained in the country until 15 October, but there were other visitors such as Louis Armstrong (sponsored by Pepsi-Cola).

The atmosphere of feting went on until the inauguration of Nnamdi Azikiwe as governor-general on 15 November, at which, says Ekwensi, "the attendance was staggering. The spirit this time was less formal, more emotional. The cars with the IND number-plates were still not sold, the Federal Palace was booked to capacity, and the whole ceremonial process was repeated with fervour. In an after-lunch speech, Dr Zik described those assembled as the greatest collection of rebels and agitators ever."

THE 1963 TREASON TRIAL

The independence honeymoon did not last long. The first big post-independence political crisis, of which some of the crucial action took place in Lagos, was the crisis over the split in the Action Group in August 1962, which put Western Nigeria under a State of Emergency. The party leader Chief Awolowo was put under house arrest a month later, and in November was arrested on charges of treason, along with 26 colleagues from the Action Group, and there were serious riots on Lagos Island, both on his arrest and after the verdict in mid-1963 before he was sent to confinement, as it turned out for three years, in Calabar.

The main scenes in this drama were in Lagos, at the High Court and at the old nineteenth-century prison in Broad Street (now the site of the Freedom Park), where he and his co-defendants were detained. There is a house in the middle of Lekki port where the chief stayed for two weeks when he was first put under restriction in the Western Nigerian State of Emergency in June 1962, which has been refurbished as a spot for visitors by the Lagos State government. He was also held under house arrest at his official residence as leader of the opposition in the Federal Parliament, 7 Bell Avenue in Ikoyi. In his memoirs *My March through Prison*, Chief Awolowo recalls the question put by his wife: "Why is it that that the first official residence in which we lived turned out to be a 'prison house' for us?" In the book Awolowo also notes that his cell in Broad Street "was reminiscent of the old slave trade. There remained, fixed to the solid concrete-like floor, an old giant iron ring, which used to form part of the chain with which slaves were held in the cell before they were trans-shipped to the Americas."

SEASON OF COUPS, 1966

The year 1966 saw two of the most dramatic happenings the city has ever witnessed. This was not just in terms of sheer tension and fast-moving events but also their political implications for the future destiny of the country. Early in the year came Nigeria's first coup d'état on 15 January. This was a coup that only partly succeeded in attaining the objectives of its perpetrators: it achieved the destruction of the previous regime, but not in the manner the plotters intended. This was in part because in a federation like Nigeria with several centers of power, coordination of something that depends on surprise as well as human capacity proved unreliable. Although the key successes of the coup were in the Northern capital Kaduna, where the powerful regional Premier Sir Ahmadu Bello was assassinated, and in Ibadan where the Western regional Premier S. L. Akintola was also killed, Lagos was still the epicenter where the key events leading to a new regime took place.

They appear to have begun about 2:30 a.m. on 15 January with the arrest and assassination of prominent politicians such as the federal Prime Minister, Alhaji Sir Abubakar Tafawa Balewa, the Finance Minister, Festus Okotie-Eboh and senior army officers including notably Brigadier Zakari Maimalari, who had entertained some of the coup-makers at a cocktail party at his Ikoyi house the evening before. There are number of accounts of these events, some bloody, some pitiful. In *The Nigerian Civil War* the British journalist John de St. Jorre relates how Sandhurst-trained Major Emmanuel Ifeajuna, a Commonwealth Games athlete who was designated leader of the coup plot in Lagos, had gone to the Prime Minister's house in King George V Road, Onikan, on Lagos Island, heading a small detachment of soldiers.

> The police guard was quickly overpowered and Ifeajuna kicked Balewa's bedroom door open and took him away after allowing him to say his

prayers. The soldiers then went next door to the house of Chief Okotie-Eboh... brushed aside his personal guard, armed with bows and arrows, gave him a severe beating and arrested him too. Meanwhile another group of mutineers had driven to the port and commercial suburb of Apapa where several senior army officers lived. Three key men in the army hierarchy had been selected to die... All three were killed by the major in charge of the group (another ringleader) with bursts of his sub-machine gun, either in their houses or out in the road. The bodies were thrown into the vehicles and the party drove back to Lagos to rejoin the main group.

The Nigerian Special Branch report on the coup contains many other factual details such as the circumstances of the killing of Brigadier Maimalari, who was not in his Ikoyi house, having been warned by phone that something was happening:

> At a point on the Golf Course adjacent to a petrol station, Brigadier Maimalari was walking towards Dodan Barracks (army headquarters since colonial days) when he saw Major Ifeajuna's car. The brigadier recognised Ifeajuna [his chief staff officer and special protégé] and shouted and beckoned him to stop. Ifeajuna stopped the car and accompanied by another officer, went towards Brigadier Maimalari and killed him.

The Prime Minister and the Finance Minister were both killed at separate locations on the Abeokuta Road. The body of Colonel Largema, who was actually killed in the Ikoyi Hotel, was later deposited on the same Ikoyi Golf Course, which in Lagos legend came to be thought of as a famous location for disposing of the victims of "collateral damage." The Ikoyi Golf Course is still a favorite elite sports venue, especially at weekends, but few of those now following the eighteen holes seem troubled by ghosts.

An hour or two later, a blocking move masterminded by the army commander, General Aguiyi-Ironsi—who, curiously, had not been scheduled for arrest by the plotters—with others who had escaped, used police headquarters in the Obalende district of Central Lagos to spearhead his operation, before driving pistol in hand to the crucial barracks of the

Second Division in Ikeja to rally their support. At this point Ifeajuna seems to have lost his nerve, and after the killings on the Abeokuta Road in which he was also involved, drove his blood-smeared Mercedes to Enugu where he went into hiding before fleeing to Ghana.

The failure of the coup in Lagos (despite its success in Kaduna) meant that Ironsi took control with the compliance of those politicians left around such as Senate President Nwafor Orizu (President Nnamdi Azikiwe being conveniently out of the country as if he were aware something was afoot), and Nigeria's first military government was ushered in. The stated intentions of the failed coup were radical/nationalist and it felt briefly like a sort of liberation, attracting massive enthusiasm from the Lagos populace and from its newspapers. However, the manner in which the coup was executed also caused suspicion, especially in the North, that this was in fact an Igbo coup designed to further the Igbo cause or at the very least a "Southern" coup. Although in the Nigerian context this could only have been the case with extreme difficulty, there was enough evidence and enough insensitivity for a gruesome backlash to develop, especially after the passing of Decree No. 34 introducing a unitary state, which rode roughshod over the Northern concept of Nigeria.

By July the mood in the country had changed and for weeks there were rumors that something was to happen. A young colonel from Kano called Murtala Muhammed had been heard boasting to that effect in places like the Mandarin Restaurant in Ikeja, and on 29 July the balloon went up. First-hand accounts of the events of that day (in less plentiful supply than those of January) focused in Lagos mainly on the Ikeja barracks; there, as in Abeokuta and Ibadan (where the head of state, General Aguiyi-Ironsi, was killed along with the Western military governor Adekunle Fajuyi), many Igbo officers were killed as perceived revenge for the January killings, only the July numbers were much more substantial.

Although most sources deny absolutely that the "flag of the North" ever flew on the barracks (it was apparently Eastern Nigerian propaganda) there is no doubt that a secessionist sentiment had gripped some of the officers from the far North. On the other hand the rank and file—mainly from the Middle Belt, a large central region of minority peoples situated between the main ethnic homelands of the Hausa-Fulani (North) and Yoruba and Igbo (South) people—were equally passionate believers in "one Nigeria." Their spokesman was the self-appointed airport commandant Captain Paul Dickson, who articulated the view that the rank and file preferred Colonel Yakubu Gowon (himself from the Middle Belt), who was at the center of high-level crisis discussions that were going on in the three days without a government between 29 July and 1 August. Key players in the talks were senior permanent secretaries, the Chief Justice and Attorney-General and, controversially, the British and American Ambassadors.

The British High Commissioner Sir Francis Cumming-Bruce (now Lord Thurlow and over one hundred years old) made a remarkable comment at the beginning of an interview with the author in April 2007: "I sometimes wonder whether I did the right thing in keeping Nigeria together." He then recounted how he and General Gowon had a two-hour tête-à-tête in Ikeja Barracks at which he had put forth the issues squarely, after which the die seemed to be cast. There was also a key moment at which Murtala Muhammed deferred to Gowon's military seniority. Thurlow appeared to discount the influence of US Ambassador Elbert Matthews in Gowon's decision to grasp the nettle. But this was the moment in which Nigeria survived, and it happened in Lagos. Captain Dickson remained in control of the airport, impossible to dislodge for many months.

EPISODE FROM A CITY IN WARTIME, 1967

In the civil war that followed the violent events of 1966, the physical evidence of warfare never touched Lagos very much although the crisis and war atmosphere initially had a dampening effect on social life. There were one or two early alarms. There was a bomb outrage in Ikoyi during talks organized by prominent people in various walks of life (called "leaders of thought"), and another at the Casino cinema in Yaba at the beginning of the war, but these were exceptional. The great set-piece of wartime drama in the capital came in September 1967 with the explosion of a Fokker Friendship airplane directly over the Motor Boat Club in southwest Ikoyi. This was a Nigeria Airways plane hijacked by the Eastern Nigerians/Biafrans before the war early on a Sunday morning. In the words of John de St. Jorre, it "suddenly appeared over Lagos, and watched by party-goers, circled slowly over the docks and oil depot dropping small bombs—despatched apparently by hand. Nigerian anti-aircraft guns opened fire. Then, as it was turning for a new run, it blew up in a series of spectacular explosions ('like a firework display,' said an onlooker) directly over the Lagos Motor Boat Club."

I was in Lagos at the time, but knew nothing until I was called out the following morning to witness the recovery of the wreckage from southwest Ikoyi gardens and body parts from the lagoon, as well as to visit the morgue in Yaba to see the mangled corpses, European and African, that had fallen from the sky. I was also almost arrested the same day, called out of a bar called the New Can Can in Customs Street after having innocently gone to inspect a hole in the side of the Ministry of Defence building close by on the Marina, apparently caused by a stray shell fired in the night by artillery over the lagoon in Apapa. Having satisfied my army questioner, I was applauded on my return to the New Can Can.

THE BIAFRAN SURRENDER AS SEEN IN LAGOS, 1970

For this historic happening I can provide my own personal eyewitness account from Dodan Barracks of the auspicious day of 15 January 1970. It began with my sighting of Colonel Olusegun Obasanjo, then in command of the army's Third (Marine Commando) Division in Port Harcourt, with a prominent Biafran, former Chief Justice Sir Louis Mbanefo, walking out of the Ikoyi Hotel. It was clear that something big was afoot as we had already been told of the flight of the Biafran leader Ojukwu by plane from Uli (where the secessionists had built an airstrip) to Côte d'Ivoire, so the place was buzzing with rumors. I was called by Bridget Bloom, then *Financial Times* Africa correspondent, who in turn had been called by the Information Minister, General Ibrahim Haruna (whom I had once made the serious mistake of beating at Scrabble). She told me to meet up and go the same Ministry of Defence building where I had previously nearly been arrested.

We mounted a military vehicle with Haruna and drove at breakneck speed through Onikan and along Awolowo Road, and then down Ribadu Road to Supreme Headquarters at Dodan Barracks to an event whose significance was not immediately explained but was clearly important. Little by little its almost mystical nature was unveiled as we noted the presence of a who's who of the country's top brass from generals to "super-permsecs." I asked Gowon's Private Secretary Hamzat Ahmadu, "who is that light-skinned man in white?" and he did not want to say. I only learned later that it was the legendary M. D. Yusuf, head of the Special

Surrender in Dodan Barracks (see below)

Branch (the top security man in the country, later to be justly famed as the main practical implementer of the post-war reconciliation). We were all ushered into a meeting room in which Gowon was surrounded by all the members of the Supreme Military Council. We realized that this was the moment as a group in civilian clothes entered the room. These were the Biafrans, and they were about to surrender.

There were three foreign journalists present—Bridget, Hugh Neville, the bearded correspondent of Agence France Presse, and myself, also sporting a trimmed moustache and beard. In the photograph of the event the three of us can be seen diligently taking notes in the background even as General Philip Effiong, recently the Biafran forces' chief, is shaking Gowon's hand, the clinching moment of the surrender.

THE ALL-AFRICAN GAMES OF 1973
One of the first prestige events of Gowon's peacetime rule was the 2nd All African Games in 1973, for which the first National Stadium was built on

158

the Lagos Mainland, along Western Avenue in Surulere. It was highly popular and attracted a number of stars, notably the Ugandan runner John Akii-Bua. I was among foreign media representatives covering the event, which proved something of an ordeal as we were all cooped up in the Hotel Excelsior near to the port area in Apapa. On paper this may have looked a practical location, not far from the stadium, but reporting proved a difficult exercise, not least because our only access to the stadium was in a bus that visited numerous locations in Surulere. Apapa had a certain Wild West atmosphere at that time, and among my faint memories over the years is of singing *You are My Sunshine* late night in the streets of Apapa with Senegalese film-maker Ben Diogaye Beye.

Another vignette in the mind's eye is of the opening ceremony at which doves were released which resolutely refused to fly upwards, so that capturing them became a spectator sport. I recall Akii-Bua's lap of honor for his gold medal at which the crowd cried vociferously "Amin! Amin!" after the then ruler of Uganda, Idi Amin Dada, who at that time had a lot of African "street cred." Journalists, I recall, arrived at the press gallery only to find it packed with large gold-bespangled ladies who were, I was told, "cash-madams," apparently a by-product of the oil boom. Another press space was found.

Assassination on Bank Road, 1976

One of the most shocking events in the whole history of the city, which struck deep into the collective imagination, was the assassination on 13 February 1976 of General Murtala Muhammed after he had been head of state for barely six and a half months. There are many who would still say that it was probably the greatest single setback in Nigeria's post-independence history as Murtala, despite his controversially turbulent past, promised when he came to power radical change that might have gone some way to meeting popular aspirations. Or perhaps this is one more of the fantasies that linger in the Lagos air like mists on the lagoon…

The assassination happened in Bank Road, a side road in upmarket Ikoyi so named because it contained residences for senior officials of what at that time was still Barclays Bank (it became Union Bank three years later when a majority shareholding was acquired by the federal government in protest at British oil trade with South Africa). The bitter irony is that the head of state's car was driving that way to avoid one of those traffic jams ("go-slows" to Lagosians) that by the mid-1970s had acquired great notoriety.

The existential arbitrariness of the whole incident is atmospherically described in *Converging City*, a short story by Ben Okri from his early period in the 1980s, which appeared in a collection called *Incidents at the Shrine*. But the story is told with a degree of poetic licence that not just obscures but reverses the facts at a certain point, to make it seem as if the head of state survived the attack. Most vividly, Okri writes of the context of the go-slow which made the assassination possible. "An intractable traffic jam resulted. Streets and main roads were blocked. Cars and lorries stood bumper to bumper. The whole traffic jam soon resembled a long and obscenely metallic centipede."

The black bullet-ridden Mercedes could afterwards be seen in a strange shrine in the Nigeria Museum in Onikan—an arresting piece of what might almost be called performance art in an otherwise downbeat display. Ever since then Nigerian leaders have ridden without fail in bullet-proof vehicles. The military ruler General Muhammadu Buhari even shipped his bullet-proof Mercedes to the Organization of African Unity summit in Addis Ababa in November 1984.

THE UNDOING OF SIR MARTIN LEQUESNE, 1976

Following Murtala's assassination, the leader of the coup, Lt.-Colonel Bukar Dimka, in an equally surreal Lagos moment, walked into the British High Commission in Campbell Street surrounded by armed soldiers, although his coup was already falling apart. Demanding to see the High Commissioner, he requested that a call be made to the former head of state General Gowon in England (presumably to ask him to return as leader). Sir Martin LeQuesne, playing by the rules, refused and reported the incident to the authorities, who requested that he hush it up. Unfortunately Reuters News Agency's office was in the same building and the agency put out a story, which angered the new head of state General Obasanjo, who had felt that Dimka should have been refused entry to the building.

This led to the expulsion of both Sir Martin LeQuesne and Reuters. It was real comeuppance for Sir Martin, a spiky and intellectual diplomat who suffered few fools gladly (*The Times'* obituary of him in 2004 said his "kindness of heart was masked by a rather peppery manner and talent for asking awkward questions"). He had also, from force of circumstance, been considered too much part of the British love affair with Gowon. After his brush with Dimka he was blamed by Nigerians for a statement demanding that Nigeria should pay for damage to the building caused by rioters protesting at the Dimka incident. Obasanjo in his book *Not My Will* contrasts this with the understanding attitude of the Americans, who had not insisted on compensation in the heated atmosphere of the time. He writes: "The time and manner of his demand were most inappropriate. Certainly it was a most unabashed display of lack of human sensitivity and feelings." It was enough to ensure that Sir Martin was almost immediately asked to leave Nigeria.

OMINOUS 1983

Fast forwarding past the return to civilian rule of 1979, there is a fascination about the year 1983 which ended in another coup. What lingers most in the mind is the mass expulsion of more than a million African "aliens" from Nigeria by the administration of President Shehu Shagari. Most of those expelled were Ghanaians. The reason was xenophobia in a declining economic situation, although the African immigrants played an essential economic role. Somehow the shadow it cast on the country was symbolized by the murky haze of the particularly heavy Harmattan dust of early 1983. One of the most cuttingly ironic accounts of the expulsion was by the award-winning poet Niyi Osundare writing at the time in *West Africa* in which he posed as an enthusiast for the expulsions, sarcastically reproducing common prejudices against immigrants:

> At last those illegal aliens are gone! Unemployment has become a thing of the past. Millionaires can now go to be with their golden doors wide open, without the fear of a Ghanaian gun or a Chadian arrow: prostitutes are now gone and our country can bounce back into moral health. What's more, since the invaders left, NEPA hasn't suffered a single bout of epilepsy; uninterrupted water supply has greeted every home; no more inflated contracts, no more gubernatorial acrimonies, no more inferno in public buildings; above all 'Africa still remains the centre-piece of our foreign policy'.

Other ominous portents early in the year were two major and never-explained fires on the Marina—one on the tallest building there, Nigerian

Telecommunications (NITEL), the other at the Defence Ministry further along the Marina in Customs Street. The year continued with the disastrous elections over a month in August, which led to violence in a number of states (although not in Lagos) and seemed to set the scene for General Buhari's coup on New Year's Eve. This was perhaps less of a Lagos coup than all previous ones, for although the coup-makers still operated out of the army headquarters at Dodan Barracks, President Shagari was arrested in Abuja and the only resistance that took place was there.

The Dele Giwa Killing, 1986

One of the most abiding unsolved political crimes in contemporary Nigerian history was the murder by parcel bomb on 19 October 1986 of one of Nigeria's leading political journalists, Dele Giwa, leading light in the crusading weekly magazine *Newswatch*. It was very much a Lagos event and remains fixed on the psyche, if not the conscience, of the city. The house Giwa was living in was 25 Talabi Street, in a quiet part of Ikeja. He was taking breakfast with his correspondent from London, Kayode Soyinka, when at 11:40 a.m. a parcel addressed to Chief Dele Giwa (although he was not a chief) was delivered marked from the Cabinet Office, with "to be opened by the addressee only" written on it. A few seconds later, as Giwa was opening the package it blew up, mortally wounding him in gruesome fashion. He cried "they have killed me" and died after he reached the hospital. Soyinka was more overwhelmed than injured, although his hearing was affected.

The shock waves of the killing reverberated through Nigeria and beyond, but in spite of a number of inquiries no one has ever been arrested. The suspicion of official involvement has lingered to this day as it was reported that Dele had come up against the security services in a possibly reckless manner, although speculations have never been substantiated. It was certainly curious in that this was the only time the expert technology of parcel bombing has ever been used in Nigeria, which suggested the assistance of an outside hand.

The assassination left a place for Dele Giwa in this book's arbitrarily chosen collection of people, not just because it happened in Lagos but also because his spirit represented the crusading nature of journalism which Lagos had come to represent from the 1880s onwards. In spite of the concealed identity of his killers, the words of his colleague at *Newswatch*, Ray

Ekpu, are bound to echo through history: "If by his death he has watered the tree of our national revival, if by his death he has fuelled our desire to toil for a better Nigeria, then his death, painful, tragic, untimely, senseless though it is, would not have been in vain."

THE ORKAR COUP, 1990

The failed coup of 22 April 1990, led by Major Gideon Orkar, was perhaps the last major political event to take place in Lagos before the power and authority of the federal government of Nigeria withdrew from the city forever. This is not to say the city then retreated into banality; the three months of demonstrations in 1993 after the annulment of elections on 12 June were among the most violent and alarming it had ever seen, and the nightmare years of General Sani Abacha's rule between 1993 and 1998 saw many dramas such as the murder of Kudirat, wife of the jailed opposition leader Moshood Abiola who won the June 1993 elections. But the main political drama had from 1990 onwards been displaced to Abuja. Lagos could concentrate on its role as commercial capital, but the political starring role faded.

The Orkar coup seemed to come out of the blue, and was motivated by radicalism apparently pro-South in motivation, to judge by the coup-makers' intention of excising the five Hausa-Fulani states of the far North from the federation. It also very nearly succeeded, in that the key unit from the Brigade of Guards that went looking for President Babangida in Dodan Barracks got to his bedroom only minutes after he had fled. The shock of near-death caused Babangida to forswear Lagos and never return after he had so narrowly escaped assassination that even his bedroom slippers were reportedly shot up. From then on the fate of the federal role of Lagos was sealed as the move to Abuja took on a new intensity. This was a key psychological moment in the city's itinerary, but it has taken it in its stride. And with the departure of the federal capital the risks of Lagos being center-stage in the theater of coups also faded.

(Postscript: Babangida may not have liked Lagos, and he was never a Lagos personality—but that did not prevent his acolytes putting up advertisements in 2006, including one on the Marina, touting him as a presidential candidate, almost mocking Lagosians in an ironic afterword to his hasty departure from the city in 1990.)

THE JANUARY 2002 EXPLOSIONS AT THE IKEJA BARRACKS

One of the strangest episodes in the story of the Fourth Republic, already submerged by the passage of time, was the series of explosions at the armory of the Ikeja Military Cantonment on 27 January 2002. Although there were few deaths among the military or their families, the panic stampede it caused in the vicinity led to over a thousand deaths, mostly in the nearby Oke-Afa Canal in nearby Isolo. I was working in Nigeria at the time, and wrote a diary in the short-lived publication I was editing, *Business Confidential*, on how I happened to witness the events from the vantage- point of the airport. The diary was called "The Cutting Edge," signed by "Cutlass," and I wrote:

> Your diarist was actually in Murtala Mohammed Airport about to leave for Senegal when the explosions started. The first one looked almost like a large firework, and I thought it to be a curiosity. But just after I checked in at the Air Gabon counter, there was a massive bang that shook and rattled the fabric of the building, and all the milling throng that usually populate the outside foyer took to their heels in a panic-stricken rush, with the instinct of getting out of the building. Armed with my boarding pass, my instinct was to get through into the departure lounge, which seemed the most secure place to be. The staff who had remained at their posts (and there were some) did not quite seem to have their minds on the job. Despite rumours circulating, there was clearly not a coup, or the airport itself would have been under attack, which it was not. In fact although the explosions were still whamming in with regularity, it was clear they were coming from Ikeja barracks, and the terminal building had a horribly fascinating ringside seat of the periodic columns of flame and fireballs—described by some as Nigeria's own September 11.

VOTING IN LAGOS, 2007

In April 2007 I chose to observe the two stages of the election in Lagos. Although in 1983 I had heard the announcement of results at the Electoral Commission there, I had not studied the voting in the streets, having gone on a fairly pointless airborne dash with American journalists around Enugu and Kaduna. In fact, in 2007, even by the time of the elections of state governors, the result was more or less a foregone conclusion in Lagos. This was because the battles between the Action Congress (ruling in Lagos State) and the Peoples Democratic Party (ruling at the federal center) for control of the streets had gone on in the run-up to the vote, which had been tense, a tension increased by political assassinations, notably that of Funso Williams, a PDP leader from an old Lagos family. In the days before the vote, especially in certain Lagos Island locales such as Freeman Street, there was a measure of gang violence in which many "area boys" were involved. The election was won by the AC candidate Babatunde Fashola, standing in succession to Bola Tinubu (see profiles of both in Chapter 8).

Most opinion soundings suggested that compared with some parts of the country, especially the Delta, it was a relatively fair and peaceful election in that the AC (and its predecessor parties) had controlled the city since the 1950s, a situation that was unchanged. My own observations, focused mainly on Lagos Island, confirmed this—there were abuses or faults such as the late opening of polling stations and the lack of transparent voting bags, but in general procedure was observed: there was no one to contest it. There was some disappointment that a popular local candidate, Jimmy Agbaje, did not attract more votes, but he lacked the powerful machines of the main parties.

I went with William Wallis of the *Financial Times* to the area around the Oba's palace in Idunganran Street where there was an almost festive atmosphere—there were Fashola posters on the walls of the palace. William attracted a group of friendly "area boys" who were baptized the "Wallis Boyz," all professed AC supporters. A week later the presidential election was more apathetic (the two main candidates were northerners, Muhammadu Buhari and Abubakar Atiku, neither of whom aroused much interest or enthusiasm in spite of Atiku's affiliation to the AC). It was hard to obtain the final figures from the Electoral Commission website, but from personal observation at polling stations they must have been much lower than in the governorship elections.

Sixteenth-century Benin ivory mask of Queen Idia, used in the logo of FESTAC

Chapter Seven

THE LONG SHADOW OF FESTAC

There are many episodes that are emblematic of the 1970s oil boom such as the already mentioned All-African Games and the International Trade Fair. But nothing recalls the *Zeitgeist* of the decade more than the delights and follies of FESTAC in 1977 and the subsequent aftermath—the sad and squalid sacking of Fela's Kalakuta Republic. FESTAC, the Black and African Festival of Arts and Culture, was one of the most glorious moments of Lagos in its capacity as federal capital, though the decision to move to Abuja came almost exactly one year before the festival began, so it proved to be the last fling of its life as capital of Nigeria.

In Nigeria there is an unusual contrast between the stultifying official view of culture and the eye-catching, head-banging reality of the streets, of the freewheeling anarchic city, excruciating in its poverty but generating a strange excitement. The juxtaposed contrast is highlighted in the story of FESTAC, held in January-February 1977. Andrew Apter's book *The Pan-African Nation: Oil and the Spectacle of Arts and Culture* has resurrected this magnificent event from the near-forgotten pages of history, and has put it in the context of the politics of Nigeria in the heady days of the oil boom and the subsequent collapse of ambition and expectation.

COLONIAL SYMBOLS

For some FESTAC was incarnated in the legendary durbar in Kaduna, one of the centerpieces of the festival. It was meant to be a re-staging—some would say even a pastiche—of the durbars introduced by the colonial British (though there had been similar events in Hausa-Fulani tradition), which had only really found favor among the horse-loving Emirs of the North and their retinues (indeed, riding displays still continue on a smaller scale in Northern cities on Sallah day, Id el-Kebir). It was significant and appropriate, given British encouragement, that the two grandest durbars in Nigerian history were held on British royal visits. The FESTAC Durbar was probably the last durbar of this kind held in Nigeria. They had always been held in the old North, even if FESTAC itself was otherwise essentially a Lagos event. The regatta, based on the regattas that had also been a feature of British colonial Nigeria, was also held in Lagos although drawing for the most part on the rich riverine culture of the Niger Delta.

Apter recalls the first durbar of the then General Lugard at Lokoja, capital of the new Protectorate of Northern Nigeria, at the confluence of the Niger and Benue rivers on 1 January 1900. This was actually to mark the handover of power by the Royal Niger Company, which had had a trading monopoly and powers of government on the river, to the administration of the British crown, but the event—a march-past and two days of sports which generated much popular enthusiasm—was also, in the words of Arch Callaway, "to display mystical authority and to incorporate the Nigerian military units and the populace into the British empire." The durbar was important in establishing the power of the crown in imperial India, where the institutionalized practice was "adapting and transferring a Mughal ritual of kingship to serve Britain's civilising mission." It was vital in the integration of India's wide and disunited diversity, using "an elaborate cosmology and culture of rule." Lugard, although he had no direct experience of India, had brought it to Nigeria where "it took root and developed in similar ways." On his return to Nigeria in 1913 he staged a durbar to mark his appointment as Governor-General of the country, whose unity was solidified by his fusion of the Northern and Southern Protectorates in 1914.

Lugard's durbars, which incorporated rituals of the Islamic Sallah, institutionalized Hausa-Fulani dominance into a kind of caste system beginning with the Emirs, passing through the Nupe and Yoruba traders, to the hill pagans of the Middle Belt as a lower order nonetheless protected from slavery by Pax Britannica. Significantly, the most impressive durbars were held on the occasion of royal visits, as with that of the Prince of Wales in 1925 when a durbar was held in Kano to which the Sultan of Sokoto, the Sheikh of Dikwa and other rulers paid attendance. The last major imperial-style durbar before FESTAC was that given in Kaduna for Queen Elizabeth II on her official visit of 1956. She had hoped there might be one in Kano for her visit in 2003, but was advised not to expect one for security reasons, a sad sign of the times.

Apter's book also treats that other manifestation of what he calls "the theatre of empire" that was reproduced at the festival, the FESTAC regatta.

He examines this in the context of the historic southern Nigerian culture of the war canoe, traditionally one of the main means of military transport and attack along the coast from Lagos via the Niger Delta to Calabar. Considering "war canoes and their magic," he believes them to have had a pivotal role in the development of the "cultural economy" of the area. Canoe regattas were an important part of the "ceremonial protocol of palavers and treaty negotiations" especially in the nineteenth century, although even in the fifteenth century the earliest Portuguese travelers identified a powerful canoe culture, which over the centuries even came to figure in the slave trade.

All the writing on Britain's military involvement in Lagos after 1851 indicate that the deposed Oba Kosoko had an imposing fleet of armed war canoes when he moved to his base at Epe. The canoe "houses" (trading households) significantly adopted European insignia and clothing as well as weaponry, a phenomenon observed at first hand in a remarkable description from the Landers' expedition to the Niger. Apter, with his social anthropologist's eye, sees the importance of the canoe regattas as a symbol of "exchange value," but the colonial power realized the ritual significance of displays by huge multi-story decorated canoes in helping to impose and maintain power. Like the durbars in the North, they helped to reinforce kingship and hence, in application of the indirect rule so prized by Lugard, the colonial authority. This was seen in the Port Harcourt regatta held for Queen Elizabeth II in 1956. Hosted by none other than Nnamdi Azikiwe, then Premier of the Eastern Region, it reveled "in the glory of imperial symbolism and pageantry," in which "the most potent icons of colonial authority figured on land and water."

Given the colonial background, what was remarkable about this aspect of FESTAC was the way in which past symbols were adapted to suit the deeper nation-building purposes of the festival in the minds of its organizers. Thus both the FESTAC regatta, which was held in Lagos during the festival, and the durbar in Kaduna were instruments of nationalist policies transforming the old colonial traditions into emblems of Nigerian nationalism and unity. The Lagos regatta was inaugurated by the then chairman of the National Council of Arts and Culture, Chief Harold Dappa-Biriye, himself a man of the Niger Delta. Wearing white top hat and robes, he poured a libation for the water gods of Five Cowrie Creek for the success of the regatta. It involved two hundred war canoes from eight states, more than two hundred paddlers and dancers and a massive crowd of spectators on the banks of the Lagos lagoons including military top brass from Head of State Obasanjo downwards, and proved so successful that it was extended from two to three days. In his speech at the opening Obasanjo had invited the assembled Nigerians and international visitors to "gain inspiration from what was left behind by our ancestors."

Looking back, I am only now aware what an unusual privilege it was to be present, as a humble journalist, at FESTAC. Nothing sticks more in my mind than traveling on the "FESTAC train" which went from the Nigerian Railway terminus at Iddo on the Lagos mainland, handsomely decorated with bunting. It carried special passengers destined for the durbar including some other journalists and a jovial Gabonese orchestra all the way to Kaduna. It was an overnight journey with frequent stops and a special Nigerian Railway packed dinner of *akara* (bean-cake), chicken parts and a sandwich, together with a standard issue pillow. Little did we know that there would never be another chance to see this kind of display, with all the emirs from all over the former empire of Uthman dan Fodio with their fine umbrellas and regalia, their horsemen and multiple entourages.

As well as the regatta, most of the major happenings in the festival were in Lagos, either at the National Arts Theatre or in the Stadium (built four years before for the All-African Games): the exhibitions, plays, concerts, and the cultural symposium were held at the glamorous new state-of-the-art National Arts Theatre in Iganmu. There was a splendid sense of elation at some of the events: I have a vivid memory of attending a rapturously received concert by the immortal Mighty Sparrow (aka Francisco Slinger), probably the most magnificent Calypsonian ever produced by Trinidad and Tobago. Then there was Fela's "alternative festival" at the cannabis-shrouded Shrine in Surulere, which cheekily became a place of pilgrimage for many of the international artists and artistes attending FESTAC. The popularity of the Shrine led to a brutal aftermath (was there an element of revenge?) when shortly after the end of FESTAC the military destroyed Fela's Kalakuta Republic compound (see Chapter 9).

The whole FESTAC concept had contained a duality from the beginning: was it an affair of governments, officials and "elites," or was it for the people? The "alternative festival" idea was also seen in the writer Wole Soyinka's suggestion that palm wine rather than champagne should be drunk at some of the celebrations (it was not long after this that champagne was officially banned in Nigeria, although that did not prevent smuggling in larger quantities through the neighboring Republic of Benin). His own observations on FESTAC in his bulky volume of memoirs *You Must Go Forth at Dawn* (2007) are brief but damning; having saved the festival by ending the threatened Senegalese and Francophone boycott, he withdrew because the FESTAC chairman Admiral Fingesi had "insisted on overriding decisions of assigned experts, remaining locked within military dictatorial arrogance." Only after the "organisational debacle" did he return to stage an event that wiped out some of the "sour taste in the mouths of most of the visitors."

This theme was enlarged on in a lecture given by Soyinka at Duke University in North Carolina titled "FESTAC Agonistes," an entertainingly acerbic insider's account of how he was not only involved in mediation by President Senghor of Senegal over the threat of a Francophone African boycott of the festival but, with senior civil servant Francesca Emanuel (who was also a professional singer), responded to an appeal from President Obasanjo (described with cruel wit as only Soyinka knows how) to help get the organization on track. Soyinka has harsh words for both military and bureaucrats. Before he was dragged reluctantly into the fray he says he could already only "lament that the spirit of the smaller scale, frugal but quality informed Negro Arts Festival of Dakar 1966 was about to be succeeded by a vulgar, unprincipled and directionless jamboree in a nation where petroleum crude had turned the brain into human crude." He derides "the chop-chop spirit, 'eat your own and I'll eat mine' that began from the very top leadership of the organisation, percolated through the entire bureaucratic set-up and, to my intense distress, infected even the artistes who had been co-opted into the organisation."

As a visitor I could see why some others might have experienced a sour taste: many were certainly bemused and bewildered. To me the dysfunctional organization came from the huge scale of the exercise and frequent administrative changes combined with the fact that it came at one of the most chaotic periods of Nigeria's boom years, when traffic congestion in Lagos was at its worst. Apart from that, I was told that some of the churches castigated it as an immoral event. But it was for me unforgettable: a profoundly existential experience that confirmed the extraordinary and unexpected nature of this city.

FESTAC was, indeed, a magnificent moment. In Sefi Atta's Lagos novel *Everything Good Will Come*, which contains some illumination of Nigerian political and social history from the 1970s to the 1990s, she writes with some irony:

> That was the year of the Festival of Arts and Culture we called Festac. Stevie Wonder came to play at our national theatre, Miriam Makeba, Osibisa, every African person in the world represented in Lagos... We had colour television for the first time in our country, and everyone was growing vegetables in their back yards in support of the government's Operation Feed the Nation. My mother grew okra, my father said the whole regime, its Operation Feed the Nation and Festival of Arts, was all nonsense.

AFTERMATH

In a way, the experience of FESTAC came to embody all the glory (and folly) of the oil era, and the hangover was severe. Intended as a national cultural booster, it probably did more to damage and warp Nigeria's view of cultural activities because it came to be seen as a symbol of waste and corruption. Apart from Festac Town (originally an artists' village constructed for the festival itself), its main legacy seems to be the still decaying National Arts Theatre. Built by the Bulgarian firm Technoexportsroy on a contract without competitive tendering (which led to some serious criticisms in a subsequent audit), when it was put up specifically for the festival it was considered an architectural wonder. At the time there was some cynical observation that the design resembled the cap of a military officer, a reminder that it had been conceived and built by two military regimes. The theater's prospects of survival have not been helped by the fact that it was built on low-lying swamps at Iganmu, and that construction of both access roads and the theater itself may have begun before infilling had properly settled. Concern is still sometimes expressed that the foundations may slowly be sinking.

A visit to the National Arts Theatre today is a sobering exercise. Compared with what it was and what it might be, it presents a pathetic sight. Only a few of the auditoria are now in use, and the whole complex has suffered from the Nigerian sin of lack of maintenance. Some see the only way out for the theater to be privatization, and it has certainly figured

The National Theatre: "high cultural vocation"

on the targeted lists of the Bureau of Public Enterprises in Abuja (responsible for selling off state-owned companies and assets).

There has, however, been a strong rearguard action fought by some in the cultural lobby who see privatization as the equivalent of selling the "family jewels" and fear that the theater—still, even in its shabbiness, a symbol of some kind of national pride—might fall into the hands of casinos or, worse, lose its high cultural vocation forever. For a time the campaigners seemed to have prevailed, and some funds were allocated through the initiative of Ahmed Yerima, director of the National Troupe, which led to some rehabilitation work. Yet there is still uncertainty given the propensity to philistinism in the national bureaucracy, as well as pressure from free-market ideologues in Abuja.

Some might say the same applies to the crumbling National Stadium in Surulere, built at the beginning of the oil boom and now in a much more advanced state of decay, especially since a new National Stadium was built in Abuja for another All-African Games in 2003. To visit it now is another mournful experience. There are a variety of fringe commercial activities that still continue on its premises, and the Lagos State government built a new sports complex on the other side of the Western Avenue as a kind of rebuke to the federal authority, but the huge and once spectacular complex has virtually abandoned its sporting vocation, although some groups such as body-builders regularly meet there and keep up the idea that it is a major sports arena. It is one more monument to the lack of maintenance culture. Moreover, the roads and medium-rent houses of Festac Town, the other symbol of modernity associated with the events of 1977, are also in deteriorating condition, with some of the most nerve-racking potholes in a city that is already riddled with them.

Yet behind it all is the thesis that the collapsed illusion of FESTAC made Nigeria look more and more like a cultural wasteland. It is true that appreciation of the broad value of culture occupies a relatively small space in the government's mindset. Lagos, however, in so many ways has been one of the main focal points of Nigeria's continuing cultural vitality, defying its own prevalent philistinism. The memory of FESTAC is kept alive by a few of those who value Nigeria's cultural heritage and are determined to salvage the good things that it represented: in 2007 there was a commemoration of the thirtieth anniversary of FESTAC by the Centre for Black and African Arts and Civilisation (CBAAC), an organization that operates from a small office in Broad Street on Lagos Island, and the legacy will be more cherished with the passage of time.

Chapter Eight

PROMINENT PERSONALITIES OF LAGOS

The early figures in the history of Lagos have a shadowy presence at best. **Aromire** was in some sense the founding father of the settlement on the island in the lagoon which became Lagos, although some might attribute that role to his father Olofin. The great figures of the seventeenth century such as Ashipa and Ado are still one-dimensional. It is only in the eighteenth that personalities begin to emerge.

Oba Akinsemoyin, the second son of Ado arrived at the throne after the death of his elder brother Gabaro, and may have been one of the longer running rulers, although there is still considerable controversy among historians as to his dates, ranging from 1704 to 1740 or even 1760. Historians do agree that, however long his reign, it was noted both as a period of increased prosperity and for the arrival of the Portuguese traders, whose presence he encouraged along with opportunities for expanding the commerce in slaves. The Portuguese had followed Akinsemoyin from the period he lived in Badagry before he became Oba. Akinsemoyin's mother was an Egun from the creeks around Badagry and Porto Novo, and he married a Badagry woman. At the same time, the fusion of the Bini and Awori traditions was furthered during his rule. Akinsemoyin is said to have had many disputes with the Idejos, and is credited in some quarters with having created the White Cap chieftaincy titles for the original Idejos who had been the sons of Olofin—awarding them to his favorites, who also received land to encourage them to move from the mainland to Lagos Island.

The historian Professor Ade Adefuye tells us in his profile of Akinsemoyin that "he was said to be a tall, well-built, light complexioned man, with a considerable energy and zeal. He had a warm and friendly disposition and was very quick at developing strong links with individuals and groups who he believed could be of use to him." He was also an "outspoken personality," which often brought him into dispute with his brother

Gabaro. Losi's description of him as "an obstinate man remarkable for his tyranny" was only half the truth: he was perhaps underlining his awareness of the royal prerogative which he reinforced and extended in a manner to help Lagos rise to supremacy over Badagry, where chieftaincy was more collegiate.

His reign also saw the development of the Iga Idunganran on its present site, but his Portuguese friends were said to have built him a palace in keeping with his wealth and way of life, including iron columns for roof supports and tiles for the roof which helped limit the frequent fires that occurred at that time. Other chiefly palaces in the vicinity of the Iga were also built around that time. Adefuye relates that Akinsemoyin not only encouraged the slave trade with the help of the Portuguese, but "stimulated commercial activities among the people so they could provide the articles which the Europeans needed in exchange for finished products" so that they became traders rather than brokers. War between Dahomey and Porto Novo also drove trade towards Lagos.

The descendants of Akinsemoyin have been one of the more controversial wings of the royal houses of Lagos. This was because it was **Ologun Kutere**, the favored child of his much-loved sister Erelu, who succeeded him. Adefuye tells us that Akinsemoyin's wish that she should look after his own children after he died was, however, ignored, and only descendants of Ologun Kutere have succeeded to the Obaship to this day. Erelu was however much revered and her tomb can be found to this day in Erelu Square. It was only after the Kassim Report of 1977 that other descendants obtained legal entitlement to put up candidates for the post of Oba.

The three critical Obas at the time of the British intervention in the mid-nineteenth century were very contrasting personalities, and have all been described by European visitors. **Oba Akitoye** ruled from 1841 to 1846, when he was deposed after a power struggle by **Oba Kosoko**; and he ruled again for two more years after his restoration with the help of the British in 1851 until his death in 1853, when he was succeeded by his son **Oba Dosunmu (Docemo)**. Akitoye has been described by Alhaji H. A. B. Fashinro as "amiable and pleasant" with a great love of peace: "His one fault was that he was weak and this was what caused the trouble he had with Kosoko throughout his reign…" In 1851, before the British bombardment, Commander Bruce of the Royal Navy West Africa Squadron observed drily that "Akitoye does not appear to me to be a man likely to maintain his place by physical influence."

Kosoko, however, was a powerful and strong-willed warrior-ruler who was always a force to be reckoned with. Giambattista Scala, the Sardinian consul whose memoirs give a vividly impressionistic if sometimes faulty account of Lagos in the 1850s, describes Kosoko in heroic mode:

It has pleased nature to shape in him the true model of an African king. He is tall, of Herculean stature, and endowed with uncommon muscular strength, a quality which is greatly prized in these countries, and which excites the admiration of his subjects, and makes him the more respected and revered by all who come into his presence... he can, when he pleases, express his inmost feelings or else remain silent and impassive according to the circumstances. His eyes are black and lively, his gaze is acute, and when he looks into the face of the person he is speaking to, he bores into his heart and easily discovers his secrets.

Scala notes Kosoko's indomitable courage and an intelligence "not only superior to that of the people around him but which can also compare favourably with that of the Europeans who come into contact with him." He was, however, on the wrong side of both history and the British. Having chased his cousin Akitoye from the throne in 1846, he found that the pincer movement of the missionaries in Badagry and Abeokuta with the West Africa Squadron was squeezing him and at the same time damning him as the arch-perpetrator of the slave trade in Lagos. If this was something in which everyone in Lagos, including at one time even the British favorite Akitoye, was involved, Kosoko proclaimed his acceptance of slavery without compromise. Scala wrote, "His principles in this respect were quite inflexible; to him slavery was by natural law a political institution hallowed by religion, and the sale of human beings was the finest prerogative of his crown and absolutely essential to his state. Anyone who argued against these principles became his personal enemy and no reasoning could prevail against his deep-rooted convictions."

After the events of December 1851 Kosoko fled to Epe with many advisers such as Oshodi Tapa and some of the Portuguese/Brazilian slavers. There he held a rival court and continued to engage in the slave trade drawing on an Ijebu-provided supply and using Lekki and Palma as outlets. Although he made attempts to regain his throne, and sporadically engaged in negotiations with Consul Campbell, it was only when the pragmatic John Hawley Glover came as Governor in 1863 that a *modus vivendi* was established and Kosoko and members of his court returned from exile.

History has not been kind to Oba Dosunmu, the man who is remembered in Nigeria above all as the unfortunate leader who was compelled by the British to sign the infamous Treaty of Cession of August 1861, in which control of Lagos passed to the British crown (see full text in Appendix on pp.255-6). He came to power at a most difficult time in 1853 on the death of his father Akitoye, when the British had already established a presence on the island (although they had not taken it over formally) and there was still a threat from the deposed Kosoko. He subsequently said he had no idea of the content of the cession treaty and two years later tried unsuccessfully to renounce it. He ruled, however, in a state of near powerlessness until his death in 1885.

Madam Efunroye Tinubu was one of the most remarkable figures to mark Lagos in the whole of the nineteenth century, with a life experience spanning the pre-colonial era of the slave trade through over 35 years of British rule until she died in 1887. She is said to have been born in 1805, probably an Egba from Gbagura district with maternal connections in Owu where she had apparently been sold as a slave to the chief, who "loved her like his own daughter," according to Scala (who appears to have known her well and provides a vivid if romanticized view of her). He also says that with her "youthful charm" she had won the heart of her owner and became "the idol of the people." Although uneducated she had developed a "boundless ambition" and soon negotiated her way out of slave status. Part of this came through marriage: she was said to have been married three times—her second husband briefly became Oba of Lagos but he too died, and her third marriage was to Yesufu Bada, a supporter of Oba Kosoko. She followed him into exile after Kosoko's deposition in 1851 although she was also believed to have been a niece of Akitoye (the British candidate who replaced Kosoko).

Madam Tinubu had a flair for business although at the time the best—though by no means the only—business in Lagos was that of slaves. She was well established as an intermediary in the palm oil trade with the interior, and returned to Lagos where she was already a major influence. In 1856, after suspecting she was involved in a rising against the new influx of Saro and Aguda "immigrants," Consul Campbell forced her into exile

Madam Tinubu statue in Tinubu Square

in Abeokuta on suspicion of slave-trading; probably more important, according to Margaret Peil in her book *Lagos*, was that Madam Tinubu was reported to have engaged in "anti-British political activities." She owed £5,000 to white merchants at the time, "which ensured that her trading activities continued." At the same time her talent as a trader had aroused jealousies among other merchants who undoubtedly pressured Campbell to secure her banishment from Lagos.

In Abeokuta her entrepreneurial skills ensured her a prominent place, even if she met some initial hostility from competitors. However, she was as proficient in trading arms and gunpowder as she had been with slaves and other commodities, and helped organize the guns and men to ward off an attack from Dahomey in 1864, as well as backing the fight against Ikorodu the next year. The grateful citizens named her Iyalode (First Lady), and although readmitted to Lagos by Governor Glover in the 1860s, where she resumed some of her former business activities, her main connections and interests were in Abeokuta, where she was eventually given a state funeral in 1887 after a long and eminent old age.

There are apparently no surviving portraits of her, but she seems to have been a woman of great presence and charisma, although as Scala rather cruelly says, "the ravages of time and the vicissitudes of a stormy life had diminished... her seductive charms." Even so he waxes lyrical about her. She was, he says,

> ... tall, slender and well-proportioned; her bearing was proud, but not lacking in grace and subtlety; she had the art of expressing by various movements of her body and by all her postures an indescribable voluptuousness which few could resist. The lines of her face were not at all delicate or regular; her nose was rather thick with very wide nostrils, her lips were full, her mouth large and her eyebrows very thin: nevertheless these features, combined with two large, black, brilliant eyes which had the fascination of a serpent, and two rows of very white teeth formed a wonderfully harmonious example of African beauty which was immediately pleasing and which continued to hold the beholder's gaze for a long time. It is not therefore surprising that this extraordinary woman endowed with so many natural gifts and with an uncommon intelligence, soon came to lord it over these rough men and to find numerous supporters and admirers throughout the tribes.

Although she was herself childless, the Tinubu name was adopted widely by Lagosians in her honor, and later the central square in the middle of Broad Street on Lagos Island was named Tinubu Square, where her statue has remained for a long time. Governor Bola Tinubu (see below) has made much of his family connection with the Tinubus, and it is still clearly a name very much to be reckoned with in Lagos.

One of the most colorful Europeans in nineteenth-century Lagos was **William McCoskry**. Although his past—even his date of birth—is obscure, he came to Lagos, probably in the 1840s, as a trader at a time when the only Europeans to show up there were adventurers. It was always said that his activities initially included slave-trading—it was, after all, what everybody there did—but he was also involved in trading in other commodities such as palm oil and a range of the European imports including alcohol, increasingly in demand. He certainly did business with slave traders of all nationalities. A canny Scot, he rapidly developed contacts in the local community including the different camps around the court of Kosoko, and survived the British deposition of Kosoko and the restoration of Akitoye. His local success and interaction with Africans rewarded him with a Yoruba name relating to his eye-catching red beard (*Ajele Apongbon*, hence Apongbon Street in Olowogbowo). Despite his acknowledged past involvement in the slave trade and his one-time business partnership with Madam Tinubu, he managed to maneuver himself into a solid position in the volatile politics of the Consular period so that he not only double-crossed his business partner Tinubu, who consequently had to flee to Abeokuta, but was able to secure the appointment as consul himself, for the short but critical period of 1860-61, and in that role was actually one of the advocates and signatories of the Cession Treaty. He was reputed to have been the initial creator of the Marina, complete with the planting of trees, when it was first laid out in 1860 as he was said to have felt the need for an evening promenade from his own residence there (although the development and expansion of the Marina were very much the work of Governor Glover) and, as has been noted, he gave his name to a street on Lagos Island.

The story of **Oshodi Landuji Tapa** (c.1800-68) was the remarkable one of a slave originally brought from the Nupe kingdom at Bida who rose through his many talents to become both adviser and leading military support for Oba Kosoko. He is said to have come to Lagos when young as a servant to Oba Osinlekun. According to J. B. Losi, the young man was, with the Oba's consent, taken by a Portuguese merchant for a time to the Americas and also to Portugal. On his return the Oba sent him to become a commission agent at the firm of G. L. Gaiser (known to the locals as Goroti). Losi tells us that Oshodi Tapa (the word *Tapa* is simply how the Yoruba described the Nupe) became a wealthy man as

> on every hundred-fold of different pieces of cloths bought from European traders for the King, he was entitled to a piece from each kind as his own profit given by the European traders; and also for other various articles bought on every occasion, whenever the Portuguese merchants' vessels arrived. By these valuable articles often received, he was able to trade. In this way he became a rich man.

When Kosoko became Oba he was designated Chief Oshodi, with the particular duty of keeping Ipeti Ayaba (the queen's apartments), and later Generalissimo of Kosoko's army. Such was his influence with Kosoko that when the latter was overthrown by the British, Oshodi Tapa left with him to exile in Epe and remained faithful to him as a war-chief through the difficult ensuing years. He was seemingly involved in the mediation between Kosoko and Oba Dosunmu, and he returned with his master to Lagos in 1862, settling in the district of Epetedo near the Oba's palace in Isale Eko (Epetedo is named after the Epe connection, as most of the Lagos Nupe were supporters of Kosoko and had fled to exile in Epe with him in 1852).

The historian Kunle Lawal says that Oshodi Tapa flew the flag of Nupe culture in Lagos and in the grounds of his Epetedo compound there was a grove for the Igbunnoko cult. Oshodi Tapa was given the traditional title of Oloja of Ereko. In this period he reportedly became a close friend of Governor Glover, who spotted his skills, contacts and immense experience of the ins and outs of the "deep" politics of Lagos, and often sought his advice before implementing any plans. Oshodi Street in Epetedo is named after Oshodi Tapa, and there is still a large related family bearing the name. After his death in 1868, while Glover was still Governor, a monument was erected in his memory in Epetedo.

Sir John Hawley Glover, although a man of his time and a Victorian of the imperial age, is still considered by some as one of the most effective colonizers to have been in charge of Lagos. Like McCoskry he was one of the few British rulers who generated a sentimental following and to be given an affectionate Yoruba soubriquet, Oba Golubbar: the "Oba" was an indication of his chiefdom, the second name a local version of his English name. He first came to the area of the Niger in 1857 as part of the expedition of McGregor Laird on board the *Dayspring*. Glover's Hausas (identifiable Northerners, some of whom may well have been Nupe) showed him considerable personal loyalty and some of them eventually even accompanied him to fight in the Ashanti Wars in 1873-74, eventually being granted land in Okokomaiko.

Among Glover's achievements were the pursuit of a policy of openness towards those who had previously been considered enemies, notably Kosoko, Oshodi Tapa and Madam Tinubu, all of whom were allowed back into Lagos during his period as Governor. He also had a vision of the kind of Lagos he wanted, and seriously took up McCoskry's idea of the Marina as a shady tree-lined promenade. He introduced pavements and gas-lamps and created a parallel thoroughfare that he named Broad Street (see Chapter 10). In Lady Glover's life of her husband, she recognized his contribution to Lagos and the appreciation of him among Africans.

Although he was replaced in 1872 by the controversial James Pope-Hennessy (who temporarily reversed some of Glover's policies), his period came to be regarded in retrospect by Lagosians as a golden age, and in the late 1880s a function room was built in Abibi Oki Street called Glover Hall, which became a great meeting place. Its reputation carried on through the twentieth century when it became a famous venue for political meetings until it was rebuilt in modern times. A bust of Glover was recently unveiled in the Union Bank foyer at their headquarters on the Marina, alongside one of his old adversary and accomplice Madam Tinubu.

Samuel Ajayi Crowther was one of the dominant figures in Lagos in the second part of the nineteenth century (even if his church activities took him mostly outside the town) and played an important part in helping to shape the Christian-educated elite that was central in defining the character of early Lagos. According to his own account of his life, he was born, probably in 1805, in Osogun, to the north of Abeokuta, but to a family mainly from Old Oyo. He tells of how he was sold into slavery when in his teens, after Osogun had been destroyed by Fulani invaders. He relates how in 1822 he was put on a Brazilian ship from which he was liberated by a British anti-slavery naval patrol shortly after embarking. He was then taken to Freetown, where such was his intelligence and ambition that he educated himself to the level where he could train for the Anglican ministry.

He was baptized Samuel Crowther in Freetown in 1822, but his middle name Ajayi was remembered from his home in Oyo. His was a heroic tale that made him an iconic figure in mid-Victorian England, especially where he returns to trace his origin back to the exact village in his homeland. He also wrote a highly descriptive account of his often high-risk missionary activity on the Niger in later years prior to his promotion as the first black Anglican bishop. His name became a household word in Christian homes as one who had not only been freed from slavery and embraced education, but had also founded schools and colleges as well as transcribing written Yoruba and driving the translation of the Bible into that language which, says Ade-Ajayi, laid the foundation for "developing the Yoruba language as a vehicle of education and communication."

Crowther's story is in some ways an inspirational one of self-help in the face of adversity, and of how even in the mid-Victorian era it was possible for an autodidact African to achieve advancement through his talents. But it also has a bitterly tragic dimension. In the twenty-first century we have to take due note of the fact that that he even wrote to Foreign Secretary Palmerston saying why it was important for the British to end slavery in Lagos, and he was taken to London in mid-1851 by Rev. Venn of the Church Missionary Society as an eloquent "native" advocate of what was effectively an imperial lobby for "sending a gunboat." It was on the occasion of his London visit that he was taken by Lord John Russell to Buckingham Palace to meet Queen Victoria and Prince Albert. It was an early example of how the British political class found an "African of choice" to suit their own purposes. With the benefit of historical hindsight, he seems now to have allowed himself to be used, but at the time he thought it to be a genuinely honorable cause. Who can fault anti-slavery as a motive? But there was a frightening honesty in his statement, presaging what was to come, when he is quoted in the letters of Queen Victoria as telling her "the slave trade on that part of the African coast would be at an end if Lagos, the stronghold of its greatest supporter, was destroyed."

He was one of the main agents who brought Christianity to Lagos after the bombardment of 1851, and as an influential figure in the Consulate period was one of the witnesses of the infamous Treaty of Cession of 1861. Although this may surprise nowadays, this was because of his continuing belief in the British as the agents of abolition rather than as an aggressive colonial power. The early West African elite, in which Crowther was a leading light, formed what Marxists would call a "comprador" class collaborating with colonialism. However, his career concluded with what must have been a measure of disillusionment in the white man and his ways. It was his dignity in the face of increasingly insulting attacks on him and his management of his diocese by uncomprehending members of the CMS that restored and enhanced his reputation in history.

One of the most illuminating written works about Crowther is the play *Ajayi Crowther: Triumphs and Travails of a Legend* by the playwright and social commentator Femi Osofisan. This is set entirely in the Macaulay house in Odunlami Street on the corner of Broad Street, near the end of Crowther's life in 1891. He had a close relationship with the Macaulay family, as T. B. Macaulay, the great educationist and founder in 1859 of the CMS school in Lagos, married Crowther's daughter Abigail, so that the great nationalist politician Herbert Macaulay was his grandson. The play has appropriate flashbacks to some critical moments in his past which highlight the tragedy of how—despite his remarkable achievement in becoming the first African bishop of the Anglican Church (he was consecrated bishop on the Niger)—the dignitaries of the CMS, influenced by the prevalent imperial racism of the latter years of the nineteenth century, charged him with falling short of Christian principles because of his views on adapting Christianity to African conditions on such issues as dress, language and even polygamy, and proceeded to remove him as bishop. The play captures the high tragedy of Crowther's story as a casualty of early African contact with the perfidious British, evoking the changing mood in race relations between British and Africans that affected particularly the churches at the time of colonization.

Professor Ade-Ajayi's *Patriot to the Core*, a collection of biographical lectures, is equally devastating, as he writes from a strong awareness of historical injustice. Using his typically measured prose, he exposes the way the sanctimonious representatives of the CMS treated the great man in his declining years and probably helped cause his demise, although he was already in his eighties. "His death marked the end of an era," Ajayi writes. "It removed the one person the CMS did not know how to handle in their determination to assert the authority of European officials over the churches in Lagos, the Yoruba country and the upper and Lower Niger missions."

After Crowther's death no African was appointed as diocesan bishop in Nigeria's Anglican Church until 1952, in itself an indictment. His treatment provoked much dissent and turbulence, as well as serving as an encouragement to the end-of-century rise of African churches as a reaction to the high-handedness and racism of the CMS authorities. The CMS official historian Eugene Stock was obliged to write: "the Bishop lived in an atmosphere of suspicion and scandal, yet no tongue of a white man or a black man, however malicious, ventured to whisper reproach against his personal reputation."

Ajayi seeks earnestly to correct the less attractive aspects of the CMS' interpretation of its own history in Nigeria: for example, he notes that one of its books was even dedicated to George Goldie, claiming that he had been Crowther's friend when he was in fact "the very man who, with his agents, did so much to undermine the work of the bishop and his staff on the Niger." Ajayi is concerned even now that the greatness of this early Nigerian, and the rehabilitation of his reputation that his fellow (white) Christians had tried to damage, have still not been fully acknowledged by history. (Which tempts one to suggest in all modesty that a fully comprehensive and accurate history of the British in Nigeria has yet to be written.)

Mohammed Shitta-Bey was the son of an eminent Sierra Leonean Muslim named Shitta. Although baptized a Christian in Freetown, when his father returned to Badagry as Imam in 1844 he reverted to his father's faith. His father died in 1847, and the young Shitta moved to Lagos in 1852 like many Saros at the time. Although a successful trader who acquired substantial wealth in the Delta, he established a great reputation for piety. Over thirty years he worked on the grand project of building a mosque, designed and built in the Baroque manner by Brazilian craftsmen, which still stands in Martins Street. It was inaugurated with much fanfare in 1892 at a ceremony attended by the representative of the Sultan of the Ottoman Empire, who conferred on him the title *Bey*, which was then hyphenated with his original name. Descendants are prominent members of Lagos professions: one became a senator in the Fourth Republic.

James Johnson, known as "Holy" Johnson, is described by E. A. Ayandele in his eponymous biography as a "pioneer of African nationalism." He was born in Sierra Leone in 1838, his father being an Ijesha Yoruba who had been freed by the British anti-slavery squadron. He passed through the newly-developed educational system there, first the CMS Grammar School and then Fourah Bay College before going into teaching and then the church, being ordained in the Anglican Church in 1866. From early on he showed his belief that Christianity needed an African form. He advocated this even while in Sierra Leone (where he was known as "Wonderful Johnson") and was hostile to the notion that white men should rule Africans. He went to England in 1873 to consult on the formation of how to achieve an independent African Church in Sierra Leone, and was sent almost immediately to take charge of St. Paul's Breadfruit Street in Lagos, apparently to try and contain nationalist feelings there, though in fact he agreed with them and made St. Paul's his base.

It was clear that the authorities in the Church Missionary Society in

London never quite knew how to handle him, for although among the powers at the CMS headquarters in Salisbury Square there was a theoretical commitment to encourage African clergy, one who took them at their word so seriously brought himself nothing but trouble. After two years in Breadfruit Street, where he found a group of influential supporters such as Otunba Payne sympathetic to his ideas (see below), he was sent by the CMS as Superintendent of the Interior Yoruba Mission in Abeokuta. This, it was said, made him a *de facto* bishop, but his pursuit of his beliefs in a much wider field of activity caused so much anxiety in Salisbury Square that he was recalled after three years. He remained in Breadfruit Street for the next twenty years, a permanent thorn in the side of an increasingly intolerant and racist CMS establishment, but his evident popularity made it hard to move him. Thus he escaped the fate of Bishop Crowther (see above). He was even brought into the Legislative Council from 1886 to 1894, and, at the same time the parsonage in Breadfruit Street was a center of theological and political discussion of issues such as education and polygamy.

Although at least two important secessionist African churches developed out of Breadfruit Street under his influence, Johnson himself always preferred staying within the embrace of the Anglicans, with a touching belief that there were Afrophiles in London while the missionaries sent out were useless. He could be dogmatic and extreme in his views against, for example, Roman Catholics or Muslims, but his enjoyment of his gadfly role made him a typical Lagosian, a kind of nineteenth-century Gani Fawehinmi.

Holy Johnson died in 1917: his obituary in the *Lagos Weekly Record* eulogized him as "armed as if with power from on high, his admonitions and exhortations seemed to breathe words of living fire."

John Augustus Otunba Payne, one of the most prominent Lagosians of the late nineteenth century, was born in 1839 in Sierra Leone. His father, an elder brother of the Awujale (Oba or king) of the important Yoruba kingdom of Ijebu Ode, had been taken as a slave but had been freed in the Middle Passage. He had recall of his origins in Ijebu and after some schooling in Freetown made his way to Lagos where after further education he established himself both as a businessman and professional. He was one of the first Chief Registrars of the Lagos courts that had recently been established by the British administration. A man of considerable erudition, he produced an annual *Lagos and West African Almanac and Diary* between 1874 and 1902. A churchwarden at the celebrated Anglican church of St. Paul's Breadfruit Street, he founded with another Saro, Charles Foresythe, the Society for the Promotion of Education and Religion in Lagos as early as 1872, to campaign for a stronger voice in the affairs of the CMS, which was considered as unresponsive to the views of members of the new Christian-based Nigerian elite. He later became closely associated with the nationalist ideas of "Holy" Johnson, vicar of St. Paul's.

At the same time, without any contradiction, he was always strongly pro-British, traveling to London to attend Queen Victoria's Diamond Jubilee in 1897, while he also rejoiced in his Ijebu origins. Echeruo in *Victorian Lagos* quotes Payne as saying in 1898, "I am a Jebu man. I am a prince of the country." Thus he tried to create a genuine kind of fusion in his names, and changed his Ijebu name Adepeyin to Payne, while incorporating the Yoruba title Otunba (meaning king's adviser) into his name. His big house, the Orange House in Tinubu Square, was for a long time considered a haven of modernity with the latest Western amenities. It was, sadly, knocked down in the 1950s as part of the modernization of the square, a modernization which effectively destroyed its ambiance and its role as a social center of the city.

THE TWENTIETH CENTURY

Although Governors Moloney, Carter and McGregor all had their Nigerian supporters because of certain recognized benefits they brought, not many liked or appreciated **Sir Walter Egerton**, Governor of Southern Nigeria from 1904 to 1912. He had also been Governor of Lagos Colony from 1903 to 1906, when it was merged with the Protectorate. Of all the British Governors he seems to have pursued a more openly racial agenda in enforcing segregation of Europeans and Africans in the capital and policies that created anger among the growing Lagos elite. From the time of the creation of the two protectorates in the 1890s and the bringing of the administration more affirmatively under the Colonial Office, which meant a considerable expansion in the number of British colonial officers, racial segregation was more likely, compounded when officials' wives started to come. The arrival of colonial officials had also meant promotion blockages for educated Africans who often had to defer to younger and less qualified men who nonetheless flaunted their superiority. It was not surprising that many African officials left government service to go into business. In his period as Governor Africans were excluded from the West Africa Medical Service, and it was stipulated that no European in the Service should take orders from an African.

Sir Frederick (later Lord) Lugard, Governor of the two Protectorates of Northern and Southern Nigeria from 1912 to 1914 and Governor-General from 1914 to 1919, made a profound mark as an agent of history, but he only belongs in this gallery of Lagos figures as a kind of bogeyman, for he hated and despised the place. In this he was typical of many of the British colonial servants who became infatuated with their idea of the North. He revealed his prejudices in his magnum opus of 1922, *The Dual Mandate in Tropical Africa*, in which he holds forth on the superior virtues of the Fulani as collaborators. There is an interesting contrast with that other British imperial figure fingered by many Nigerians as one of the villains in the conquest of the area which became Nigeria, George Taubman Goldie, who rarely had anything to do with Lagos, being above all a man of the Delta.

In the eyes of his British contemporaries and admirers Lugard had a distinguished and courageous career, as he was not afraid to take decisions that were to profoundly influence the whole course of Nigerian history and which indeed created the entity we know as modern Nigeria, for good or ill (and there are many Nigerians who still say his influence was profoundly for ill). It is a matter of chagrin for some that it was Lugard's future wife, the journalist Flora Shaw, colonial editor of the *Times*, who coined the name "Nigeria" in a letter to her paper on 8 January 1897, surely the only case of a country being baptized via a letter to a prominent newspaper. After remarking that since the name "Royal Niger Company's Territories" was "not only inconvenient to use but to some extent also misleading," she suggested that it might be "permissible to coin a shorter title for the operation of pagan and Mohammedan states which have been brought by the exertions of the Royal Niger Company within the confines of a British Protectorate and thus need for the first time in their history to be described as an entity by some general name." She went on to suggest that "the name 'Nigeria' applying to no other portion of Africa may, without offence to any neighbours, be accepted as co-extensive with the territories over which the Royal Niger Company has extended British influence." The letter also contained in very blatant form the racist view that the Hausa and the Fulani were superior to "other Negroes," which, as we have seen, permeated Lugard's own thinking.

Lugard's main opponents, who were inevitably concentrated in Lagos, were the political elite and their colleagues in the press, for the most part very closely linked including through ownership. The idea of political success depending on newspaper proprietorship (which later became a rule of thumb for the Nigerian political elite as a whole) developed further in the Lugard period. Fred Omu tells us in *Press and Politics in Nigeria 1880-1937* that even before the start of his occupancy of Government House on 3 October 1912 he was viewed in Lagos with suspicion and resentment, mainly because of uncertainty over his much-forecast plans for amalgamation of the two Nigerias.

"The thinking was like this," says Omu. "Lagos was a stagnant community as part of the Gold Coast colony, and it was not until the 1886 separation that the economy began to grow. The 1906 amalgamation resulted only in the expansion of the European bureaucracy imbued with racial bigotry and enjoying vast sinecures." Indeed, several newspapers warned of conflict to come, such as the *Nigerian Chronicle* which said that the amalgamation plan would be awaited before any reaction: "We promise him that we shall do so fearlessly, conscientiously, constitutionally and with the powers we possess."

Lugard had one strike against him from the start, that he had been responsible earlier for the North's system of government, Indirect Rule, which would have been, in Omu's words, "inconceivable and dangerous" in Southern Nigeria, and attempts to introduce it in modified form never really worked in the manner intended. He did not help his cause by proposing early in 1914 (perhaps as a piece of wishful thinking) that the capital of the new amalgamated state should move from Lagos to Kaduna or Zungeru. Omu speculates on how the Nigerian press and people would have reacted if a popular Governor like Gilbert Carter had been given the task of implementing the amalgamation. As it was, Lugard's record and his autocratic style cast a shadow on the amalgamation, which set the tone of his whole period of rule.

There were other issues that fueled animosity such as the enduring problem of water rates, and after 1914 there was significant unhappiness in Lagos at Lugard's brutal repression of Egba independence, especially in view of the strong Lagos-Egba connections: the continuing autonomy of Egbaland in spite of British conquest had been a token of hope that the colonial situation might change.

Although after the outbreak of the First World War the newspapers went through a period of support for the endeavors of the British Empire, this in no way inhibited the attachment of politicians and press to their rights. Some of Lugard's subordinates tried to establish a dialogue with Lagos' budding political class, yet Lugard himself was entirely insensitive to such moods, owing perhaps to his dislike of what he referred to contemptuously as "the educated African." Margery Perham, his sympathetic biographer and former secretary, acknowledges this dislike and quotes him saying of the "educated African": "I am not in sympathy with him. His loud and arrogant conceit are distasteful to me." It was also absolutely typical of Lugard that he had a very poor view of Herbert Macaulay, the prototypical Southern politician and educated African, even if the imprisonment of Macaulay in 1912 on probably trumped up charges was prior to Lugard's arrival. It did not help that Lugard referred to him later as a "jail-bird."

At a crucial period in 1915-16 he introduced a number of draconian political measures calculated to give offense, notably a revival of the controversial water rate that had caused a rash of protests when Governor Egerton had tried it in 1908; a new version of the rigid criminal code of 1899, which had produced such opposition from politicians and newspapers for its "abstruseness and elasticity" that it had to be withdrawn; and the Provincial Courts Ordinance. The last-named measure seemed to limit the powers of the Supreme Court in Lagos in favor of an abhorred Lugardian decentralization, but there was particular objection to the introduction of flogging, which was considered alien to Yoruba culture.

Above all, Lugard waged war on the by now highly combative Lagos press, which had already cut its teeth in a series of acrimonious conflicts with Governor Egerton. These focused on the 1909 Seditious Offences Act, which had proved so unpopular that Egerton never chose to begin any prosecutions from it. Lugard's problems, initially eased by the coming of the First World War, reached breaking point in the Bright Davies trial of 1916 (see Chapter 6). This case proved to be an important event in the annals of Nigerian nationalism, and in the long view of history is scarcely to Lugard's credit in any way. When Lugard retired in January 1919, Omu says that "never in the history of Lagos had the news of a retirement created such great excitement." The *Record*, for example, said: "Sir Frederick is a huge failure... a hopeless anachronism... the victim of exaggerated personality... Opinionated, unswerving from a purpose even if it be irrational when it was once formed, and brooking no interference with his imperious will."

Herbert Heelas Macaulay was one of the most spectacular figures of Nigerian nationalism, whose career spans more or less the whole colonial period from the late nineteenth century period, before Nigeria was officially created, through to the beginnings of nationalist politics. He died in 1946, just as the full blast of nationalism was to hit Nigeria in the wake of the Second World War. Macaulay was a trained surveyor and in his youth had designed a number of Lagos buildings, but he was one of the major casualties of the arrival of the new breed of arrogant colonial officials in the 1890s who disapproved of "natives" holding senior positions. It was after he left government service in disillusionment at his situation and took up private practice that he became more politically conscious, part of a mood that affected a whole generation.

Herbert Macaulay

There is a statue of him, mustachioed and in stylish pose, in the long street running through Yaba that bears his name. It had originally stood outside the CMS on the Marina, which was fitting, as he was Bishop Crowther's grandson, although he was known more for his political than his religious virtues. Obafemi Awolowo in his autobiography described Macaulay's *Lagos Daily News* as "ultra-radical, intensely nationalistic and virulently anti-white." He was a flamboyant, occasionally mischievous figure, the bugbear of successive Governors who styled himself the "Gandhi of Nigeria," but he incarnated Nigerian nationalism for thirty years or more. Even if his political vision for Nigeria rarely extended beyond Lagos (although he was an ardent advocate of West African unity through the West African Congresses of the 1920s), his Nigerian National Democratic Party (NNDP), which contested the very limited elections of African members of the Legislative Council starting in 1923, called for universal compulsory education for Nigeria, and he was at the center of most of the political dramas from the water rate riots of 1908 to the prolonged controversy over the British handling of the Eleko affair.

Piers Brendon in *The Decline and Fall of the British Empire* describes Macaulay in later life as "an angry old man in a white suit and a white moustache that stuck out like cat's whiskers" who became increasingly discontented with British rule. He was in a way the political godfather of the pioneer nationalist Nnamdi Azikiwe who came back from his long pilgrimage to the US to pick up Macaulay's West African dream (see below).

Lugard had been Macaulay's most considered adversary and frequently passed bitter comments on him. If Lugard saw him as constantly duplicitous, Macaulay was certainly a Machiavellian player in the cause for which he was fighting. Even in 1931 Margery Perham in *West African Passage* referred to him as a "so-called agitator." She visited him in Odunlami Street, where she described "a strange house, full of antimacassars and shell-covered boxes reminiscent of a bygone England." Of their conversation she says, "there was much sense, some extravagance, but most of all personal obsessions about his grievances. But he is one of the ablest Africans I have met and at once a potentially dangerous and rather pathetic figure."

Henry Rawlinson Carr, Macaulay's contemporary, was also his great enemy and antithesis, although both men, essentially Lagos figures, were in their different ways giants of the colonial period. He was born in 1863, his father being Amuwo Carr, a freed Saro popularly known as "Daddy

Shope" who had left his wife to go and live in Abeokuta as what Dele Cole calls "a happy polygamist." He was educated at the Wesleyan school, Olowogbowo, and proceeded to the Wesleyan High School in Freetown from where he went to Fourah Bay, graduating with a Durham degree in mathematics and physical sciences. When he was sent by the colonial service to the United Kingdom in 1899 for training, Governor Carter observed unkindly that "Mr Carr is a very intelligent Negro with a very good opinion of his own abilities and such a person is apt to be spoilt in England." Specializing in education, Carr rose in the colonial service, against the trend of the times, to be eventually appointed by Lugard as Provincial Commissioner for Lagos in 1918. He retired from the colonial service in 1924 and then became for some years a member of the Legislative Council. He died in 1945.

It is interesting and revealing that both Carr and Macaulay were men of great culture who were deeply involved with their remarkable personal libraries, both of which were bequeathed to the University of Ibadan by their families and still provide an unrivaled archive of the period. Carr's personality was also a very contrasting one to that of Macaulay, and he was seen by some as the very model of an Uncle Tom, always trying to ingratiate himself with the British. He was a devout Christian, an admirer of the British public school system and an assiduous reader of Matthew Arnold. According to Dele Cole he was a man of remarkable intellectual erudition, but was extremely sensitive to criticism and made himself unpopular both for advocating the banning of polygamy and for his hostility to Islam, neither of them wise postures in a city like Lagos. Macaulay, it has to be said, knew exactly how to fuel that criticism.

Eleko Eshugbayi, Dele Cole records, was the only Oba of Lagos to be called "Eleko," although in the official biography of the present Oba of Lagos (see below) we are told that after the Benin implantation the title of the ruler installed there was Oloriogun (leader of the Benin warriors in the area), but became Eleko later. It means "owner of Lagos" and was adopted to stress political control, so it was understandable that it was not continued in view of the entanglements surrounding land ownership. Even so, the title became wholly identified with the Oba in the reign of Eshugbayi, who had reasons for emphasizing ownership in his long dispute with the British authorities. The Lagos elder statesman Femi Okunnu described him in conversation with the author as "a thorn in the flesh of the British."

He reigned as Oba from 1901 to 1925, when he was deposed. He had already been suspended in 1920, as he was caught up in the growing conflict with the government (especially a faction in the Executive Council led by Henry Carr). This was Macaulay's most ebullient period and he played politics with both the division in the Muslim communities in Lagos and the position of the Eleko (although Eshugbayi was not himself a Muslim). The deposition was done through a petition from members of a part of the ruling families but gave Macaulay a huge issue on which to campaign against the colonial administration. The Eleko was eventually restored to office in 1931, only to die a few months later.

Governor Hugh Clifford (1919-25) was one of the better-remembered representatives of the British crown in Government House. Cole says, "After the dictatorial rule of Lugard, Lagos could hardly have hoped for a better Governor than Sir Hugh Clifford… he was enlightened, liberal and entirely free of the racial prejudice." Even so, because of the period in which he was Governor he had to face a great deal of turbulence in the volatile era after the First World War. He had particular problems with the rise of Herbert Macaulay (founder of the NNDP political party), with whom he was not at ease, but it was mainly his deputy and successor Sir Donald Cameron who often had to cope with the crisis around the Eleko's support for Macaulay, which led to the ruler's 1925 deposition.

Sir Adeyemo Alakija (1884-1952) was one of the most stylish Nigerian figures of the colonial period, whose family had returned from Brazil with the Portuguese name Assumpçao but still knew of their origins in Abeokuta. This allowed him to re-adopt his original family name. He attended St. Gregory's Catholic Grammar School and the CMS Grammar School, then joined government service as a clerical officer, but in 1913 qualified as a barrister at London's Inner Temple. A distinguished lawyer, in politics he was a conservative figure, very hostile to Herbert Macaulay who accused him of complicity with the British (who knighted him in 1945). He was one of the establishment figures favored by Lugard and his successors, so it was not surprising to see him on the Legislative Council.

Sir Adeyemo was known as an owner of racehorses, which were kept in stables in his big house in Customs Street just off the Marina. He had a strong interest in newspapers and was a co-founder in 1926 of the *Daily Times*, then serving as a director of the company publishing that newspaper, a position which his wife inherited up to the time of her death in

2005. His daughter Aduke Alakija has recollections of growing up in the house in the 1920s. Interviewed by the author in 2008 she recalled with great clarity his large house, his horses which raced on the Lagos racetrack and his interest in growing grape-vines. The spread of his widely-talented descendants includes Kofi Annan's first wife Titi Alakija, also Sir Adeyemo's daughter.

Sir Kitoye Ajasa was another of the figures in the early years of the twentieth century who were favored by the British, thus earning knighthoods. He was unusual in that he was a noted pro-British conservative, a friend of Lugard (who secured for him his knighthood, the first ever awarded in Nigeria) and an ally of successive Governors. His newspaper the *Nigerian Pioneer* consistently gave what James Coleman in his *Nigeria: Background to Nationalism* called "unqualified support to the British connection" while making "suggestions for reform and improvement." He was originally called Edmund Macaulay, from a branch of the Saro family who had migrated to Lagos from Ajase in Dahomey, and he decided to change his name after he had spent twelve years in London and qualified as a barrister at the Middle Temple. He married Oyinkan Moore, granddaughter of the celebrated Abeokuta trader Osanyintade Williams (not a Saro, having taken his name Williams from his supplier in Manchester)— one example of the extent of interlocking relations among "old Lagos" families and an indication of how a European name is not necessarily a clue to origin.

Nnamdi Azikiwe (1904-96), although a national figure, had so many connections with Lagos that he can be considered in part a fundamentally Lagosian character. Indeed, it is hard to encapsulate the many-sided career of Nigeria's foremost nationalist politician who, after three years as Governor-General, became the country's first president in 1963, a non-executive president (though he sometimes thought he had some powers). He subsequently had a long career in the very forefront of politics although he was never again to hold high office. He strongly merits inclusion here because although an Onitsha Igbo he had the mentality of a "Lagos boy." His experience in the city helped make him a nationalist; even if he was later compressed into an Igbo ethnic pigeonhole by circumstance, this did not diminish the splendid aspects of his long career and life.

His description of life in Lagos in the years 1916-20 in his autobiography *My Odyssey* contains some vivid descriptions of growing up in central

Lagos, to which he moved at the age of ten. He writes that 139 Bamgbose Street "will ever remain green in my memory," recounting his links and friendships with the local boys, many of whom bore Brazilian names—the street was in the Brazilian quarter. The boy who lived in the house next door was Francis Alaba whose family came from Abeokuta and who encouraged his own interest in printing and photography. "I remember dreaming with him how we would own a printing press and a cinema theatre where both of us could work together and make jobs possible for a great number of people."

A student at the Wesleyan Boys High School in Broad Street, Zik—as he was generally known for most of his life—recalls winning a prize, a deluxe edition of the Methodist Church hymn book, which was presented to him in 1917 by Lord Lugard at prize-giving day in the Glover Memorial Hall. He only returned to Lagos, after many years' educational experience in different colleges in the US which he justly described as his Odyssey, in 1937, having returned first of all (1934-37) to the Gold Coast, where he made fire-raising declarations in support of African independence. These were among the formative experiences of the young Kwame Nkrumah, who saw Zik as a role model and followed his example in going to study in the US. In 1937, from a base in Accra where he edited a nationalist newspaper, he acquired funding to get the presses to launch the *West African Pilot*, the most important newspaper in the history of Nigeria's nationalist movement, first published on 22 November 1937. The *Pilot* and the wider Zik Group of Newspapers had their Lagos base for a time at 100 Broad Street, then at 34 Commercial Avenue in Yaba, and formed the base for Zik's emergence as a Nigerian politician during and after the war, which changed and matured his choices.

In 1944 he teamed up with the veteran politician Herbert Macaulay, by then over eighty and a national and nationalist icon, to found the National Council of Nigeria and the Cameroons (NCNC). It was in fact not very long before Macaulay's death in 1946, but it was a symbolic association of age and youth. In its early days it was a genuinely nationalist political party (Nigeria's first) and was not a little disturbing, especially, it seemed, to British colonial officials who more often than not could not abide Zik. It was feared that with his flamboyant eloquence he was another Kwame Nkrumah, a figure who filled many colonial officials with irrational terror. These fears were mainly triggered by the often vehement anti-

British sentiments of Zik's frequently banned newspapers (see Chapter 4).

Azikiwe's years as a true Lagos politician, beloved by so many of its inhabitants, were between 1937 and 1955 when, with constitutional advance bringing real devolution of power, he switched from national politics to become the Premier of Eastern Nigeria. But the extent to which an Igbo politician could hold the national stage, alarm the British and carry a large part of the Yoruba Western Region with him was the measure of his magic. It was true that his strength in Lagos came from its sizeable non-Yoruba (especially Igbo) population who were among his most fanatical supporters, but there was a period when he wore the clothes of a real nationalist politician. His departure from the national platform in 1955 also helped enable the British to cut him down to size. He always reproached Awolowo for not staying in the same camp with him, a resentment that lasted for the whole of their long political lives. This separation was one of the seminal moments in Nigeria's nationalist politics, which dominated the next 35 years. Although they and their parties occasionally came together in tactical alliances it never lasted long as they were personally antipathetic, with contrasting personalities and political styles, as different as chalk and cheese.

With regret, it seems inappropriate for this section to dwell as much on Azikiwe's great rival **Obafemi Awolowo**, although in many ways the latter was deeply involved with Lagos politics when he was Premier of the Western Region and later leader of the opposition in the federal parliament. He built a party structure there that has never been disbanded, even if the parties themselves changed their names. Awolowo was tried for treasonable felony in 1963 in a great set-piece trial in the High Court in Lagos, which led to riots outside the prison in Broad Street. Although after his sentence he was sent to distant Calabar to serve out his term, for a brief period after his arrest he was detained in a house in Lekki town (see Chapter 2). Chief Awolowo held high office under General Gowon, and like Zik remained in the forefront of political life until his death, rising to receive the courtesy title of Leader of the Yoruba. But while he too must certainly be considered as one of Nigeria's founding fathers, he was not really, and never could be, a Lagos personality in the way that for a period Azikiwe had been, both in his youth and as a budding politician. Pauline Baker says of him that from the days when he was Secretary of the Nigerian Motor Transport Union and incurred the wrath of Herbert Macaulay,

Awolowo was "contemptuous of Lagos politics, with its petty rivalry, its lack of discipline and its opportunism." Lagos was for him for the most part only a trophy, a political football to be kicked around.

A short examination is useful of two highly contrasting Governors, **Sir Bernard Bourdillon** and the already mentioned **Sir Arthur Richards** (later Lord Milverton), both of whom have streets in Ikoyi named after them: in the case of Bourdillon Road, it is now a dual carriageway that spans much of the south side of the peninsula and no attempt has been made to change the name, nor that of Milverton Road nearby. Bourdillon (1935-43) was one of the more popular of the later Governors, as evidenced by the fact that he stayed eight years in part at his own request and in part because of the Second World War. He had come to Nigeria from Ceylon (Sri Lanka) and seemed to enjoy the climate of Lagos more than Colombo. His biographer says he was in general popular because of his "outgoing attitude and gentlemanly mien" and his apparent recognition that the future of the country lay in the hands of educated nationalists. The pork pie hat which he frequently wore became *à la mode* in Lagos and was known as a "Bourdillon."

His affectionate biographer R. D. Pearce says he had "formidable powers of relaxation" devoted mainly to sports, and recounts some of his eccentric ways: he liked to travel viewing the Nigerian countryside from a seat placed in front of the engine pulling his train, or, when he voyaged by boat from his stern-wheeler *Valiant* which had a skittles alley on the upper deck. He drove his Railton sports car round Lagos so fast that he once killed a young Nigerian. Some of the locals found him "swanky," and the elderly Herbert Macaulay disliked him intensely. The Colonial Secretary in London thought he suffered from *folie de grandeur*. But at least he had flamboyant style, while his successor Richards was colder and more conservative, although he was said to have had a strong private sense of humor.

Richards was much more out of sympathy with the nationalists, especially Azikiwe, and like many others in the British colonial service had a more instinctive sympathy with the traditionalist Northerners. Martin Lynn, in his introduction to the two fine volumes in the *British Documents on the End of Empire Project (BDEEP) 1943-1960*, observes that "he had little time for the educated African, and little vision of what was needed in the situation facing Nigeria after 1945." The

Richards Constitution of 1947 was introduced "with little consultation" although he had the difficult task of ensuring national unity in face of the growing pressures for regional autonomies from North, West and East. The draft constitution was eventually withdrawn, to be replaced by the painstakingly negotiated Macpherson Constitution in 1953. Richards' proposals were attacked by Azikiwe's newspapers, two of which Sir Arthur banned for alleging the British had been plotting to assassinate him. It was a kind of re-run of Lugard's clashes with tormenting editors during the First World War.

Richards' constitution was eventually rejected and an extension of his term was refused by the Colonial Office, which was sensitive to Richards' limitations, although he in turn continued to attack "the intellectual dreamers of Whitehall." He had his supporters, as is evidenced by a short biography of him written in 1980 by Richard Peel called *Old Sinister*, the apparently sympathetic nickname only given to him by European civil servants in Nigeria, for which there were several explanations. "One was that it derived from the scar at the corner of his mouth, which he acquired in his youth and which increased the severity of his countenance." He also had "an extraordinary capacity for sitting motionless." Another explanation given to Peel by Ralph Grey (who later became Chief Secretary) was that the name derived from "the habit, which could be alarming to lesser mortals of making from his gubernatorial eminence a remark which closely resembled the wildly outrageous premises of a 'Saki' story in order to make a serious point, following it up after a perceptible interval by a chuckle that wound its alarming way up from below his diaphragm and caught the nervous listener still undecided about His Excellency's intent." He was the only British Governor of Nigeria apart from Lugard to have been elevated to the peerage, as Baron Milverton of Lagos and Clifton (suggesting that, unlike Lugard, he might, after all, have had some affection for the city, although his preference, as with many of the British colonial officials, was for the culture of the North).

Sir James Robertson, one of the more respected of the British rulers, was not as unloved as some of his predecessors. This was perhaps because he was the last Governor-General before independence who actually carried on after independence from October to December 1960 as head of state of Africa's most populous country before handing over to Zik. Professor David Anderson has reported interestingly in the BBC program

Document that there are 100-year blocked files in the British National Archives on both Robertson and Zik, possibly because of revelations of untoward political dealings at the time of the 1959 federal elections. Robertson was probably too shrewd and diplomatic ever to express views on Lagos though some of his dispatches were fairly candid and were often worth reading, even if sometimes revealing of his own prejudices. Robertson recorded his worthy and rather banal thoughts on African nationalism in his memoir of 1974, *Transition in Africa*.

A whole group of businessmen who came to prominence with the independence era are catalogued by Tom Forrest in his highly informative 1994 study *The Advance of African Capital*, which takes the story from the 1950s and the impact of oil wealth on the business class where old money is still competing with new. Although it is invidious to make a small selection from such an impressive body of entrepreneurs, I feel I should highlight the story of **Sir Mobolaji Bank-Anthony**, born in what was then the Congo Free State, son of "Pa Alfred" who ran a successful firm of undertakers. From education at several of the top Lagos schools he became a general merchant moving from palm oil and patent medicine to German watches and finally to fountain pens, becoming the third largest dealer after the United Africa Company and the United Trading Company and using his undertaker business to import marble Italian angels for tombstones. Although he only briefly dabbled in politics he was prominent in business organizations, including the Committee of All Nigerian Businessmen of 1956. This led to his association with a number of foreign companies helped by frequent visits abroad, especially to Europe, securing a British knighthood before Nigeria became a republic. He was also a founding father of the Nigeria-America Chamber of Commerce as well as Chairman of the Nigerian Stock Exchange, and engaged in a wide range of philanthropic activities.

Another of his generation to make a lasting mark in the promotion of local enterprises was **Chief Adeyemi Lawson**, who was educated as a lawyer and entered business via chairmanship of first Lagos City Council and then the Lagos State Development Board. His first major business was West African Breweries in Abeokuta, which competed with the international brewing firms, followed by the Agbara industrial estate off the Badagry Road with 27 factories and a large residential area. His main place in the history of Nigerian enterprise is the role he played in helping to build the West African Chamber of Commerce, which led him into his key role as a founding father of Ecobank. Originally a project involving the ECOWAS Fund (set up by the regional economic grouping the Economic Community of West African States), Ecobank international became essentially a privately-owned bank, with participation from a growing range of African countries, now more than thirty, in each of which there is an Ecobank company. Its diverse ownership, which now includes non-African capital, helped it to survive the recent global recession and it is one of the most successful pioneering Pan-African corporations. Lawson's son Kolapo became Chairman of Ecobank International in 2009.

Alhaji Isma'il Babatunde Jose (1925-2008) was one of independent Nigeria's most significant media figures. For nearly fifteen years he ran the Daily Times Group from the period of independence to the moment in 1975-76 when the military government took over the group and eased him out. The irony was that only three years before, Jose had presided over what was called "indigenization," the acquisition of a foreign-owned company by Nigerian shareholders. The newspaper had been acquired through the takeover of its publishers in 1947 by the Mirror Group in London as the linchpin of the corporation's West African media empire in which Cecil King, head of the group from 1951 to 1968, took a particular interest. Jose was King's star protégé, and the two remained in close touch until the latter's death in 1987. Jose and his former deputy managing director Laban Namme attended King's funeral in Dublin.

Born in 1925 in Lagos, Jose was the son of a trader and educated at Yaba Methodist School and St. Saviour's College. A devout Muslim, he was connected to the Nigerian wing of the reformist Ahmadiyya movement. He joined the *Daily Times* as a trainee at the age of sixteen. Although he moved to other papers, he returned to the *Times* after the Mirror Group takeover and rose through the ranks, becoming editor in 1957 and a board member in 1958. With the coming of independence and Africanization, he was appointed the company's first African managing director in 1962, becoming chairman as well in 1968.

The Mirror Group sought to bring modern tabloid production and distribution techniques to African newspapers, and in Nigeria it worked wonderfully. By 1975 circulation was 275,000 for the daily and 400,000 for the *Sunday Times*. After the change of military regime in 1975, the new rulers found the paper too powerful and independent and were uncertain of Jose's loyalty. So they first forced the sale of sixty per cent of the shares and then engaged in a conflict which obliged him to resign. The story of this crisis is recounted in detail in his autobiography *Walking a Tight Rope*. Although the telling is restrained, his feelings occasionally show through. The *Daily Times* had been his life and his monument, and he watched over its experience as a government-owned newspaper with increasing alarm.

Although non-partisan, Jose was highly politically aware and also believed firmly in the power and virtue of newspapers. Although not a university man himself, having learned on the job, he had great belief in the importance of educated journalists and went out of his way to set up a training school and employ graduates. There is a whole generation of Nigerian journalists who came under his influence and who still talk of him with enormous respect. In his later years his white beard reinforced his elder statesman image. He was already a prominent member of the Nigeria media establishment before 1976 and went on to a full life as a businessman and media guru, holding such positions as chairman of the Nigerian Television Authority, but it is for his *Daily Times* experience that he will be remembered. His influence has been profound and his memory in the Nigerian media, often turbulent but always vibrant, will surely endure. He died on 3 August 2008.

Mobolaji Johnson was born in 1936 into a family of Saro descent. From Methodist Boys High School he chose to go into the army, first to cadet training in Ghana, then at Sandhurst. After rapid promotion he was in the right place at the right time in 1967 as he became the first military Governor of the newly created Lagos State.

The story of his eight-year administration has certain epic qualities as the architects of the state were beginning from nothing. Despite being starved of funds by the federal government, it is said he oversaw the establishment of the State government and administration with authority and vision, and those who succeeded him knew that he built well even though, at the age of forty and without a house to call his own, he was given seven days to leave his office after the 1975 coup. Modern developments started at that time included notably the mainly federally funded overhead motorways. While Johnson was Governor he developed close relations with Julius Berger, the German construction company that based its strong position in Germany on its fantastically successful track record over forty years in Nigeria (see Chapter 2). Only in 2008 did Mobolaji, now in his seventies, resign as local chairman of Berger Nigeria. At six feet and four inches and still an imposing figure, he is now one of the State's elder statesmen.

Teslim Olawole Elias was one of the most distinguished sons of Lagos, who achieved considerable international eminence as a lawyer. Born in 1914 into an old family in Isale Eko, reputedly related to one of the Lagos royal families, he showed prodigious educational aptitude especially in law, and his family (despite their adherence to Islam) sent him to the CMS Grammar School and Igbobi College before he went in 1935 to work for the Nigerian Railway Corporation. Aspiring to study law, he enrolled with Wolsey Correspondence College, winning interim qualifications in 1943 of a standard that encouraged his family to find the funds for him to go to London to further his studies. There he obtained a Bachelor of Laws with distinction and a scholarship to the Inner Temple.

His first inclination was to be an academic lawyer and he pursued research in Manchester and Oxford: in 1951 he published *Nigerian Land Law and Custom* and between 1954 and 1956 he brought out three more books on Nigerian law, the beginning of a vast corpus of works on the subject. In 1956 he was a visiting professor at the University of Delhi, lecturing in other Indian universities. Nigerian politics was increasingly calling him, however, and in 1957 he became constitutional and legal adviser to Azikiwe's NCNC party, which role he played par excellence at the constitutional conference of 1958. He became one of the architects of the independence constitution, so that on independence T. O. Elias was an inevitable choice to become Attorney-General through the whole of the First Republic.

Although he lost that post after the coup of January 1966, he was never far from the center of power, and after the July coup of that year he exercised considerable influence in the political and constitutional crises that followed. By November he was back at the Justice Ministry as well as being Dean at the Law Faculty of Lagos University and an influential force in setting up the Lagos Law School and instituting the Nigerian Bar with its qualification Senior Advocate of Nigeria (SAN).

T. O. Elias' long and immensely effective period in politics was well summed up by George Okoro in the *Daily Times* in 1972: "Looking back today, I see him in that intricate game of skirting the whirlwind which only masterminds can play well. Before his own eyes constitutions were made and constitutions were destroyed by men of bizarre emotions and hopes. All through a decade of chaotic instability, he remained a legal draftsman, the constitutional adviser whose words could be ignored by politicians and putschists but who knew how well tacturnity could serve a reputation founded on hard won knowledge."

In 1972 he reached the top of the Nigerian legal tree when he was appointed Chief Justice. At the same time he was developing further his international reputation, serving on a number of UN legal bodies, while also playing an important role in Africa—for example helping to draft the charter of the Organization of African Unity (OAU). After he was removed following the 1975 military coup his international reputation prevailed over Nigerian political shadows and in 1976 he became a judge at the International Court of Justice in The Hague and in 1982 its President. He served until 1985 when he retired and returned to Nigeria, where he enjoyed elder statesman status in the Lagos that was his home as one of its most distinguished sons. He died in 1991.

The politician and journalist **Lateef Kayode Jakande**, born in 1929 into a Lagos Muslim family, started at the now-defunct *Daily Service* in 1949 but made his career with the *Nigerian Tribune*, the party paper of the Action Group of which he became editor and then editor-in-chief before moving into newspaper management. He was one of those put on trial with Chief Awolowo, the Action Group leader, for treasonable felony in 1963. He was indeed one of Awolowo's most loyal lieutenants and later wrote a book about the trial.

Although in later life he and Awolowo experienced a certain political estrangement, loyalty was rewarded when in the 1979 return to civilian rule he was selected to be candidate for Lagos State Governor on behalf of the UPN, the United Party of Nigeria, formed from the AG whose hold on the State had always been very secure. In office for more than four years—he was re-elected in the elections of 1983—he was one of the most loved of all the Governors, called the "Action Governor" and responsible for promoting the much-needed Lagos Metroline, a project killed off by the Buhari regime. In old age Jakande became a respected elder statesman of the city.

Colonel Muhammed Buba Marwa was one of a succession of military Governors (or "administrators") of Lagos State in the second and most oppressive period of military rule from 1983 to 1999. Some of the others left an alarming reputation in Lagos, such as the hated Col. Raji Alagbe Rasaki, the Ibadan man who razed Maroko to the ground (see Chapter 4). Chief Michael Otedola, the only civilian Lagos State Governor in this period, suffered from the lack of fulfilment of the Third Republic in 1993 (it only lasted for a few months of that year). His military successor (as Military Administrator) was the unloved Olagunsoye Oyinlola, who according to the journalist Uthman Ademilade Shodipe in his book *From Johnson to Marwa*, "alienated Lagosians from governance" with his reign of fear and insecurity at the time of Abacha's dictatorship (1993-98). Marwa, however, managed to raise some genuine support in the city, partly through personal modesty and charm. Although his family originally came from Adamawa State in a far-off part of north-eastern Nigeria, he had grown up in Lagos and was fluent in Yoruba although the story that he had a mother still living in the Hausa quarter of Idi-Araba proved mythical; his mother had died forty years before. But this stage of his career was an illustration of how Lagos can sometimes take strangers to its heart.

Asiwaju Bola Ahmed Tinubu was one of the two Lagos State Governors of the Fourth Republic. The two (the second being Governor Fashola) should be taken as a continuum as Fashola was chief of staff for five of Tinubu's eight years as Governor from 1999 to 2007. Tinubu saw himself in a line of political descent from Gandhi and Awolowo (observers even noted that his round glasses were similar to those worn both by the Mahatma and by the venerated late leader of the Yorubas). Although he was by his own choice not a federal politician, he made his mark on Lagos in his eight years, drawing up plans for the development of the city which his successor began to implement, and pronouncing "zero tolerance" against crime, mainly in the areas of "the Island" occupied by foreigners and the wealthy such as Ikoyi and Victoria Island. Crime was always threatening to get out of control, and on the mainland led to the development of local vigilantes for community policing (sometimes these took on alarming connotations as in the case of the Odua People's Congress which thrived particularly in Tinubu's first term but has since been largely tamed as a separate vigilante organization). Tinubu regards the nickname of "Area Boy Governor" as a badge of honor and he has not been afraid of street politics. In order to maintain power he had to develop relations with some of Lagos' fractious trade unions, especially those in the transport sector such as the powerful National Union of Road Transport Workers (NURTW).

His political success depended above all, however, on the well-oiled party machine he inherited. It had been maintained from the Action Group onwards, which ran Lagos from the 1950s and 1960s, via the Unity Party of Nigeria in the Second Republic, to the Action for Democracy and the Action Congress in the Fourth Republic, still essentially the same political organization. Although he also dreamed dreams for the city and laid the foundation for developments that began to bear fruit under his successor, his lasting contribution was probably in using his skills as an accountant to introduce an efficient taxation system in the state, which helped to maximize revenue from its own sources. This was especially important as for almost the whole of his tenure he was at war with the federal government and in particular with President Obasanjo, who throughout his eight years as President deprived the State of much-needed revenue in a dispute over the creation of additional local government councils and whether they should receive federal government funding.

Some found Tinubu's slogan for Lagos as a Centre of Excellence ironic, but the response of its apologists was that there is nothing like saying something enough to make it happen. When asked about investigation of his finances by the Economic and Financial Crimes Commission (EFCC), he told this writer he was open to any inquiry; his critics cite his own palatial house in Bourdillon Road, one of Ikoyi's main arterials, and other properties as evidence of wealth. The house always seems surrounded by masses of people, who, one is always told, include a host of "area boys." In an interview with the author about this aspect of his politics he replied with feeling, "They are my boys: I care for them, we have to retain them… I relate to them, I communicate with them, I share their pains." Showing his streak of populism, he feels it is important to treat the "area boys" as human beings and has been responsible for ensuring jobs for them in State agencies such as traffic control, waste management and even security ("they give information and are paid for it").

Babatunde Raji Fashola, Tinubu's successor, is in a different league. Tall and imposing, with an articulacy that speaks of his training as a barrister, he comes across as a technocrat rather than a politician. It was possible to observe a number of changes when Fashola came into office— not just of style but of serious management of the city. He was lucky to have arrived when civilian rule was becoming more stabilized, and the foundation of better finances was something he pursued with vigor, but it did permit him to begin to implement a number of planned programs and in so doing make them very much his own, even though they originated in Tinubu's eight years.

What has been important under Fashola has been the impression created that Lagos had a guiding hand that was trying to plan for its future despite all the chaos and piles of problems. The conscious attempt to improve the appearance of the city was widely noticed with the planting of trees and the clearance of rubbish (Lagos now has its first litter bins). His lasting contribution lay in the grand long-term projects—notably the developments on the Lekki Peninsula and along the Badagry Road, but also finally getting off the ground the plan to give the city the long dreamed-of light rail mass transit system. There is a feeling with him of commonsense rather than megalomania, as when he says: "Even as we build more roads, we cannot build our way out of congestion. So the solution is management—making what exists work, that is, management for the greatest number for the greatest good."

The poor relations with Abuja which had obtained under Tinubu and Obasanjo for the time being seemed to come to an end with President Yar'Adua, owing to Fashola's apparently improved contact with the new President, until July 2009 when political pressures caused new tensions over the same issue of extra local government councils. The background to this deterioration was the unsuccessful efforts of the ruling PDP to snatch the great prize of Lagos in the 2007 elections and the federal ruling party's hope, with the approach of the next round of voting, of achieving the almost impossible task of defeating the highly popular Fashola and his tendency. The elections of April 2011 demonstrated this conclusively, as Fashola won with a large majority.

There were some suggestions that Tinubu was unhappy that Fashola was receiving the praise for developments which he (Tinubu) felt he had originated, but major efforts were made to continue to present a united front as the two, with their contrasting styles and personalities, so evidently needed each other. In his interview with the author Tinubu accepted that they had a certain complementarity, that Fashola was not so interested in "political idiosyncrasies." Fashola seems to most observers to have shown less taste for the hurly-burly of the political arena than his predecessor, preferring to concentrate on the techniques of governance.

There has been a great groundswell of popular support for Fashola's evident sincerity of purpose and the fact that he is a Governor who has finally been effecting physical changes in the city. The dramatic nature of some of the changes introduced have sometimes brought concern at the human cost of slum clearance or, for example, the removal of street traders from the expressway at Oshodi, but this was a notorious traffic blockage and the obvious improvement of traffic flows through such schemes as the Bus Rapid Transit (BRT) was seen as contributing to a greater public good. It was never going to be another brutal slum clearance like Maroko in 1990.

Oba Rilwanu Akiolu I, the current traditional ruler of Lagos, was crowned in August 2003. He was born in October 1943 and grew up in Isale Eko in the shadow of the Iga Idunganran. Although his education was somewhat disrupted by the deaths of his parents, he survived thanks to benevolent relatives, and his official biography says it was his own "perseverance" that took him to both the National College of Commerce and the Ansar-ud-Deen College in Surulere. After sampling the Inland Revenue and the railways, he went to the Police College at Ikeja, passing out in 1970. After serving in Cross River and Yola, he was assigned first to the mobile police in Lagos and then to a number of different positions in

His Majesty Rilwanu Akiolu I, present Oba of Lagos

209

police headquarters. On promotion to Commissioner he moved to the sensitive Criminal Investigation Department at Alagbon Close. After a spell in charge of the police force in Kebbi State he then served as Commandant of the Ikeja Police College in 1999 (at this time becoming Assistant Inspector-General). After a year at the Nigerian Institute of Strategic Studies he retired in 2002 after 32 years' service.

He says he developed an ambition to become Oba at the age of 21, aware of his own lineage—his official literature says he is a direct descendant of Ologun Kutere, ruler for thirty years at the end of the eighteenth century. His coronation (iwuye) as the 21st Oba took place on 30 August 2003. Perhaps because of long service in the police, he has shown that in many ways he has more of a modernizing temperament than some of his predecessors, but he is still very much involved in upholding the ways of traditional Lagos, which are remarkably deep-rooted. In an interview in 2006 he explained at length the traditional background of the different chieftaincies in Lagos, and criticized strongly the 1861 Treaty of Cession, over which he says that even now legal actions have been continuing. When the Queen and the Duke of Edinburgh visited Lagos in 2003 he had raised the issue with the Duke, who told him the British interest had been purely commercial. While the British had brought administration and education, "in politics they gave us divide and rule." He also personally showed me round his palace; this had been modernized extensively at the time of independence, but I saw the location of the shrines of Ashipa and Akitoye. In an adjoining palace I saw the door of a secret room where elders planned each traditional eyo ceremony, which takes place after the death of an Oba or another prominent Lagosian, the most recent being for a leading politician of the 1950s and 1960s, Chief T. O. S. ("Tos") Benson.

Gani Fawehinmi was a maverick firebrand civil and human rights lawyer, much loved as an icon in both Lagos and in wider Nigeria for his restless energy and turbulent outspokenness. The very same characteristics meant that he had to qualify as a "Lagos boy" although he was in fact born over seventy years ago in Ondo, an important Yoruba city, and really only came to Lagos after he had been to London to study law. Part of the Gani legend has it that while in London his struggle to survive financially as a student was so tough that he worked for a time as a toilet cleaner at the Hotel Russell in Bloomsbury. He qualified in 1964 and returned to complete his qualification as a barrister at the Nigerian Law School in

Lagos, before beginning a long career taking on a wide variety of high profile and controversial cases. He was once sued for defamation by one of Nigeria's most eminent lawyers, Chief Rotimi Williams, and he crossed swords with the highest in the land, notably the military leaders Babangida and Abacha.

Gani received international awards for his campaigning integrity long before he finally received his much merited SAN (Senior Advocate of Nigeria) title, but he continued his critical view of government, witheringly taking on President Obasanjo over his ambitions to seek a third term. I well recall attending the ebullient launch of his election campaign as presidential candidate for the National Conscience Party in 2003 in the heart of the historic ghetto of Ajegunle, after having called on the traditional ruler of Ajegunle before the rally. There was never a chance of his winning, but it was a noble and memorable campaign. In 2008 he was diagnosed with lung cancer and was taken to a clinic in London amid many messages of sympathy and support; he died the following year.

Chapter Nine

FELA ANIKULAPO-KUTI
ARCHETYPAL LAGOS BOY

"Lagos exercised a powerfully determining influence on Fela's imagination, but Fela also actively sought to reshape the city in his own image, compel it to accommodate his eccentricities, and firmly imprint his footprint."

Tejumola Olaniyan, *Arrest the Music!*, 2004

"On the day the people said goodbye to Fela Anikulapo-Kuti the sun shone and the heavens rained at the same time. When this happens, a Nigerian might observe that a tiger has given birth to a child."

Knox Robinson, "The Father, the Sons and the Holy Ghost," in *Fela: From West Africa to West Broadway*, 2003

The life of Fela Anikulapo-Kuti (1938-97) is a quintessential Lagos story, the tale of a Lagos boy who became an international icon and in death a world-class African legend as well as a metaphor for the city where impossible dreams are dreamed. It is a story that begins with two remarkable Egba Yoruba parents, early protagonists of the Nigerian middle classes in Abeokuta. His father, the Rev. Israel Oludotun Ransome-Kuti, was a strict Christian headmaster from whom he inherited the musical gene; indeed, he was the most important influence in Fela's musical education. His emancipated mother Funmilayo was a fearless politician who was the first

Funmilayo Ransome-Kuti

213

woman to smoke in public in Nigeria, and to visit China. She was also the first woman in Nigeria to have driven a car. Her activism and political commitment had a profound influence on Fela's own evolution.

Fela went to London in 1958, ostensibly to study medicine, but he switched to music at Trinity College and formed the Koola Lobitos, a band playing a fusion of the kind of modern jazz which had been dominant in London while he was there and the highlife which was the music for youths in Nigeria in the 1950s. On his return in 1963 he persevered with Koola Lobitos at a variety of clubs on the mainland, but he really only found his direction after a visit in 1969 to the United States, where he was radicalized politically. A strong influence was Sandra Smith Isidore, a former Black Panther member who introduced him to the Black Power thinking prevalent at the time, but he also absorbed the wider-ranging thought of Malcolm X, all of which motivated him to want to play truly African music.

Having initially criticized the hold of James Brown on the Nigerian popular imagination, he realized the force it represented and it helped provide the aesthetic for his own brand of music, Afrobeat (a name he had coined the year before). It was a fusion of Yoruba rhythms and declamatory chants, highlife, jazz and the "funky soul" of which James Brown was the main protagonist. Afrobeat was the music of the newly defining record *Jeun Koko* (chop and quench) released in 1971 by his new Afrika 70 band, which set him on his unique path in that decade as agent provocateur, rebel and musical genius. It was around this time that for the same reasons of African identity he changed the first part of his last name from Ransome to Anikulapo or "he who carries death in his pouch." Thereafter he came to be known (possibly self-baptized) as *abami eda* ("the strange one").

The central drama of the Fela saga was the destruction in February 1977 of the Kalakuta Republic, the building where he lived in communal style, as he said "outside the jurisdiction of the military regime," and where he was eventually joined by his 27 wives. It was alongside his celebrated Shrine, a club constructed in the courtyard of the Empire Hotel in that area where Mushin, Surulere and Yaba converged, where he had earlier had his first club, the Afro-Spot. The attack on Kalakuta by 1,000 soldiers (it was alleged that the army was used because the police could not be trusted) had been in part in revenge for his boycotting of FESTAC in early 1977 and the attracting to the Shrine of visitors such as Stevie Wonder,

Gilberto Gil and Sun Ra. The attack was a defining and terrible moment in his life and generated great sympathy for him, especially as the troops who perpetrated the act threw his 78-year-old mother Funmilayo from a first floor window, causing injuries that led eventually to her death the next year.

Sympathy for Fela had always existed, but with a measure of ambivalence because of his scandalous drug-related lifestyle and the arrogant parading of his wives, which shocked the Nigerian middle classes (especially the religiously-minded) as did some of the blatantly sexual lyrics of his early songs. His quixotic bid to stand for the presidency in 1983 was not taken seriously, even if it generated some affection. But his eventual death in 1997 from AIDS, which had limited his creative output for some time before though he denied its existence—even in the last song he wrote—brought him a new wave of sympathy and built an unassailable mystique.

In Lagos Fela had, in any case, achieved certain immortality (irrespective of his international celebrity) because of his central role in the psyche of true Lagosians and his place in the international perceptions of the city. Tejumola Olaniyan in his profound study *Arrest the Music!* has a whole chapter on Fela's relationship with Lagos ("Fela, Lagos and the Post-colonial State"), pointing out that Lagos features in a large corpus of Fela's songs (he calls them "metro songs"), which were commonly sung in pidgin. Even where the subject matter is not specifically Lagosian, "it is impossible," says Olaniyan, "to know the city and not recognise it in the imagery of the lyrics." However, after Fela's serious brush with authority in 1974, spelled out bitterly in the number "Alagbon Close" (the security headquarters in Lagos where he was held in detention) the songs become less humorous and more vitriolic, and depart from the early Lagos subject matter such as "Eko Ile" and the poignant "Monday Morning in Lagos." The sack of Kalakuta was particularly reflected in the song "Sorrow Tears and Blood" and the later "Unknown Soldier" (so titled because a mealy-mouthed government inquiry into the affair concluded that any criminal acts were committed by "unknown soldiers").

The potent satire of his songs spared no-one, attacking for example the rising businessman M. K. O. Abiola, against whom Fela's 1979 song "ITT International Tief Tief" (referring to the American multinational ITT, and using the pidgin term "tief" rather than "thief") was directed, or his old adversary (but fellow Egba, like Abiola) General Obasanjo (whom he referred to as "fat belly" and whom he held directly responsible as head of state for the assault on Kalakuta). Ironically, Abiola's death in detention in 1998 (the year after Fela's death) came when he was in the hands of the military so abhorred by Fela. The anti-military song "Zombie" (1976) proved immensely popular with the Nigerian public and contributed to ensuring that the army withdrew from power on time in 1979.

The profound anger was always there, however. There is one track recorded in 1971, probably his most typical Lagos song, full of burning criticism of the city's blatant social divisions and pinpointing another aspect of the multiple dualities of Lagos. It is the second track on the CD titled *Why Black Man Dey Suffer* called "Ikoyi Mentality Versus Mushin Mentality" (refined five years later in "Ikoyi Blindness"). It conjures up potently the class rivalry portrayed in the "Party of the Rich" and the "Party of the Poor" in the unnamed city of Ben Okri's *The Famished Road*, but for those who know the deep contrasts between the two areas, the song is a poignant illustration of some of the hidden intolerances in Lagos society, for all its warmth and unity. To me it is one of Fela's most powerful statements about the city.

The lyrics begin with an announcement: "Some people dey Ikoyi, Some people dey Mushin." The goes on to say that Ikoyi man "him travel all over the world," adding "him bring civilisation for us/ him civilisation we no understanding." On the other hand Mushin man "dey for house/him never travel anywhere" but the song makes the point that "him understand people language/the language of Africa." The number then highlights even more trenchantly the social and class difference between the two areas. Ikoyi man rejoices in a fork and knife and spoon but when "Mushin man dey hungry/Him go say give me my chop." Ikoyi man talks "big big English/ him go wan talk like oyinbo man," while Mushin man "him go talk him broken English/Him go talk like the way him know/ the original African way of life."

When it comes to a song embodying the spirit of Lagos, however, there is none more potent than "Confusion" (1975) where Fela epitomizes the crazy area of the Ojuelegba roundabout at the convergence of the Agege Motor Road with Western Avenue. This is described as "a symphonic hymn to the infrastructural nightmare of Lagos" by Jeremy Weate and Bibi Bakary-Yusuf in a long essay from 2003, "Ojuelegba: the Sacred

Profanities of a West African Crossroad." (These authors use Fela's song as a text for a whole thesis on the special synchronized disorder of Lagos, which Olaniyan calls the "aborted *civis*," seeing it as a kind of sum of the significance of Fela's canon of lyrics.)

Weate and Bakary-Yusuf are wary of the "aestheticising afrophilia" which they observe in the work in Lagos of the Dutch architect Rem Koolhaas (see Chapter 11). The way they use the meaning of the place (it translates from Yoruba into "the shrine of Eshu Elegba," the communicator-trickster, one of the more ambivalent figures in the Yoruba pantheon) nevertheless fits in to the Koolhaas thesis of the vital place in the city of the informal economy. The Eshu shrine has been moved to the Apapa Road, but the Weates see the place as still bearing the mark of Eshu Elegba. It is hard to communicate the buzz which the historical association with Fela has given to Ojuelegba, but it lives on in the Lagos of the imagination. As Fela sings:

> *For Ojuelegba, for Ojuelegba*
> Moto dey come from south
> Moto dey come from north
> Moto dey come from east
> Moto dey come from west
> And policeman no dey for centre
> Na confusion be dat-o

Fela embodied in both his life and his music the deep spirit of anti-authority that is essential to the Lagos ethos, for it is a city permanently in rebellion. There was said to have never been a Lagos funeral like it as an emotional experience when he died in 1997, with a huge number of people on the streets estimated at well over a million. Trevor Schoonmaker, in his introduction to the book of essays and interviews he brought out in 2003 called *Fela: From West Africa to West Broadway*, includes a moving description of the funeral in which he records the lying-in-state in Tafawa Balewa Square on 12 August 1997, where hundreds of thousands of people filed by the coffin, while Fela's Egypt 80 orchestra and his son Femi Kuti's band The Positive Force played Fela's music. "The enormous crowd sang and swayed as he lay before them in tight yellow tailored trousers and with a joint between his fingers to ease his journey into the afterlife. This was

Tribute to Fela, "the best-known of all Nigerians on the planet"

the same site where Fela had once performed for loving fans, launched his political party and was sentenced to a term in prison by a military tribunal." A procession covered the twenty miles to the Afrika Shrine at Pepple Street in Ikeja, where a private family service was held. He was buried there outside the Kalakuta Republic.

LEGEND AND LEGACY

Fela's legend has grown larger and larger since his death, as seen, for example, in the exhibition on "the Black President" at the Barbican in London and in New York in 2004. A musical celebration of Fela staged in 2008 in New York was followed in 2009 by a musical presentation on Broadway called *Fela!* This was heaped with praise and enjoyed a similar success in London at the National Theatre at the end of 2010.

The Nigerian Director of the Centre for Conflict Resolution at the University of Cape Town, Dr. Adekeye Adebajo, wrote in the Johannesburg *African Mail and Guardian* of the Shrine as "a commune of debauchery in my childhood city of Lagos, where the humorous Fela entertained and educated the country's middle and lower classes, often singing in the pidgin English of the masses to speak for the voiceless and the powerless." He adds, however, that "many of Nigeria's conservative middle classes saw Fela as a Pied Piper of Perdition, leading the youth astray." Adebajo also makes the important point that Fela's relations with women were "complex and paradoxical," pointing out that "while feminists criticised his misogynistic views on the traditional role of women in songs like *Lady*, he married his 'Dancing Queens' as a potent protest against women being physically attacked and widely depicted as prostitutes."

Every year around the time of his birthday in October there is a huge event commemorating the man and his work known as the "Felabration" at the New Afrika Shrine in Ikeja. I was there in 2009 with a group from Nimbus, having traveled there in the back of the "Nim-Bus." The group included a couple of *babalawo* (local practitioners of native medicine) with braids bedecked with cowries. We were immersed in the mass fervor that rose from the large and packed warehouse-like hall.

Fela and Nelson Mandela appeared on lists of the greatest Africans of the twentieth century, and in 2005 Fela was one of three Africans to appear in *Time* magazine's list of "60 years of heroes." There is also a whole body of literature from Carlos Moore's *This Bitch of a Life* and Michael Veal's *Story of an African Musical Icon* to Sola Olorunyomi's *Afro-beat: Fela and the Imagined Continent* and the already mentioned *West Africa to West Broadway* and *Arrest the Music!* as well as sheaves of material in music magazines, academic articles in learned reviews and doctoral theses galore.

His sons doubtless capitalize Ziggy Marley-style on their father's reputation, but their music is still some of the best coming out of Nigeria at the moment and has the immense tradition of Afrobeat to draw on. The music of Femi, the older son, is an adapted version of his father's punchy style, but critics call it Fela-lite, and some fans see his younger brother Seun as the true musical heir. They seldom appear together.

Apart from the legend of his outsize personality, Fela Kuti left a real musical legacy, seen in the impact of Afrobeat and Afrofunk on more than

Femi Kuti

just Nigerian music, and also in the way the development of that music weaves in to his own political evolution—the more iconoclastic the music, the greater the venom of the social criticism. Nicholas Shaxson in *Poisoned Wells*, his entertaining study of the dread impact of oil on the politics of a handful of states in the Gulf of Guinea, uses Fela as an indomitable emblem of Nigeria in all its chaos. This had the purpose of demonstrating, through the extremes of his political philosophy, the "curse of oil." It shows how much Fela has become an international icon, arguably the best-known of all Nigerians on the planet.

Chapter Ten

STREETS OF THE IMAGINATION
EVERYDAY MYSTERIES OF THE CITY

"The history of Lagos is on its streets."
Kanmi Olatoye, *Lago de Curamo: Histories and Personalities behind the*
Ancient and Modern Streets of Lagos, 2001

Another way of exploring the city is to take some of its individual streets, roads or byways and look for their individual personalities. In the course of research I have visited or revisited many of these streets, using the example of how their names speak of history and culture, as demonstrated in Kanmi Olatoye's richly detailed book *Lago de Curamo*. This work is devoted to explaining the origin of Lagos street names, in particular providing biodata of even the most obscure among those who have achieved immortality in this way. It is a book to which one pays due homage, to be recommended to all those who have even the remotest curiosity about their environment, and are seeking to understand the mysteries of the city.

CHANGING NAMES
On the whole there has not been a wholesale changing of street names in Lagos, and even those streets that have been given new names are still often known by ones that went before. If Victoria Island is top-heavy with Lagos dignitaries, there are a few roads in the old colonial quarter of Ikoyi that still bear the names of former Governors. Lagos Island in particular has a number of examples of unusual street names (although very few Brazilian names apart from Campos Square) and one of the oldest, Breadfruit Street. Some names are brutally functional, such as Reclamation Road on the north side of Lagos Island where swamps were drained, or Wharf and Warehouse Roads in Apapa, but most, as Olatoye makes clear, are named after a range of historic, or not so historic, figures.

The renaming of roads is also an ongoing process, sometimes moving with political trends and originally depending very much on Lagos City Council and then the State government. There was a rash of name-changing at independence when some leading politicians were commemorated such as Chief Obafemi Awolowo in Awolowo Road (in southwest Ikoyi), and President Azikiwe in Nnamdi Azikiwe Street (formerly Victoria Street), while the racecourse became Tafawa Balewa Square only after the former Prime Minister's death.

Broad Street, named in the 1860s, was changed to Yakubu Gowon Street in 1970 in honor of the victor of the civil war, only to be changed back to Broad Street after Gowon lost favour in the late 1970s. But such reversals have been exceptional. Again, the road in which Murtala Mohammed was assassinated, Bank Road, was renamed after the murdered leader, although taxi drivers still know it as Bank Road, perhaps simply because of its brevity. Under Governor Tinubu's administration local councils made quite a few name changes to reflect the struggle for democracy in the 1990s, with the names of both the late Chief Abiola and his murdered wife Kudirat gracing roads in Ikeja. Both also have statues at the same locations. Kingsway in Ikoyi was renamed after Alfred Rewane (see below).

IKOYI

There are some Lagos streets particularly redolent with history and memories. **Oyinkan Abayomi Drive** (formerly Queen's Drive), Ikoyi, which runs alongside the lagoon (the stretch of water south of Ikoyi named in the early nineteenth century as Five Cowries Creek), is named after the wife of Sir Kofoworola Abayomi, an Edinburgh-trained ophthalmologist originally from a Saro family named John, prominent in both politics and philanthropy and knighted in 1954. When the British laid out Ikoyi in the early years of the century it was named Queen's Drive and was the most snobbish address in Lagos, from the British High Commissioner's residence to the Navy chief's house which has large anchors on the gates. There is also what used to be the Lagos residence of the foreign minister originally built to house the secretary of a now-forgotten organization called the CCTA (Council for Technical Cooperation in Africa) whose most prominent incumbent was Claude Cheysson, an unconventional and brilliantly bilingual Frenchman, later European Development Commissioner and foreign minister in his own country. For a period, indeed, it was known as the "Cheysson House"—Cheysson himself, on an official visit in 1977 while at the European Commission in Brussels, broke from his program to look at his former home and was chased away by security guards as it had by then already become the residence of the Nigerian foreign minister, and remained so until the capital moved to Abuja. (I can verify this story as I accompanied him on the visit.)

Business premises had been rigorously kept out of residential Ikoyi, but in 2001 British Airways installed themselves in a lagoon-side property further down Kofo Abayomi, defying the ban on commercial properties, although Lagos State apparently tried unsuccessfully to evict them. Since then there have been further intrusions. MTN likewise now has a glittering Ikoyi HQ on Glover Road, and Accenture (ex-Arthur Andersen, whose name change in itself marks a small footnote in the business history of the city) has premises on Gerrard Road. A powerful residents' association strives to help preserve the residential atmosphere, although Victoria Island (which is part of the same association) has not been able to exercise the same clout.

There is a cheap ferry connecting Oyinkan Abayomi across the lagoon to the Lekki motorway, more specifically to a speed-boat station/restaurant called Tarzans (see profile of Tarzan and his brother Fiki in Chapter 2) which is the take-off point for those who wish to go to Tarkwa Bay, one of the few safe popular bathing beaches with tranquil waters, since it is sheltered from the Atlantic. It is on the other side of the promontory from Lighthouse Beach, facing the ocean not far from where the notorious "bar" used to be, the first of a long stretch of mostly undeveloped coastal beaches running westwards all the way to Badagry. If Lighthouse Beach is bleak and forlorn, strewn with rubbish and old plastic pure-water containers, Tarkwa Bay, where there is a placid and sheltered beach much favored by locals for weekend outings, is a somewhat artisanal local tourist venue. There are pony-rides, local snacks and Star and Gulder beer readily available, as are rented deckchairs under home-made canopies. There are also a few private and company houses in the vicinity.

Behind the lagoon-side splendor of Oyinkan Abayomi are other famous streets of Ikoyi; one thinks particularly of **Lugard Avenue**, which has never been subject to the indignity of a name

At lighthouse point

change in spite of the bitterness that the name of the dread Governor-General still provokes in Nigerian breasts. Not so, however, Chief Ernest Shonekan, who for eighty days was head of state in the turbulent year of 1993. When he retired as managing director of the United Africa Company in 1989 he bought the MD's residence, built in the 1920s, and proudly kept the name Lugard House. He made a number of embellishments, and in the well-laid-out gardens you can still see one of the original gas lamps introduced by Governor Glover on the Marina in the 1860s.

36 Lugard Avenue, an old style rambling Ikoyi colonial residence with heavy beams, is a government residence inhabited for a few years at the beginning of the twenty-first century by the former Commonwealth Secretary-General Chief Emeka Anyaoku. It was once occupied by General Obasanjo in 1975-76 when he was number two to Murtala Mohammed in the military regime that overthrew and replaced Gowon.

Mekunwen Road, named after a prominent businessman of the 1940s and 1950s, is full of the unexpected. I know it because one of my oldest friends in Nigeria, Alhaji Abdulaziz Ude (Boroji of Lagos, businessman, publisher, Igbo Muslim and much else besides) has a residence with a courtyard and a tower block within, on top of which is his own sitting room with a panoramic view over Ikoyi. Just along Mekunwen you cannot miss the palatial white building of the Xenon oil magnate Otedola, which locals will readily identify. They will also point out former Governor Tinubu's house on nearby **Bourdillon Road**. Nearby is **Ilabere Avenue**, where I lived for two memorable years just after the turn of the twenty-first century and around the time that Jim Ovia, the big boss of Zenith Bank, one of the most successful products of Nigeria's banking boom, built in the same road not only his own massive mansion but an adjoining block of luxury apartments called Marcell's Meadows (although it is hard to see the meadows).

In the major and sometimes reckless transformation Ikoyi has undergone because of the unceasing rise in real estate values, many of the old colonial houses with their broad eaves and large well-tended gardens have been destroyed. The Lagos State Government says that it does have a policy on preservation of some of the classic Ikoyi buildings, and although they have accepted that roads like Bourdillon (which has become a dual carriageway) have been more or less sacrificed to modernity, there are a few that can be conserved. The incursion of highways into Ikoyi will increase as Banana Island develops and the planned Lekki-Ikoyi Bridge (described in *Business Day* as linking "two highbrow areas") is built. There are those who feel Ikoyi's definitive character was lost when the already mentioned Ikoyi Park was given over to developers in the 1990s and became the upmarket Park View estate. The Banana Island development has already reportedly been causing problems with the flow of water in the lagoon, as it is connected to Ikoyi by a causeway and not a low bridge. More infilling is increasing the problem by deepening the lagoon, which threatens the bridges and increases the risks of flooding in lagoon-side properties. As it is said, "nature is not endlessly forgiving."

Kingsway (now officially **Alfred Rewane Road** after a prominent Action Group politician who was assassinated in the troubled 1990s) is the main north-south arterial in Ikoyi. It divides Ikoyi proper, which was once an all-white colonial residential area developed initially in the period of Governor Egerton, from south-west Ikoyi, a more heterogeneous area, some of which was built on land only reclaimed in the 1930s. The court-yard of the now-vanished Ikoyi Hotel, scene of so much history, was a fa-vorite gathering-place where one of its permanent residents, Chuma Azikiwe (son of the former president), often liked to chat with visiting journalists. You could drink local beer and eat *suya*, Hausa peppered beef (the best *suya* can be found in the boisterous mini-ghetto area of Obalende situated between Ikoyi and Lagos Island).

In the 1990s the Ikoyi Hotel became decrepit and cockroach-infested. It was knocked down in 2005, except for the shell of what was called the Atlantic block, which used to have on its twentieth floor a restaurant that was a smart Lagos meeting-place. In its place was built, with South African partners, the Southern Sun, opposite where once the French Cultural Centre used to hold swinging events (mostly Nigerian bands with very little to do with French culture) that knocked spots off the more prosaic and less inclusive British Council further down the road: both have now both moved deeper into Ikoyi. Some cognoscenti came to feel there was more action at the Goethe Institut on the other side of the lagoon at the beginning of the Lekki motorway.

AWOLOWO ROAD

One particularly evocative highway is the long, curving mainly commer-cial **Awolowo Road**, the soul of southwest Ikoyi. It was built to take the colonial servants and their business counterparts from the business quarters of Lagos Island to the safe dormitory of Ikoyi. The road was named only in the 1950s as independence approached (like its tributary streets **Okoti-Eboh** and **Ribadu**, both independence-era politicians). If one begins at the western end, as the slip roads come off the overhead motorway by the Motor Boat Club, one can move all the way to the Police Barracks at Falomo by way of sundry restaurants and bars, some of which are ephemeral (others such as the Bacchus restaurant and an Indian establishment strangely named the Sherlaton, however, have been there since the 1970s).

Let me quote from my "back page" column in *Business Day*, on the subject of Awolowo Road, to me always a place of pilgrimage:

> It was always between somewhere and somewhere else, and development around it was unplanned and higgledy-piggledy. The houses were much closer together than the roomy properties of true Ikoyi, and it still retains a random feeling in all its long length, from the military hospital by the McGregor Canal at one end, to the Falomo roundabout at the other. It has always been a mix of small shops, restaurants, which are now interspersed regularly with banks and filling stations.

Given its central location, land in Awolowo Road's side streets is now hugely expensive, and one may well expect serious residential and commercial changes in the next few years. But where does the imagination come in, since this is such a manifestation of basic materialism? Not long ago it was entirely resurfaced by Julius Berger (who else?), and on a Sunday you can see it as it was meant to look, although on weekdays its broad pavements are entirely occupied by cars so that unfortunate pedestrians have to take to the road. Being an eccentric *oyinbo*, I took my own walk… down the segment between Keffi Street, and the Polo Club. It was scarcely a walk on the wild side, in spite of *okada* darting like wasps interspersed with the increasingly popular yellow covered tricycle rickshaws known as *keke-napep*, all blending restlessly with the relentless regular traffic.

My main objective in this pedestrian peregrination was the Jazz Hole, more of a magical library than a bookshop, deliciously un-commercial, selling myriad African music CDs as well as stocking an enticing collection of books, so that when one leaves one is poorer financially but richer intellectually and spiritually. It is a true cultural haven in the wilderness, a little like the Interpreter's House in John Bunyan's "Pilgrim's Progress." With the Quintessence gallery/shop, selling cloth, cushions, books and jewelery at the Falomo Shopping Centre, and the already praised Bogobiri Guest House, these shining lights justify making Awolowo Road, against all inconsequential appearances, a true street of the imagination.

The Polo Club, founded (not surprisingly) in colonial times is nowadays a trifle shabby, which is not how I recall it in the early 1970s when it was a smart social spot. There was a period just after the birth of the twenty-first century when it was the scene of pop concerts by performers including the US rappers Naughty by Nature, but these became increasingly rowdy and were stopped after the singing star Usher had to call off his concert because of exceptionally unruly turbulence from "area boys." I was also told a strange story by a resident of the Oniru Estate (which replaced the celebrated Maroko ghetto) of how retired polo ponies were at one time simply put out to grass on Lagos streets and could be seen wandering in a somewhat distressed condition in the estate.

At the Falomo roundabout end is the Falomo Shopping Centre. Built in the 1960s long before anyone thought of shopping plazas let alone malls, it has a pleasingly retro air. Once upon a time journalists used to come here for the Cable Office (when journalists used to have to send press cables in difficult and sweaty conditions) but its main attractions are two typically disorganized bookshops, Glendora (a smaller version of the Jazz Hole) and Bestseller, as well as the already-mentioned Quintessence.

The side roads off Awolowo Road are also atmospheric. In Okotie-Eboh Street, for example, you can find the Ambassadors Hotel, a typical Lagos guesthouse decorated in best Nigerian kitsch (which is only surpassed on the African continent by its South African equivalent). The historic Ribadu Road leading to Dodan Barracks was raced down many times by coup-makers and once used to link directly to Kingsway but was swallowed up by the endlessly spreading military enclave. Keffi Street was where Agence France Presse held out through all the good and bad years when most foreign journalists were discouraged—although, no condition being permanent, even they have moved.

BROAD STREET AND THE MARINA

These are the two great thoroughfares of the city center dating back to the beginnings of British rule, and are surrounded by a network of other historic streets on Lagos Island (**Martins**, **Breadfruit**, **Catholic Mission**, **Campbell**, **Oil Mill**), the old landmarks of the Island in the days when Lagos was the federal capital. Here in Catholic Mission Street is the City Hall built in fine modernistic style for Lagos City Council in the early 1960s, which fell into disrepair (although it was recently refurbished by the Lagos State government as a public function space). It is in the heart of the area which the State government is trying to see revitalized as the main business district, although to some extent that process is defying market forces.

Broad Street still has a few fine buildings such as the government printers and St. George's Hall. It passes through **Tinubu Square**, curving down to Olowogbowo, and was once the veritable hub of Lagos Island and its business district. Of the fine buildings of the early years of the century such as the houses of Henry Carr and Otunba Payne, only the Ilojo Bar, the house of the Olaiya family, remains. It was the first building "listed" for preservation by the Lagos State government, but I am told that only now has the first phase of work begun. The fine colonial Supreme Court building, which had been one of the glories of Tinubu Square, was knocked down just before independence and replaced by fountains. It is now dominated by the Central Bank building, which resembles a bunker, and one fears the square's original soul has been lost.

The Marina was one of the pivots of the city in colonial days, dreamed up in the mid-nineteenth century by McCoskry and Glover as a place to promenade on a previously insalubrious part of the Island. When I first saw it in 1964 it was still a pleasing street, which it was possible to walk along from Christ Church Cathedral via the Post Office to Kingsway Stores. It faced directly on to the lagoon, looking over to the port in Apapa (although already full of the ubiquitous street traders

The Ilojo Bar building on Tinubu Square

who are a permanent feature of the city). Yet the landfill that occurred in the lagoon alongside the Marina in order to build the overhead motorways from the late 1960s onwards destroyed the street's purpose. It also offered a large new area for the same street traders, who burgeoned and multiplied, and although they are regularly cleared away they somehow keep returning. There was once a green space called the Lovers' Garden in the Onikan area, where the Island Club (once a great social center that embodied the post-independence spirit), the old football stadium and the Nigeria Museum now lie. Here is also the City Mall, originally a part of the Nigeria Museum and now one of the new shopping malls that have sprung up in the last ten years, and the ocher-colored building of the MUSON Centre (built for the Music Society of Nigeria through private sector sponsorship, notably from Shell) of fine concert halls.

The Marina ceased many years ago to be a promenade. There is a stretch near to the Governor's current residence that has been planted with young palm trees as part of plans to re-beautify the city, although because of incessant traffic it is fairly inaccessible to the general public. Central to the present-day Marina is the CMS bus station/motor park—a hub of both *danfo* (minibuses), *molue* (bigger buses) and now the red rapid transport buses—which has been moved onto the reclaimed area where the car park is gradually given over to other uses such as a Coca-Cola depot and a private power station for the Governor's residence. The spot is named after the Church Missionary Society whose original building on Lagos Island was located nearby, and the name has clung on, in part through the bookshop (renamed CSS or Church and Schools Supply in the 1970s). What the CMS once was has long since been forgotten, living on only in the cries of the bus touts.

IGBOSERE ROAD/BAMGBOSE STREET

These two arteries of the old Lagos seem mostly stuck in a time warp of small single-story establishments. They were among the central streets of the Brazilian quarter, still the most evocative part of the old city, even if some of the most classic examples of Brazilian architecture have been destroyed. They all lead to **Campos Square**, symbolic heart of the Brazilian quarter, but like Tinubu Square a shell compared to what it was in its heyday. Campos Square leads to **Kakawa Street** and **Odunlami Street**, both of which have witnessed the loss of many magnificent buildings (with some such as the Water House lovingly restored). Campos Square itself (named after Ramao Campos, one of the first Brazilian repatriates) is where the head of government even from colonial times, so it is said, always had to make a speech confirming Lagos as the federal capital. The last one was reportedly delivered by President Shehu Shagari in 1982.

Both **Igbosere Road** and **Bamgbose Street** offer the same profusion of barbers, workshops and snack bars, to which are now added cyber-cafés, all in the same single-story buildings of the stone-fronted Portuguese/Brazilian style dating back to the late nineteenth century, in poor repair but still showing characteristic architectural detail. Once this area was mainly residential, and a surprising number of people still live there in houses long inhabited by the same families. Igbosere has begun to see higher buildings, including the offices that once housed *Next* newspaper in its brief life. In other circumstances the whole segment could be restored as a heritage area, but it is hard to see that happening now.

AHMADU BELLO WAY

This is the best-known major road on Victoria Island. It begins at the old bridge over Five Cowrie Creek and passes by the Bonny Camp, which in the era of coups housed the presidential guard, having previously been the site of the International Trade Fair staged at independence in 1960. The road moves past the Silverbird building, with popular cinemas, shops and cafés, and the Federal Palace Hotel before entering a different, more open phase with on one side the shoreline and on the other a series of former State Government lodges (some in a state of disrepair) and other sundry blocks such as the striking electric blue pyramidal headquarters of the IMB (International Merchant Bank) built in 1985. The Way then sweeps inland to meet one of the city's most celebrated landmarks in a commanding position by the Kuramo water, the Eko Hotel. This was for a long time in splendid isolation, but now it has not only extensions to the Kuramo Lodge and the Eko Suites but also in its vicinity boutique hotels like the two Proteas.

Above all, this highway is home of the legendary Bar Beach, the least touristy stretch of metropolitan sand in the world, often lovingly photographed, scene of execution squads for coup plotters and armed robbers and home of the white-clad evangelical groups, especially the Cherubim and Seraphim who feature in films like Ola Balogun's *Money Power* and in Talib Kweli's Lagos-filmed music video "Deliver Us." It also appears in novels like Okey Ndibe's *Arrows of Rain* and Soyinka's *Trials of Brother Jero*.

The beach has now become a giant land reclamation project, described on its placards as the "permanent solution" to its problems. I visited the site in 2006, facing the single-story palace of the Oniru—one of the Idejo, the historic landowning White Cap chiefs of Lagos—and was told then that the objective, through land-filling with vast quantities of sand, was to re-structure the groin/mole and push the shoreline back to its 1908 position in preparation for the intended site of the Eko Atlantic City. Although alongside the improvised cluster of bars and restaurant, the new, more effi-cient but bleaker Bar Beach, with almost military fortifications, has already changed forever.

The work has put an end to the notorious Bar Beach ocean surges that had grown more and more frequent, threatening increasing flooding in Victoria Island and serious erosion of Ahmadu Bello Way, contrasting sadly with the dream of a marina comparable to the Victoria and Alfred Water-front in Cape Town. The plans for the new Eko Atlantic City, self-sus-taining in utilities such as power and water and complete with shopping malls and condos, are going ahead, and much of the reclaimed land has been bought, but the whole concept still arouses criticism and scepticism (one friend of mine ironically calls it "Eko Atlantis City") and it is likely to be a long journey. How will this vast new urban complex, sometimes spoken of as an African Dubai, relate to the rest of the mega-city? And another question is beginning to be asked more anxiously: will the ocean surges simply be pushed further eastward along the shoreline towards Lekki?

Nearer the port area of the creek is the Federal Palace Hotel, with its amazing views across to Apapa, and other structures like the Maersk build-ing, the Leventis family home and that harbinger of change the Silverbird Mall with its cinemas and bookshop. One should also mention the two large blocks on Adeola Odeku—the icy azure towers built by Ocean Oil and the Globacom office with gold-plated portico and a massive cast-iron bull outside (said to symbolize the business powers of Mike Adenuga and the tearaway success of his mobile phone company).

Apapa, Ajegunle, the Badagry Road

On the mainland, perhaps unfairly, I find myself descending on **Wharf Road**, Apapa, probably because I once wrote in *Business Confidential* that it was a seriously bleak introduction to the port suburb, with its "graveyard of lorries, and rubbish tips that sometimes resembled a nuclear winter." There is, however, much more to Apapa than meets the eye, especially in its quiet residential areas where I used to stay in an agreeable *Daily Times* 1950s house on Marine Road with a view of the creek at the bottom of the garden. Because of the proximity of the port and a cluster of industries also dating back to the 1950s, it was considered "trade" and socially inferior to "the Island," but there are many who prefer the relative calm of Apapa to the hurly-burly of Lagos proper.

Beyond Apapa is the aristocratic ghetto of Ajegunle (not so much a collection of streets, more a concept) where visiting filmmakers go with their hand-held cameras if they want to do slums, but which still has a kind of pride in its populism. A friend describes it thus: "Ajegunle, a slum, a melting-pot, innovator of pidgin, and of musical styles with outdoor stages, home of mob justice and workshops that can break a stolen car down to parts in half a day." The British High Commission has a capacity building project there (ajegunle.org) offering work experience to disadvantaged youths, which had been personally encouraged by the then High Commissioner Bob Dewar. It was at a sports ground in Ajegunle that the late great political activist Gani Fawehinmi (a crusading lawyer called to the bar in the London Inns of Court) launched his quixotic presidential campaign in 2003 for his National Conscience Party, which I followed with a small group of journalists both Nigerian and foreign to hear the immortal "Gani" launch his manifesto, reasserting his claims as an anti-corruption crusader but knowing he was never going to make it.

Leading to Ajegunle is the **Malu Road** in Apapa, noted as the place where herders from the north bring their livestock (*malu* is cow in the Yoruba language). Once in the early 1970s I was to go meet two friends from the *Daily Times*, Angus Okoli and Tony Momoh, at the Peoples' Hotel in Ajegunle, a creek-side establishment where you could knock back a chilled Gulder or two. I took a taxi to get there but became blocked by a herd of long-horned cows on the Malu Road, and the herder came and slapped the side of the cab saying, *Oyinbo, wey you dey go* (White Man, where are you going?), a question of such philosophical intensity that it became my own catchphrase. Some thirty years later, frequenting Chike Nwagbogu's cultural hub Nimbus, I combined on special occasions with musician Tunde Kuboye to use it as the chorus of a song:

> Oyinbo wey you dey go? [repeated three times],
> na Peoples' Hotel Ajegunle.

It was a vehicle for improvisation, almost a kind of rap monologue with Tunde's own lines "You've got your technology, we have our history" developing further the philosophy, as well as the musical frame. Alas, it was never recorded.

Beyond Ajegunle lies one of the most sinister places in Lagos, the high-walled maximum security prison of Kirikiri, built around the time of independence but only fully operational when Nigeria's political crisis began in 1966. It is mentioned in more political memoirs than you can count (Bola Ige, Alex Ekwueme) including those of the former Biafran leader Odumegwu Ojukwu, who during 1984 was detained after the Buhari coup having by then returned to Nigerian politics from exile in Côte d'Ivoire. In his memoir *Because I Am Involved* he writes with his usual visceral flair: "In Kirikiri there is no privacy. Leaders belch and fart, sometimes louder than armed robbers. We scratch and pick our noses. In Kirikiri we are constantly in battle with the animal in us. In this place there is no justice, there is no beauty, there is no pleasure and there is no satisfaction."

Kirikiri's notoriety is also handled memorably by writers who were inmates under Abacha. The TV journalist Chris Anyanwu in her grueling book *Days of Terror* tells of time she did in Kirikiri among other Nigerian prisons. The writer Chris Abani's book of poems *Kalaluta Republic* was named after a cell in Kirikiri, which, it seems, inspired Fela Kuti to baptize his home as the Kalakuta Republic (see Chapter 9). The prison takes its name from the slum of Kirikiri, described by one Lagos newspaper as "where every resident is considered in prison."

The **Badagry Road** is a great arterial heading westwards to the border of the Benin Republic and has always been one of the main routes out of the city. The mega-city is now increasingly developing along it on each side, even if there are still some stretches of green space towards the border. It is at present a dual carriageway constructed in the early 1970s, but work has already begun on converting it to a ten-lane highway in a major project that is currently being undertaken by the Lagos State government. For the past thirty years this segment of road has been planned to be part of the Pan-African Highway stretching from Dakar to Nairobi (via Abidjan, Accra and Douala across the tropical forests of Cameroon and Congo). The plans can all still be viewed at the headquarters of the African Development Bank in Tunis and the UN Economic Commission for Africa in Addis Ababa. This beautiful vision still has many unrealized stretches, but it is from Abidjan to Lagos, always intended as one of its major hubs, that most serious efforts, if still incomplete, have been made.

There are a number of landmarks along the Badagry Road from its beginnings in Apapa where it winds past creeks and the industrial shapes of Tin Can Island, Lagos' second and modern container port built with oil money in the 1970s. The road runs past the astonishing baroque structures of the Eleganza shopping mall along to the huge spare parts markets at Alaba and the International Trade Fair site, now also partly used as a market. These are universes of the "sector beneath," the subculture of the informal sector. On this part of the Atlantic coast there are also some under-publicized resort hotels such as Whispering Palms near Badagry, not as well-known as some on the Lekki coastline, and secluded coves where rich Lagosians have built beach houses and park their motor boats.

YABA, IKEJA, SURULERE

Still on the mainland, we move northwards to Herbert Macaulay Street in Yaba, one of the most historic streets on the mainland. Macaulay's statue, already cited and complete with trademark moustache, stands on the corner of Commercial Street, where the famous early highlife venue the Ambassador Hotel was located. This was near the old Casino cinema and the Yaba and Ojuelegba roundabouts. The Ikorodu Road used to be the main highway out of Lagos if you were traveling either north to Ibadan or east to Benin. It is still the beginning of the Ibadan Expressway.

It also used to lead to the once-international airport which became "internal" only after Murtala Mohammed International Airport was built in the 1970s. The old single-story sheds I saw in 1964 when I first came to Lagos remained in use for a remarkably long time, perhaps because a replacement that had been built was destroyed by fire. It has now been

Makoko, "stilt city"

handsomely rebuilt as Murtala Mohammed II. The Yaba coastline stretches from the faded modernism of Lagos University at Akoka to the iconic stilt city of Makoko, now under threat from Lagos State planners.

For those arriving and departing by air the Ikorodu Road was a highway of the memory, and there were always a number of familiar landmarks to look out for such as the modern (considered positively futuristic in 1964) Methodist Cathedral in Yaba, the enticing entrance to the Palm Grove estate or the Hotel de Bobby, built by the musician and bandleader Bobby Benson, which housed a much-loved, long-running night club, the Caban Bamboo. A few tears were shed among old friends when the Hotel de Bobby building was only recently finally demolished; I used to wonder if it was the inspiration for the open-air club in the first scene of Soyinka's *The Interpreters*, but that is never identified and is not even definitely in Lagos.

One used to know when it was time to turn left to the airport when one saw the illuminated sign of the compound of the evangelist Jesus of Oyinbo, who was even commemorated in an erudite social anthropologists' article in *New Society* in 1964. The road also passes the entrance to the Ikeja barracks (scene of so much bloody action in the July coup in 1966, and of the ammunition explosions of January 2002), then the Mandarin Chinese restaurant, one of the city's earliest Chinese restaurants. The Ikorodu Road, more impersonal with fewer recognizable points of memory, is now mainly notable for leading on to the major highway, the **Ibadan Expressway**— home of many of the religious campsites which are now so much a feature of Lagos and whose preachers both local and international are advertised on a multitude of hoardings. (On which subject, there are certain motorway hoardings that have survived for as long as I can remember, such as Dr. Meyer's Gripe Water and Orheptal, still capable of giving me an emotional pang of nostalgia until finally removed in 2009.)

One street in Ikeja that acquired notoriety in the 1980s was **Allen Avenue**, which runs for a relatively short distance from the roundabout on **Awolowo Way** (near the airport hotel) down to the **Opebi Road**. It was at that time reputed to be the home of the notorious local drug barons who had thrived in the heyday of the cocaine business during the economic downturn of that decade. The barons perpetrated a famous shootout at the picturesquely named fast food joint Chicken George (named after Kunta Kinte's grandson in the hugely popular TV series *Roots* which had a devoted following in Nigeria), long since renamed. It was also not so far from the luxury homes of the Ikeja Government Residential Area (GRA), originally built for expatriate company executives, but the street itself, with nothing very spectacular in it building-wise, has nevertheless inspired poetry and even fiction, although my Lagos friends tell me that it has lost some of the rakish glamour it used to have. There are still popular joints such as Club Do It All, Storm Night and Club Unique. Bankong Obi in the poem "Apparitions on Allen Avenue" captures something of its louche ambiance:

Flashy bikinis of liberal minds
Unleashing flickers to tame broods
Of lech, love and life, about 'want' and 'norm'
We chase as NEPA calls,
Haste to chastise as cockerels herald daybreak

A corrosive poem by Helon Habila also evokes the red light seediness of the street in its heyday, while Ahmed Maiwada's poem, also called "Allen Avenue," waxes even more lyrical about its shady quality:

Curling breeze from the palms' nostril:
The final push on my stumbling heart.
I wear my naked eyes, shaded:
Wildcards to help download the night…

Both poems feature in Odia Ofeimun's brilliant anthology *Lagos of the Poets*.

One should also mention that there was even a popular rap number called "Allen Avenue" which featured on the first CD in 2005 of the lesbian rapper Weird MC. The last word, however, has to come from Maik Nwosu's haunting Lagos novel *Alpha Song*, where he describes "the famous Allen Avenue" as "so long on promise, so short on redemption."

The **Agege Motor Road** must also be classified as a street of the imagination, bizarrely immortalized in a French song of the 1970s called—less imaginatively—"Agege Motor Road" and recorded by a now forgotten *chansonnier*, Jean Mauzac. I am grateful to the filmmaker Ola Balogun, who worked at that time in the Nigerian Embassy in Paris, for this unusual recollection, an illustration of how something unexpected can become a source of inspiration anywhere in the planet. Adventurous musicians like Ginger Baker began to make their way to Nigeria in the 1970s, and in 1973 Paul McCartney's Wings recorded much of the *Band on the Run* album there.

The Motor Road is one of the oldest highways on the mainland, built at the same time as the railway to Otta in the 1890s and long predating the Ibadan Expressway. The road, which winds through the turbulent district of Mushin, is uninspiring for much of its length, as is suggested by the very name "motor road," but its appeal to the imagination comes in part from its connection to the Fela Anikulapo Kuti myth, especially at the iconic roundabout Oju-Elegba commemorated in Fela's lyrics.

Another "street of the imagination" on the mainland has to be **Panti Street** in Yaba, home of the Criminal Investigation Department headquarters immortalized by brutally frank stories about sensational crimes of all kinds in the popular weekly newspaper of the 1960s and 1970s *Lagos Weekend*, a paper like no other. The innocent way the most disgraceful offenses were reported in a cool matter-of-fact way, many of them by the mild-mannered reporter Chinaka Fynecountry, has never been equaled.

Although Yaba was once the main focal point on the mainland before Ikeja, one should also take account of Surulere, built alongside the new highway **Western Avenue** as part of the pre-independence expansion of the 1950s. It was a getaway for the middle classes from the hustle of Lagos Island before Victoria Island became a serious residential proposition. Peter Marris in *Family and Social Change in an African City* even refers to the "bourgeois idyll" of the estates built at the time by the Lagos Executive Development Board in Surulere. The name means "patience is rewarded" in Yoruba, a suitable motto for the upwardly mobile. It was still a pretty good place to live in the 1970s, especially as the spanking new National Stadium was built there and the new National Theatre was not too far away. Although there are still many comfortable residences, it gives an air of having seen better days, as do both stadium and theater. Western Avenue has been renamed **Funso Williams Avenue**, after a popular politician assassinated in 2007.

MILE TWO AND AMUWO ODOFIN

Although the long **Apapa Expressway**, which connects the Third Mainland Bridge to the Badagry Road, scarcely excites the imagination, there is a point at which it reaches its climax on joining and crossing the Badagry Road, where the Lagos addict might stop and linger. It is **Mile Two**, the nightmare spaghetti junction of loops, access roads and bridges where Julius Berger's handiwork got seriously out of hand, a scene of armed robbery and fights between gangs of truckers, yet passed through (epileptically) by thousands of motorized Lagosians each day, and also the home of the main food retail markets for the city. For me it is still synonymous with frustration, but I recall its dazzling mix of idiosyncratic signs, shacks and *bukka*s, and wrecked lorries from the time when I passed through it every day on my way to the Amuwo Odofin offices of *Business Day*, Nigeria's first financial daily where I played a modest role in its early days.

This was an unusual Lagos experience in that it gave me familiarity with the mainland, with areas that are somehow considered wilderness but are nothing of the kind. **Amuwo Odofin** is a very ordinary local government area with a number of housing projects and its own commercial areas such as the bustling **Maza Maza** (a Hausa word for confusion). I found the real Amuwo Odofin when I talked to the local Rotary Club in a hotel. The place figured in a number of diaries which I wrote in *Business Day*, including one titled "The Alligators of Amuwo Odofin," based on some fictitious alligators that were imagined to have been spotted in a patch of swampy waste ground next to Wordsmithes, the printing works on the **Festac Link Road** where *Business Day* started its life in 2001. I would gaze from the window hoping to see them, my imagination fueled by all the stories of manatees (mamy-watas) lurking in the creeks. The possibility of alligators in Amuwo Odofin alongside such an ordinary office became transmuted for me into a symbol of journalistic aspiration—that anything is possible if you can make it so. Thus presented, this conceit came to represent all the impossible ambition and irrepressible optimism that you breathe in the air in Lagos. While on the subject of Amuwo Odofin, I must note my surprise and pleasure at spotting the Taiwo Okutubo bus stop, recalling the first Lagos bureau chief of *West Africa*, ex-*Daily Times* newsroom veteran and prominent figure in the Island Club.

The link road leads to **Festac Town** itself. This was a major urban housing development built to house participants during the FESTAC of 1977. In its present condition it can no longer be said to be the new town dreamed of in the 1970s and is yet one more symbol of the dream deferred. "Festac," as it is known, has become in many respects a case history of urban dilapidation, particularly notorious for the size and longevity of its potholes. Nothing, however, is beyond restoration. The creek-side Durbar Hotel that was built for FESTAC was spectacularly refurbished a couple of years ago and became first the Novotel FESTAC, and then Golden Tulip FESTAC, while charmingly retaining the Amuwo Odofin address.

Street scene, Broad Street

Chapter Eleven

THE FUTURE CITY?

"If we can change this place, everywhere else will change."
Governor Babatunde Fashola, interview with the
author, August 2008

"Nothing is impossible in this town."
Valentine Okogwu, Lagos architect

"Lagos survives. It pulsates. It grows. It works."
Richard Dowden, *Africa: Altered States, Ordinary
Miracles*, 2008

"DELIRIOUS LAGOS"

The challenge for Lagos today is that of the ever-expanding city, the twenty-first-century megalopolis, soon to be one of the world's largest. Its population is now estimated conservatively, by the UN among others to be anything between fifteen and eighteen million, and is expected to reach a possible 25 million by 2015. By 2025 it is expected to be the third largest city in the world.

The 2006 census, we have seen, produced the curiously low figure of some nine million. It is true that this figure was for Lagos State only, not taking into account the numbers in the Lagos conurbation that are found over the border in Ogun State. Even so, it still looks like a serious under-counting. Another explanation was that many of the immigrants from other states living in Lagos went to their home states to be counted. There was still concrete evidence, however, of imperfection in the census exercise and perceived inefficiencies in the count, although there was no proof of deliberate under-counting. Governor Fashola told me in a 2008 interview that Lagos State rejected the figures and produced its own figure of over seventeen million compiled by its own parallel census officers, which he insisted was the authentic figure that could be used as a basis for planning. This figure is certainly more in line with international estimates, even if the National Population Commission hotly contested the Lagos State figure.

The image of Lagos often presented outside Nigeria is that of one of

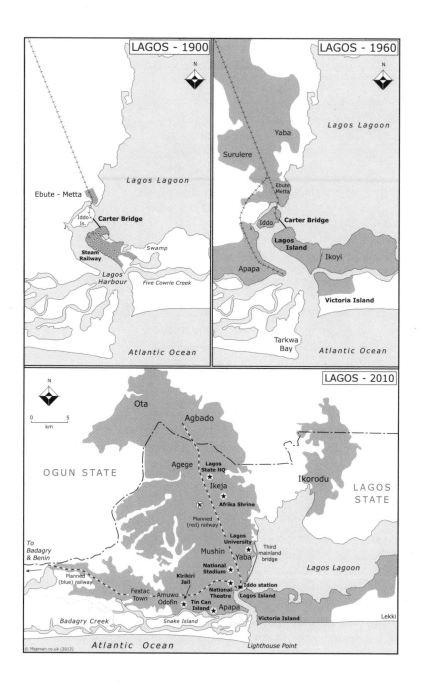

the world's most turbulent and alarming cities, bringing a shudder at its mere mention, but is not the reality different? Rem Koolhaas, the controversial avant-garde Dutch architect, for example, has put forward a different perspective: he finds the idea of Lagos as a hyper-anarchic twenty-first-century city intolerably exhilarating, in keeping with his general thrill at the nature of cities seen first of all in his book on *Delirious New York*, a title he could equally have applied (and may yet) to our present subject matter, as *Delirious Lagos*. But behind some of his more eccentric hyperbole he has hit on one truth—the logic of the city's profound sense of autonomy.

In a recent article in the *New York Review of Books*, Koolhaas is (somewhat improbably) quoted as saying that on his first visit he had been too nervous to get out of his car, and obtained use of a presidential helicopter: "What seemed on the ground an accumulation of dysfunctional movements seemed from above an impressive performance, evidence of how well Lagos might perform if it were the third largest city in the world." He identifies that what helps Lagos work is a myriad of functioning ad hoc structures, a lot of them dependent on and interwoven with the informal sector but with their own set of official relationships, such as the deeply influential market organizations and different forms of trade and professional unions from market women and transport workers to cab drivers.

IMAGES OF A CITY

Lagos has always been a vivid subject for photography, a medium particularly responsive to the immediacy of the city, and there has always been good photography of Lagos, even going back to the earliest days of the "seventh art" in the nineteenth century. There is an excellent collection of old photographs of Lagos in the book called *Eko: Landmarks of Lagos, Nigeria*, published with the enlightened sponsorship of Mandilas Group in 1999. Back in the 1960s and 1970s professional photographers such as Peter Obe working mainly with newspapers and magazines produced pictures in which Lagos featured dramatically and unsentimentally in publications like *Drum*. Another well-known photographer, Sunmi Smart-Cole, has unremittingly recorded major political events and Lagos society for the past thirty years: at one time he had a newspaper called *Lagos Life*. But there are many who have excellent collections of photos going back to the 1950s, such as the architects John and Jill Godwin, although earlier pictures are rarer.

It is only more recently, it seems, that the idea of Lagos as subject matter for more conscious "art photography" has emerged with a transforming effect. The Jamaican photographer Armet Francis saw the potential at the time of FESTAC, as is clear in his book *The Black Triangle*. Increasingly, however, some of the best work in this regard has been done by Nigerian photographers. The Lagos photos by Bode Akinbiyi shown in the "Africa Remix" exhibition at the Hayward Gallery in London, staged as part of the Africa 2005 celebration of African art and culture, are a good example. The event also included the exhibition at the gallery of the Camberwell School of Art titled "Depth of Field." This showed the work of six Lagos photographers operating at the time as a cooperative, which, said a critic at the *Times*, was "filled with the fructifying energy and psychological liberty of ordinary people cheek by jowl in their growing millions…" They covered chaotic transport scenes, markets at night, the prostitutes of Kuramo Beach—all "life on the edge." Mention should also be made of the pictures of Jide Alakija which were shown at the Lagos Future City exhibition organized by the Bukka Collective in London in early 2006, and which featured humdrum but intrinsically Lagos sights such as the façade of a Mr Bigg's fast food store.

The realization by the new school of photographers in Lagos that there is amazing subject matter in their city is entirely in keeping with contemporary ideas of photography as a medium for our times. Indeed, they have increasingly found that the camera can be used as a weapon of social concern: see, for example, the series of photographs by Jide Adeniyi-Jones, a seasoned practitioner of the art (originally shown in 2002 in an exhibition at the Nimbus Gallery and still to be found on the walls of Bogobiri Guesthouse in south-west Ikoyi) of advertisement hoardings for MTN, one of the most successful of the new purveyors of the ubiquitous mobile phone. One picture shows, symbolically, mud plastered over one of the hoardings.

The large and handsomely presented coffee table book *Lagos: A City at Work*, published by Glendora Books in 2005, makes full and effective use of photos (all by Nigerians) as artistic items. It is almost as if the text chapters, noted elsewhere, are subordinate to the physical excitement of the image on the printed page. Some may feel this is beginning to come dangerously close to the notion of what one may call "Lagos chic," the attraction of the wild side for a new and select breed of international travelers, products of the globalization of international tourism. This heresy (for it is a kind of *trahison des clercs*) is articulated in the blatantly arty volume *Lagos la tropicale* (2001) by two French photographers, Tony Soulié and Dominique Sigaud, some of whose pictures appear to have been erratically smeared with paint, using the city as merely a self-conscious background for the artist's own graffiti.

"ONE OF THE BEST KEPT SECRETS IN AFRICA"

For a long time the hidden attractions of the "city by the lagoon," as Ofeimun likes to call it, have been one of the best kept secrets in Africa, especially the existential energy and excitement that it releases as seen in its music, its art, its literature. It is something that the more adventurous tourist guides are beginning to dwell on, but, as we have seen, it has not really penetrated the compartmentalized official mind of the Nigerian tourist authorities. This may be changing with the development of the sub-cultures of the electronic age. For example, a more imaginatively practical awareness of all that Lagos has to offer could be detected on the website www.lagoslive.com. This was the joint creation of Jeremy Weate, an Abuja-resident British expatriate, and his wife Bibi Bakary-Weate. The website, born in 2005, contrived to be an up-to-date take on the upside of social life for the new internationally-minded middle classes, combined with reviews of cultural activities, but has for the time being fallen dormant. Alive and active is www.lagoscityphotos.blogspot.com, a mixture of cultural news and images.

Among all the ephemeral websites an even more unusual one, currently it seems bearing the domain name www.14thMay.com, (formerly www.lagosstateofmind), was devised by the graphic designer Emeka Ogboh. He was one of the artists included in a remarkable show of paintings and photographs at the Lagos Civic Centre in February 2008, which had the title "The Unbreakable Nigerian Spirit," and subsequently went to both Abuja and Amsterdam. Ogboh's website unusually concentrated on recording the sounds of Lagos, which the creator finds are already changing so fast as the city evolves that they are hard to keep up with. He predicts with certainty that the cries of the touts for the yellow *danfo* and *molue* buses—"CMS," "Obalende" and other noted bus stops—will eventually be phased out as the traditional vehicles are replaced by the Bus Rapid Transport (BRT) system with its red buses. The yellow vehicle brand is as much

The BRT bus route on the Marina

associated with Lagos as red buses with London, although there is less sentimental attachment. But will there eventually be some museum piece *danfo* and *molue* survivors like the Routemaster buses in London?

Many of these talents to be found in Lagos are struggling and underrated, but "unbreakable" is not a bad word to describe their persistence in finding ways to express themselves. The 2008 show was notable for being carefully selected for quality, which is not always the case in art exhibitions in Nigeria, partly because the yardsticks for what is good art are sometimes fuzzy.

This points the way to one of the striking features of this constantly surprising city—that behind the mask of relentless functional philistinism and the apparent lack of awareness of how crude and ugly a city can be, one constantly comes across islands of cultural activity. These have been described as havens in a previous chapter, but it is worth repeating that they form a core of the "city of the imagination."

A Theory of Lagos?

Is it permissible to try and formulate a theory of Lagos, or even to presume to enter the city's soul? We have already looked at the Lagos of the poets, who always knew that the city had a soul, but we also are obliged to turn back to the architects, who have the keenest understanding of what a city might be. From the colonial period onwards there have been various attempts to devise a plan for Lagos, especially after the creation of the Lagos Executive Development Board (LEDB) in 1932, which sought to balance the peculiar problems of Lagos Island with organized expansion on the mainland. While plans are only guidance documents, without statutory authority, the constant resort to them is an indication of the scale of the dilemma the city represents.

The first coherent multi-dimensional plan for Lagos was that of Otto Königsberger for the UN in 1964, which concentrates as much on basic facilities such as sewerage, waste disposal and low-cost housing as on a futuristic gaze at the stars. The plan of Doxiades in the early 1970s, taking account of the astonishing growth of population and the pressures it placed on infrastructure, especially roads and transport, formed the basis of subsequent plans including those made for adjustment after the withdrawal of the federal capital leading up to the grand designs of the Tinubu/Fashola continuum under the Fourth Republic. These include the fantastic configurations generated by the 2006 Presidential Task Force on the Mega-City, a federal project which goes beyond Lagos State to include Ogun State (significantly calling itself the Gateway State), increasingly a part of the Lagos conurbation.

The small but unusually creative collective of architects in London with whom I am happy to be associated and who have called themselves Bukka (after the Nigerian street cafeterias) have certainly been trying to pursue the subject of a theory for the city, the "problematic" of Lagos as an uncontrollable mega-city being their principal preoccupation. This has been explored in both exhibitions and workshops in which ideas of how rapid and uncontrolled growth in a setting such as Lagos can lead to its own generic. Giles Omezi, one of the leading lights of Bukka, provides examples of how the simplistically conceived expressways of the 1960s evolved into "marketspace" or sites where "it seems the dispossessed and new urban arrivals advanced their collective claims and right to the city." This poses the dialectic of elitist versus populist that was already there in the colonial period. Adebayo Lawal, in his essay on "Markets and Street Traders in Lagos," says: "the perspective of the silent commoners on the urban problems was at variance with that of the affluent European class, who by bylaws and fiscal policies were bent on turning Lagos into a modern utopia or garden city." This is a contradiction that lurks at the heart of the new Lagos now being conceived.

Any broad discussion of architects and Lagos somehow returns to the subject of Koolhaas, although certainly not in isolation—where, to do him justice, he has never sought to be. His Harvard project on Lagos is nothing if not a cooperative effort and has consistently worked against dogmatism and preconceived ideas in a constant state of existential revisionism. It was Kunle Adeyemi, an architect with Koolhaas' office in Rotterdam, who uttered a dictum at a Bukka meeting in London: "Lagos is a state of mind." It has to be a holistic theory of people, incorporating the writers and the musicians, the Lagos boys, the okada drivers, the market women, the "managers of the night," the socialites and "big girls" from the pages of the schlock journals, the financial analysts and the guerrilla journalists— all Lagos characters—into a theory of the city.

The already mentioned *Lagos: A City at Work* has rich content among the photos including an interview with Koolhaas as well as with the god-father of urbanism in Nigeria, Professor Akin Mabogunje, and the architect David Aradeon. All underline the importance of architecture and design in the theory of the city, the true channels of the imagination. A growing body of literature looking at this aspect of Lagos has been developing including some of the work that Bukka has been doing drawing attention to the possibilities offered by the increasingly central position of the city in global society, seen in the symposium *Lagos: Mega-city or Crisis City* at the School of Oriental and African Studies (SOAS) of London University in June 2010.

How to situate the much touted idea of the "mega-city"? Lagos has been changing before one's eyes—once again taking in land from the lagoon as has happened since the middle of the nineteenth century, the most spectacular part being the Bar Beach reclamation scheme on which work has already begun with Eko Atlantic City as the goal. The infilling up to the 1908 shoreline is the most ambitious maritime scheme since the building of the mole and the opening up of the port area in the first decade of the last century. As we have noted, there are some fears that changes to the mole may have pushed the ocean surges further along the coast to the Lekki beaches, but nothing is proven and the dream of a new self-sufficient modern quarter in the heart of Lagos, with hotels, malls and condos seems enough to drive the ambition forward.

The same development on the basis of reclamation has already happened on Banana Island at the eastward end of Ikoyi. The eastward expansion on the Lekki Peninsula, the new Badagry highway and the light rail mass transit projects are all ambitious schemes devised in the post-1999 period. Some have seemed like fantasies when first mooted, but so much of what was planned is already happening that anything may now look possible. Governor Fashola, interviewed by the author in 2008, referred in different places to both Dubai (which he had studied "intensely") and, a little surprisingly, Disneyland. Nigeria is a country where people go on dreaming dreams, even if they sometimes have unintended consequences.

From Tinubu to Fashola

Can we look forward to Lagos State becoming a completely urban area, a vast conurbation evolving into a proper city state, made all the more unusual because of the peculiar geographical arrangements of creeks, islands and lagoons? What are the chances of the long dreamed for special status for a very special city? It certainly now appears to have the backbone and the financial means for such aspirations. For, as one of the richest of Nigeria's 36 states, it has considerably capacity to provide funds from its own resources.

Above all, in the post-1999 civilian dispensation there have been great strides in improving revenue collection. Governor Fashola says that his predecessor Bola Tinubu took it as a personal challenge, and from 600 million naira a month in 1999 revenue increased to seven billion a month in 2007 and since then to fourteen billion a month. An aggressive tax compliance campaign has put in place facilities for self-assessment and removing bureaucratic difficulties. Revenue from the federal government budget represents thirty per cent of the annual Lagos State budget, so the State is contributing seventy per cent from within. Although this might seem to position Lagos advantageously vis-à-vis other Nigerian states, in his interview Governor Fashola reminded me that "we are per capita the poorest state in the country." Every other state is multiplied four times in

Lagos, which is a magnet to the rest of the country. "We are our own worst enemy for our hospitality and our successes."

The idea of an overhead railway, I am reliably informed by Odia Ofeimun, who was once Chief Awolowo's private secretary, goes back to the time when Awolowo was Premier of the Western Region in the late 1950s. Although Lagos had then reverted to being federal territory after its brief spell in the Western Region earlier in the decade, it was still considered a part of Yorubaland, and Awolowo's party under a succession of names (from the Action Group to the Unity Party of Nigeria to the Social Democratic Party to the Alliance for Democracy to the Action Congress) was always able to control it, usually against the influence (and sometimes manipulations) of whichever was the ruling party.

The railway project only took solid form when Awolowo's party won the first democratic election in Lagos State in 1979 and Lateef Jakande became Governor (see profile in Chapter 8). The overhead Metroline running from Ikeja to Lagos Island was a popular if costly project, and with the economic downturn of the 1980s was killed off, it was said on the advice of the World Bank—although there were those who said that the military government of General Muhammadu Buhari which came in after the 1983 coup was happy to sabotage what was seen as a political and populist project. The idea was dormant through the worst years of military rule, but was only revived with the return to civilian rule and the "natural" rule of the Alliance for Democracy and its successors.

Work has begun: Governor Fashola's current project is for two lines, the red line from Okokomaiko far to the west on the Badagry Road, and the blue line from beyond Agege in the northwest (near the international airport) joining together to go over the lagoon next to Eko bridge, ending in a new terminus on the Marina. And there are five more linked rail lines in the pipeline for the next thirty years. Of great interest is a number of new planned bridges, notably the link between Lekki and Ikoyi (already well advanced) as well as a second Falomo bridge not far away—both to relieve pressure on the new Lekki toll road which risks heavy congestion. More dramatic is the planned Fourth Mainland Bridge linking Lekki and Ikorodu on the east side of the lagoon, which effectively creates a circular road giving two different routes from eastern Lagos to the airport. This bridge, to be privately financed, has a two-tier design with shops and markets on one level on the principle of the Ponte Vecchio in Florence.

Oshodi before the clearance

This takes on board elements of the fantasizing of one Lagos architect who sees Five Cowrie Creek (between Ikoyi and Lekki) as a network of bridges like Venice or Amsterdam. For a long time these were pipe dreams, but Fashola at least has made some of them seem attainable.

Thus dreams of a "Lagos renaissance" entertained by planners and academics have begun to be taken up again by politicians, faced with the remorseless and continued growth of the Lagos conurbation into the southern part of Ogun State and westward along the Badagry Road and eastward into the open spaces along the Lekki Peninsula. The question has to be asked, how much further can it expand? And can there be urban planning any more in this situation? Indeed, it is impossible to imagine how Lagos might be even in twenty years' time.

MEGA-CITY OR WORLD CITY?

In this context we need to look at the important concept of "world cities," which tends to be favored by the UN, rather than that of mega-city which was first posed by Bola Tinubu when Governor of Lagos. P. J. Taylor, in the 1999 Annual Political Geography lecture in London, said: "world cities are the loci not just of services in the central place sense, but of unique knowledge complexes" such as financing, accountancy and corporate law, where practitioners are not just servicing global capital but creating new products. This puts them very much in the context of the global economy, but they also have a political and cultural dimension that makes them sometimes quite easy to define.

Thus, according to Taylor, "Amsterdam and Zurich are not mega-cities but are certainly world cities, while Calcutta and Lagos are mega-cities but not world cities." Similarly "the smallest two economies incorporating world cities are Hungary and Czech Republic and there are only two countries above them with no evidence of world city formation [Pakistan and Nigeria]." To which one might add that Tokyo is among several world cities that can also be counted as controlled mega-cities, while Mumbai is a mega-city that has, in the age of globalization, developed serious aspirations to be a world city. I put the question of the difference between the two to Governor Fashola in an interview in August 2008, and he acknowledged that mega-city was the term that had been adopted because a "mega-city" is what Lagos is, while a "world city" is what it should be.

Giles Omezi asks whether the wealth of problems of the mega-city should not still take priority over trying to impose a world city "aesthetic overlay" (à la Singapore) on what may be a "systemically flawed skein." This, he says, is the seduction of the "global city" (as defined by Saskia Sassens, author of *Globalisation and Its Discontents*) or the "world city" as envisaged by the pioneering Californian urban theorist John Friedman. "The emergence of the 'world' or 'global' city," says Giles, "is linked to the proliferation of market liberalising tendencies post-1989 [after the collapse of the Soviet bloc] and is therefore an urban aspiration that affirms the success of capitalism." But the Fashola vision goes beyond the modernism of the Eko Atlantic City, which can only be part of a much larger and holistic concept of Lagos if it is not to risk self-destruction. Dubai on the Bight of Benin can only happen in the context of the thriving of its huge hinterland. He sees a city where people can work and play in health and security, which links in with his legal and policing reforms as well as his attempts to introduce a viable transport system (crucially depending on mass rail transit) and his stress on the environment, admitting that immigrant capital will not come in to a "dirty economy." For example, he speaks of Lagos having a million new trees by 2012.

One should put this debate in the context of all the current international (UNFPA, UNESCO, Habitat) talk of cities and their culture in the framework of the future. I recall a big exhibition on cities called "Century City" at London's Tate Modern in 2001, which had the imagination to include Lagos (along with Tokyo, Rio de Janeiro, New York, Paris, Moscow and Vienna) and then, in spite of choosing it over Cape Town as representing post-colonial Africa, made a disappointingly one-dimensional presentation of the wonderfully rich period of 1955-70. A much better treatment of the subject came from the already-mentioned Bukka collective, which organized a small but imaginative exhibition in Clerkenwell called "Lagos: City of the Future," the name of a workshop the following year at London University. Despite all the apprehensions, the exhibition summed up all the hope for the future of this place: sometimes impossibly contrarian but still somewhere to dream dreams. It also showed how its unique experience will surely have more than a little to contribute to the philosophy of the global city in ways we cannot yet know—a true city of the imagination.

Treaty of Cession of August 1861

Treaty between Norman B Bedingfield, Commander of her Majesty's ship Prometheus, and Senior Officer of the Bights Division, and William McCroskry Esquire, Her Britannic Majesty's Acting Consul, on the part of her Majesty the Queen of Great Britain, and Docemo, King of Lagos, on the part of himself and Chiefs.

ARTICLE I

In order that the Queen of England may be the better enabled to assist, defend and protect the inhabitants of Lagos, and to put an end to the Slave Trade in this and the neighbouring countries, and to prevent the destructive wars so frequently undertaken by Dahomey and others for the capture of slaves, I, Docemo, do with the consent and advice of my Council, give, transfer and by these presents grant and confirm unto the Queen of Great Britain, her heirs and successors for ever, the port and Island of Lagos, with all the rights, profits, territories and appurtenances whatsoever thereunto belonging and as well the profits and revenue as the direct, full and absolute dominion and sovereignty of the said port, island and premises, with all the royalties thereof, freely, fully entirely and absolutely. I do also covenant and grant that the quiet and peaceable possession thereof shall, with all possible speed, be freely and effectually delivered to the Queen of Great Britain or such person as her Majesty shall thereunto appoint for her use in the performance of this grant; the inhabitants of the said island and territories, as the Queen's subjects, and under her sovereignty, Crown, jurisdiction, and government, being still suffered to live there.

ARTICLE II

Docemo will be allowed the use of the title of King in its usual African signification, and will be permitted to decide disputes between natives of Lagos with their consent.

ARTICLE III

In the transfer of lands, the stamp of Docemo affixed to the document will be proofs that there are no other native claims upon it, and for this purpose he will be permitted to used it as hitherto.

In consideration of the cession as before-mentioned of the port and island and territories of Lagos, the representatives of the Queen of Great Britain do promise, subject to the approval of Her Majesty, that Docemo shall receive a pension from the Queen of Great Britain equal to the net revenue hitherto annually received by him; such pension to be paid at such periods and in such mode as may hereafter be determined.

LAGOS, August 1861

(signed)

DOCEMO   x his mark
TELAKE   x his mark
ROCAMENA   x his mark
OBALEKOW   x his mark
ACHEBONG   x his mark
NORMAN B.BEDINGFIELD
Her Majesty's ship Prometheus, Senior Officer,
Bights Division
W. McCOSKRY

Further Reading

Ade-Ajayi, J. F., *A Patriot to the Core: Bishop Ajayi Crowther*. Ibadan: Spectrum Books, 2001.

Ade-Ajayi, J. F., *Christian Missions in Nigeria 1841-1891: The Making of a New Elite*. London: Longmans, 1965.

Adefuye, Ade, Agiri, Babatunde and Osuntokun, Jide (eds.), *History of the Peoples of Lagos State*. Ikeja: Lantern Books, Literamed, 1987.

Aderibigbe, A. B. (ed.), *Lagos: The Development of an African City*. Nigeria: Longmans, 1975.

Ajayi, E. A., Ajetunmobi, R. O. and Akindele, S. A. (eds.), *The Awori of Lagos State*. Ikeja: Literamed, 1998.

Akinsemoyin, Kunle and Vaughn-Richards, Alan, *Building Lagos*, published for the All Black Festival of Arts and Culture [*sic*], 1977.

Alaja-Browne, Afolabi, *Juju Music: A Study of its Social History and Style*. University of Pittsburgh: Dissertation for PhD thesis, 1985.

Aniagolu, Charles, *Despatches from Lagos: Nigeria in Crisis*. London: Excalibur Press, 1996.

Anikulapo, Jahman, *Collapsing Borders: Tinubu Square as a Metaphor for a Multi-cultural Society*. Lagos: paper published by the Goethe Institut, 2005.

Apolo, Edia, *Lagos Na Waa I Swear*. Lagos: Heritage Books, 1982.

Apter, Andrew, *The Pan-African Nation: Oil and the Spectacle of Culture in Nigeria*. Chicago: University of Chicago Press, 2005.

Awolowo, Obafemi, *My March through Prison: Adventures in Power, Book One*. Lagos: Macmillan, 1985.

Ayandele, E. A., *Holy Johnson: Pioneer of African Nationalism*. New York: Humanities Press, 1970.

Ayandele, E. A., *The Educated Elite in the Nigerian Society*. Ibadan: University of Ibadan Press, 1974.

Azikiwe, Nnamdi, *My Odyssey: An Autobiography*. London: C. Hurst, 1970.

Baker, Pauline H., *Urbanisation and Political Change: the Politics of Lagos 1917-1967*. Berkeley: University of California Press, 1974.

Barnes, Sandra, *Patrons and Power: Creating a Political Community in Metropolitan Lagos*. London: Manchester University Press for the International African Institute, 1986.

Bender, Wolfgang, *Sweet Mother*. Chicago: University of Chicago Press, 1985.

Brendon, Piers, *The Decline and Fall of the British Empire 1781-1997*. London: Jonathan Cape, 2007.

Burns, Sir Alan, *History of Nigeria*. London: George Allen and Unwin, 1963.

Burton, Richard E., *Wanderings in West Africa from Liverpool to Fernando Po*. London: Tinsley Brothers, 1863.

Coker, Folarin, *A Lady: A Biography of Lady Oyinkan Abayomi*. Nigeria: Evans Brothers Publishers Ltd, 1987.

Cole, Patrick Dele, *Modern and Traditional Elites in the Politics of Lagos*. Cambridge: Cambridge University Press, 1975.

Coleman, James S., *Nigeria: Background to Nationalism*. California: University of California Press, 1965.

Collins, John, *West African Pop Roots*. Philadelphia: Temple University Press, 1992.

Dare, Sunday, *Guerrilla Journalism: Dispatches from the Underground*. Ibadan: Kraft Books, 2007.

Deuber, Dagmar, *Nigerian Pidgin in Lagos: Language Contact Variation and Change in an African Urban Setting*. UK: Battlebridge, 2005.

Duyile, Dayo, *Makers of the Nigerian Press*. Published by the author, 1987.

Echeruo, Michael J. C., *Victorian Lagos: Aspects of Nineteenth Century Lagos Life*. London: Macmillan, 1977.

Ehling, Holger and Holste von Mutius, Claus-Peter (eds.), *No Condition is Permanent: Nigerian Writing and the Struggle for Democracy*. New York: Matatu Journal for African Culture and Society, Rodopi, 2001.

Eko: Landmarks of Lagos, Nigeria. Nigeria: Mandilas Group 1999.

Evaristo, Bernadine, *Lara*. Tunbridge Wells, UK: Angela Royal Publishing 1997.

Falola, Toyin and Heaton, Matthew, *A History of Nigeria*. Cambridge: Cambridge University Press, 2008.

Fashinro, Alhaji H. A. B. OFR, *Political and Cultural Perspectives of Lagos*. Published by the author, 2004.

Flint, J. E., *Sir George Goldie and the Making of Nigeria*. Oxford: Oxford University Press, 1960.

Forrest, Tom, *The Advance of African Capital: The Growth of Nigerian Private Enterprise*. Edinburgh: Edinburgh University Press, 1994.

Gailey, Harry A., *Clifford: Imperial Proconsul*. London: Rex Collings, 1982.

Geary, Sir William, *Nigeria under British Rule*. London: Methuen, 1927, reprint London: Frank Cass, 1965.

Hargreaves, John D., *Prelude to the Partition of West Africa*. London: Macmillan, 1963.

Huxley, Elspeth, *Four Guineas: a Journey Through West Africa*. London: Chatto and Windus, 1954.

Johnson, Rev. Samuel, *History of the Yorubas*. London: Routledge & Sons, 1921.

Johnson-Odim, Cheryl and Mba, Nina Emma, *For Women and the Nation: Funmilayo Ransome-Kuti of Nigeria*. Champaign: University of Illinois Press, 1997.

Kopytoff, Jean Herskovits, *Preface to Modern Nigeria: The Sierra Leoneans in Yoruba 1830-1890*. Madison: University of Wisconsin Press, 1963.

Lawal, Kunle, *In Search of Lagosians: Socio-political Issues of the 21st Century*. Lagos: Adeniran Ogunsanya College of Education, 2002.

Lawal, Olakunle, *Urban Transition in Africa: Aspects of Urbanisation and Change in Lagos*. Nigeria: Longmans, 1994.

Loynes, J. B., *The West African Currency Board 1912-1962*. London: WACB, 1963.

Mabogunje, Akin, *Urbanisation in Nigeria*. London: University of London Press, 1968.

Macmillan, Allister (ed. and compiler), *The Red Book of West Africa*. Collingridge, 1920, reprint London: Frank Cass and Company, 1968.

Mann, Kristin, *Slavery and the Birth of an African City*. Bloomington: Indiana University Press, 2007.

Maringues, Michèle, *Nigeria: Guerrilla Journalism*. Paris: Reporters sans Frontières, 1996.

Marris, Peter, *Family and Social Change in an African City: A Study of Rehousing in Lagos*. London: Routledge and Kegan Paul, 1961.

Marshall, Ruth, *Political Spiritualities: The Pentecostal Revolution in Nigeria*. Chicago: University of Chicago Press, 2009.

Miller, N. S., *Lagos Steam Tramway 1909-1933*. Privately published, 1958.

Moore, Carlos, *Fela Fela: This Bitch of a Life*. London: Allison and Busby, 1982.

Morel, E. D., *Nigeria: Its Peoples and Its Problems*. London: John Murray, 1911.

Olatoye, Kanmi, *Lago de Curamo: Histories and Personalities behind the Ancient and Modern Streets of Lagos*. Nigeria: CICS, 2001.

Olojede, Dele and Adinoyi-Ojo, Onukaba, *Dele Giwa*. Ibadan: Spectrum Books, 1987.

Olorunyomi, Sola, *Afrobeat! Fela and the Imagined Continent*. Ibadan: IFRA, revised edition, 2005.

Omu, Fred I. A., *Press and Politics in Nigeria 1880-1937*. London: Longmans, 1978.

Page, Jesse, *Samuel Crowther: The Slave Boy who Became Bishop of the Niger*. London: S. W. Partridge, 1888.

Peel, J. D. Y., *Aladura, a Religious Movement among the Yoruba*. Oxford: Oxford University Press, 1968.

Peil, Margaret, *Lagos: The City is the People*. London: Belhaven Press, 1991.

Perham, Margery, *Lugard: Vol. 1 The Years of Adventure 1858-1898; Vol. 2 The Years of Authority 1898-1945*. London: Collins, 1960.

Robertson, Sir James, *Transition in Africa: From Direct Rule to Independence*. London: C. Hurst, 1974.

Schoonmaker, Trevor, *Black President: The Art and Legacy of Fela Anikulapo-Kuti*. New York: New Museum of Contemporary Art, 2003.

Schoonmaker, Trevor (ed.), *Fela: From West Africa to West Broadway*. New York and Basingstoke: Palgrave Macmillan, 2003.

Shodipe, Uthman Ademilade, *From Johnson to Marwa: 20 Years of Governance in Lagos State*. Lagos: Malthouse Press, 1997.

Sklar, Richard L., *Nigerian Political Parties: Power in an Emergent African*

Nation. New Jersey: Princeton University Press, 1963.

Smith, Robert, *The Lagos Consulate 1851-1861*. London: Macmillan 1978.

Soulié, Tony and Sigaud, Dominique, *Lagos la tropicale*. Paris: Garde-Temps, 2001.

Spitzer, Leo, *The Creoles of Sierra Leone*. Madison: University of Wisconsin Press, 1975.

Stewart, Gary, *Breakout: Profiles in African Rhythm*. Chicago: University of Chicago Press, 1992.

Tejuoso, Olakunle (ed.), *Lagos: A City at Work*. Lagos: Glendora Books, 2006.

Thorp, Ellen, *Ladder of Bones: The Birth of Modern Nigeria from 1853 to Independence*. London: Jonathan Cape, 1956; Ibadan: Spectrum Books, 2000.

Veal, Michael E., *Fela: The Life and Times of an African Musical Icon*. Philadelphia: Temple University Press, 2000.

Waterman, Christopher Alan, *Juju: A Social History and Ethnography of an African Popular Music*. Chicago: University of Chicago Press, 1990.

Weate, Jeremy and Bakary-Weate, Bibi, *Ojuelegba: The Sacred Profanities of a West African Crossroad*. Privately published paper, 2003.

Webster, James Bertin, *The African Churches Among the Yoruba 1888-1922*. Oxford: Oxford University Press, 1964.

FICTION, POETRY AND DRAMA

Abani, Chris, *GraceLand*. New York: Farrar Strauss and Giroux, 2004.

Abani, Chris, *Kalakuta Republic*. London: Saqi Books, 2000.

Achebe, Chinua, *No Longer At Ease*. London: Heinemann, 1960.

Atta, Sefi, *A Bit of Difference*. Northampton MA: Interlink, 2013.

Atta, Sefi, *Everything Good Will Come*. Northampton MA: Interlink, 2005.

Atta, Sefi, *News from Home*. Northampton MA: Interlink, 2010.

Atta, Sefi, *Swallow*. Northampton MA: Interlink, 2010.

Cole, Teju, *Every Day is for the Thief*. Abuja: Cassava Republic, 2007.

Cole, Teju, *Open City*. New York: Random House, 2011.

Ekwensi, Cyprian, *Jagua Nana*. London: Hutchinson, 1961.

Ekwensi, Cyprian, *Jagua Nana's Daughter*. Nigeria: Spectrum Books, 1987.

Ekwensi, Cyprian, *People of the City*. Harlow: Heinemann Educational Books, African Writers Series, 1963.

Habila, Helon, *Waiting for an Angel*. London: Hamish Hamilton, 2002.

Ndibe, Okey, *Arrows of Rain*. Harlow: Heinemann Educational Publishers, 2000.

Nwosu, Maik, *Alpha Song*. Lagos: House of Malaika and Beacon Books, 2001.

Ofeimun, Odia, *Lagos of the Poets*. Lagos: Hornbill House, 2009.

Okri, Ben, *Dangerous Love*. London: Phoenix House, 1996.

Okri, Ben, *The Famished Road*. London: Jonathan Cape, 1991.

Olinto, Antonio, *The Water House*. London: Rex Collings, 1970.

Osofisan, Femi, Ajayi Crowther: The Triumphs and Travails of Legend - a Play. Ibadan: Bookcraft, 2006.

Saro-Wiwa, Ken, *Basi and Company*. Port Harcourt: Saros Publishers, 1987.

WEBSITES

lagoscityphotos.blogspot.com

www.lagosstate.gov.ng

BGL and Lagos

BGL (originally Bank Guaranty Limited) has been an involved denizen of Lagos State for the better part of two decades, as it evolved from banking turnaround to being a fully-fledged investment bank, similar to the Royal Bank of Scotland. This time-frame gives us a useful perspective on the remarkable way this inspiring—if often maddening—metropolis has sought to meet the massive developmental challenges it faces, even as nearly twenty million inhabitants threaten to burst the physical infrastructural and geographical boundaries simultaneously with a figurative swelling of ideas, ideals and aspirations seeking solace, guidance, funding or just a listening ear.

BGL is headquartered in Lagos because the former capital of Nigeria remains the financial hub of Africa's largest country. We in BGL see a bold future in which Lagos becomes the surging commercial heart of a sustainably resurgent African economic watershed. However, in reaching for this bold future we must properly contextualize the rich history of Lagos. This is where Kaye Whiteman's book takes a high level of importance.

Within the Lagos metropolis, BGL maintains offices in the courageously reclaimed Central Business District of Lagos Island; the historic, attractive but aquatically-threatened Victoria Island; the ever-entertaining Nollywood hub of Surulere; the environmentally challenged port-town of Apapa; the State capital of Ikeja and the densely populated, working-capital melting pot that is Alaba, bordering the planned town of FESTAC. There are rich back stories, characters, challenges and communities to each of these, and Kaye has sought to bring the rich histories of these to life here: Lagos Island for instance has always had colorful monarchs, administrators, business gurus, shopkeepers, merchants, activists and even criminals who have made the lives of the thousands who live in its packed housing tenements, and millions who throng the offices, richer by their actions.

Victoria Island and Ikoyi have somehow maintained their "highbrow" status (and house prices!) despite the pressures of military upheaval, coups and expropriations, as well as a vulnerable environmental situation exacerbated by the battles against flooding from the sky, the lagoon, and the sometimes unforgiving Atlantic. But we, as capitalists, also note with fondness the fact that Victoria Island and Ikoyi have retained their cachet for nuggets of posh offices and the upper reaches of real-estate denominated reward for the successful entrepreneur from all over Nigeria, irrespective of tribe, creed, religious or partisan leanings. In this regard, BGL's story mirrors the aspirations of the hustling/bustling millions of Lagos. We too have grown a firm that, from zero inhabitants of these nooks of comfort, is gratefully blest to have more than a dozen BGL members keeping homes here.

Lagos retains a singular importance to Nigeria: it occupies inordinately large market share (often as high as 30-40 per cent despite representing only 10-12 per cent of the population) of products in sectors as strategic as telecommunications, banking, entertainment and FMCGs. BGL's reach also extends to other parts of the country, and with this background we can argue that the Golden Square of Lagos-Abuja-Port Harcourt-Kano illustrates the centrality of the Finance/Trade fulcrum of Lagos as an integral part of a four-legged epicenter which is the pillar of stability for Nigeria (also involving the Federal Capital Territories' central government location, Port Harcourt's arguable claim as median for the Oil/Gas sector as well as Kano's claim as Nigeria's most historic and continuously-inhabited city).

Index of Historical & Literary Names

Index of Places & Landmarks

Fiction by leading Nigerian novelist Sefi Atta

A BIT OF DIFFERENCE
"[A]t once an American successor to classic Nigerian literature and a commentary on how the English-speaking world reads Africa. ... the story feels extremely modern while excelling at the novelist's traditional task: finding the common reality between strangers and rendering alien circumstances familiar." —*Publishers Weekly*, starred review
hardback • ISBN 978-1-56656-892-0 • $25.00
e-book • ISBN 978-1-62371-021-7

EVERYTHING GOOD WILL COME
Winner of the Wole Soyinka Prize for African Literature
"A literary masterpiece... *Everything Good Will Come* put me into a spell from the first page to the very last... It portrays the complicated society and history of Nigeria through... brilliant prose." —*World Literature Today*
hardback • ISBN 978-1-56656-570-7 • $24.95
paperback • ISBN 978-1-56656-704-6 • $15.00
e-book • ISBN 978-1-62371-016-3

NEWS FROM HOME
Winner of the 2009 NOMA Award for Publishing in Africa
"Atta demonstrates a fresh, vital voice in these 11 stories that move fluidly between pampered Nigerian émigrés and villagers grinding out a meager subsistence. Atta's characters are irrepressible... Atta movingly portrays these conflicted lives and gorgeously renders a wide spectrum of humanity and experience." —*Publishers Weekly*
paperback • ISBN 978-1-56656-803-6 • $15.00
e-book • ISBN 978-1-62371-009-5

SWALLOW
"In Atta's spirited and largehearted second novel, two young woman office workers navigate the rapids of the urban jungle of Lagos. [This] tale encompasses towns and villages, corruption and superstition, deceit and loyalty, all beautifully layered and building toward a wallop you never see coming." —*Publishers Weekly* (starred review)
paperback • ISBN 9781566568333 • $15.00
e-book • ISBN 978-1-62371-007-1